Healing Through Deliverance

The Practical Ministry

Healing Through Deliverance

The Practical Ministry

Peter J. Horrobin

Director
of
Ellel Ministries

Centres for Training and Ministry
in Christian Healing and Counselling

Sovereign World

Sovereign World Ltd
P. O. Box 777
Tonbridge
Kent TN11 9XT
England

First Edition 1995

All scripture quotations, unless otherwise stated, are from:

NIV   New International Version.
            © 1973, 1978 International Bible Society,
            published by Hodder and Stoughton.

Other translations used include:

GNB   Good News Bible.
            © American Bible Society, New York.

NASB   New American Standard Version.
            © The Lockman Foundation 1960, 1962,
            1963, 1968, 1975, 1977.

AV   Authorised (King James) Version
            Crown Copyright

British Library Cataloguing in Publication Data
Horrobin, Peter J (Peter James) 1943–
        Healing Through Deliverance 2

        ISBN 1-85240-039-0

Printed in England by Clays Ltd, St. Ives plc

For
Mum and Dad
who taught me so much,
gave me such a solid foundation for life
and,
above all,
gave me a Godly heritage.
I thank God for them and pray that they will
see this book as part of the harvest from
their years of sowing.

This book is also dedicated
to the team of people in Ellel Ministries
whom God has called together to establish and
nurture a special ministry of evangelism,
healing and deliverance.

Contents

PART B: UNDERSTANDING DEMONIC ENTRY POINTS

PART C: THE PRACTICE OF DELIVERANCE MINISTRY

About the Author

Peter Horrobin is the International Director of Ellel Ministries which, although based in the United Kingdom, is now working in a number of different countries. Peter was born in 1943 in Bolton, Lancashire, and was later brought up in Blackburn, also in the north of England. His parents gave him a firm Christian foundation with a strong evangelical emphasis. His grounding in the scriptures was to equip him for future ministry. After living in the south for a while he eventually returned to his native county after periods of living in Surrey, Oxford and Manchester.

After graduating at Oxford University, where he studied chemistry, he spent a number of years in University lecturing before leaving the academic environment for the world of business. He founded his own publishing and bookselling companies and then, after fifteen years of writing, publishing and bookselling, the doors opened for the ministry at Ellel Grange to be established in 1986. Throughout his university and business career he had known that he was only 'marking time' until his calling into Christian ministry would lead him into a different way of life.

Peter first knew this calling as a young teenager, but he had to wait nearly thirty years before his life's work was to begin at Ellel Grange! It was through trying to help a person in need that God opened up to him the vision for the healing ministry. He prayed daily into this vision for ten years before God brought it into being. Since then a hallmark of Peter's ministry has been his willingness to step out in faith and see God move, often in remarkable ways.

A Prayer Support Group was first established and the purchase of Ellel Grange was completed in November 1986. Since then Ellel Ministries has grown very steadily - there is now a full-time team of over 140 people, running a continuous series of healing retreats and training courses. Additionally there are over 300 trained Associate Counsellors serving the Lord through the different centres.

In 1991 a teaching and ministry centre was opened in the South of England at Glyndley Manor, near Eastbourne and in 1993 a centre in Canada was added to the work at Orangeville, just north of Toronto. In 1995 Pierrepont was acquired, an estate in Surrey, convenient for both Heathrow and Gatwick international airports. This centre is to become the International Training School for longer term training opportunities with Ellel Ministries as well housing a major new care and ministry centre.

The International Teaching Conferences at the Brighton Centre served to bring the teaching to a much wider audience. They were also instrumental in extending the horizons of the ministry into Eastern Europe and beyond.

There has been a steady growth of teaching and ministry conferences in Russia and Eastern Europe and plans are now well advanced for a major teaching and ministry centre in Hungary, near Budapest. This will serve Pastors and Leaders from the whole of Eastern Europe. Ellel Poland and Ellel Estonia have also been initiated under local leadership.

Under Peter's leadership the teaching and ministry team has grown considerably in size, gaining much experience along the way. They have seen God move dramatically in many people's lives to bring healing and deliverance. Through them, and in a relatively short period of time, God has built a work of international significance. They have responded to many invitations to teach on healing and deliverance throughout the United Kingdom and in many different countries. The work is a faith ministry, depending totally on donations and income from training courses for maintaining and extending the work.

Peter was one of the compilers of the amazingly successful and popular *Mission Praise*, the first volume of which was originally compiled for Mission England in 1984. He is also an enthusiast for fishing and Alvis cars. His *Complete Catalogue of British Cars*, which was published in 1975, has long been the standard reference work on the history and technical specification of every model of every make of British car manufactured before 1974!

Preface

Many people have contributed to the contents of this book. Although the title page bears my name, it could not have been written without the determined commitment of all those who have shared in the work that God has brought into being through Ellel Ministries.

Neither could it have been written without the many thousands of people who have sought God's help through Ellel Ministries, and, in so doing, have trusted members of the team to minister Jesus into their lives. I want to thank every single one of them for the living contributions they have made.

When Ellel Grange was acquired in 1986, none of the pioneering team could have anticipated the pilgrimage that was to follow. It has not been easy. We have experienced both joy and pain as the fruit of the ministry has slowly matured. No-one expected that deliverance ministry would be such a strategic part of healing. Perhaps if we had known, the team would never have come together!

Time and again members of the team have been thrown on the Lord in difficult personal ministries, and scripture has come to life under the anointing of the Holy Spirit. On occasions the dramatic thrill of the Gospel stories has been experienced first hand. At other times we have been more conscious of the long list of pressures and problems that Paul described to his friends in Corinth (2 Cor. 11:22-29)!

Neither had we any idea then, that God would take the teaching and ministry to areas far removed from our roots in the North of England. So much so that there is now a centre in the South of England at Glyndley Manor, one in Canada at Orangeville, just north of Toronto, and a developing centre at

Budapest in Hungary for the Pastors and Leaders of Hungary and Eastern Europe.

The opportunities God has given for teaching and ministry, both in England and abroad, have served more to demonstrate the relative ignorance about healing and deliverance that there has been in the Body of Christ at large, than draw attention to anything special about the work of Ellel Ministries.

For those who are not familiar with Ellel Ministries, the work is administered by a registered charity, *The Christian Trust*. The objectives and basis of faith of the work are as follows:

Objectives:

To fulfil Christ's command to preach the Gospel, make disciples and heal the sick in the widest sense. This is achieved through prayer, teaching, preaching, personal ministry to individuals and by training others to be involved in this ministry, especially in their local churches.

Basis of Faith:

God is a Trinity. God the Father loves all mankind. God the Son, Jesus Christ, is Saviour and Healer, Lord and King. God the Holy Spirit indwells Christians and imparts the dynamic power by which they are enabled to continue Christ's ministry. The Bible is the divinely inspired authority in matters of faith, doctrine and conduct and the basis for teaching.

At the present time there is a full-time team of over one hundred and forty people and a total of over three hundred part-time Associate Counsellors.

Those in need are usually ministered to on Healing Retreats where Jesus' practice of *"welcoming the people, teaching them about the kingdom of God and healing those in need"* (Luke 9:11) is the normal basis for ministry. After the welcome, teaching and ministry always go hand-in-hand.

Many people really need to hear and understand the basics of the Kingdom of God before they are able to receive

14

ministry. Often, the reason why they are still in need is directly related to not having applied the vital foundational principles of forgiveness, acceptance and repentance to their lives.

New training courses are in a constant process of development. Those currently available through Ellel Ministries are as follows:

Residential Courses (*normally 3 days in length*):

Battle for the Soul

Building a Ministry Team
  in the Local Church

Claiming the Ground

Deliverance Ministry

Developing Gifts in
  the Healing Ministry

Developing Your
  Prophetic Gifting

Dynamic Praying

Equipped to Serve

Evangelism and Healing

Foundations for
  Christian Counselling

Foundations for
  Healing Abused People

Foundations for
  the Healing Ministry

Freedom from Addiction

Freedom from Fear

Freedom from Stress & Anxiety

Freedom in Christ

Healing and the Sacraments

Healing for Victims of
  Accident and Trauma

Healing and Leaders' Retreats

Healing and Prophecy

Healing from Spiritual Abuse

Healing - The Jesus Model

Healing through Deliverance

Healing through Deliverance
  for Men

Healing through Deliverance
  for Women

Inner Healing and
  Emotional Wholeness

Intercession and
  Spiritual Warfare

Living in Wholeness

Ministry to the Childless

Ministering to the Rejected

Ministry to Marriage

Ministering to the
  Sexually Abused

Moving Under the Anointing
  of the Holy Spirit

Preparation for Marriage

Rejection & How to Overcome it

Restoring the Rejected

Specialist Aspects of
  Deliverance Ministry

Spiritual Protection

The Prophetic Ministry

Understanding Deception

Understanding Sex & Sexuality

Walking in the Anointing

Teaching Conferences

Healing and Wholeness

A training conference designed to help local fellowships establish the ministries of healing and deliverance in their church community.

The Battle Belongs to the Lord

A comprehensive 4 day conference on: How to minister evangelism, healing and deliverance in the power of the Holy Spirit.

The Church Ablaze

A relevant and challenging four day conference to equip and build up the Body of Christ, warn of dangers and teach on the weapons and tools needed to keep the Church strong.

The Day of His Power

A follow-on conference to 'The Church Ablaze' providing more in-depth teaching on how to be ready and willing to be the people of God in an increasingly difficult spiritual environment in which to declare that Jesus is the only way.

There is also a residential *International School of Evangelism, Healing and Deliverance* which embodies the main teaching elements from all the above courses. This is especially suitable for those coming from overseas or those who are able to set aside nine weeks for a more concentrated time of teaching and practical experience. The school lasts for two months. The first month is devoted primarily to teaching the foundations and the second month to the application of the teaching in personal ministries.

A new development in 1995 has been the acquisition of Pierrepont - an estate in Surrey close to both Heathrow and Gatwick airports - as the International Training Centre for Ellel Ministries. One and two year courses are expected to begin there in the autumn of 1996.

Full details of the current programme of courses, events and ministries, as well as books and teaching tapes, are available on request from:

Ellel Ministries,   or   Ellel Ministries,
Ellel Grange,   Ellel Canada,
Lancaster,   RR #1, Orangeville,
LA2 0HN,   Ontario, L9W 2Y8,
England.   Canada.

I am tremendously grateful to the various members of the team, and other friends and colleagues, who helped so generously with the preparation of the manuscript and made many useful suggestions. I especially thank Jonathan Cansdale, Ed Pirie and Lissa Smith for their painstaking work in editing and preparing the text for publication. Without their help the book would not yet have been published!

I also thank the many others who made helpful suggestions, many of which have been incorporated in the text. I thank them all for their support and encouragement. I apologise to the many others who have lovingly endured my lateness for meals, lack of immediate response to letters, and apparent likeness to a hermit at critical stages of the writing process!

This volume covers the practical ministry of healing through deliverance. Volume One covered the vital scriptural basis. My prayer for each person who reads these books is that their commitment to Christ will be deepened and that they will respond afresh to the calling God has put before each and every believer: *to preach the Gospel, heal the sick **and** cast out demons.*

Peter Horrobin
Ellel Grange
May 1995

PART A

FOUNDATIONS FOR DELIVERANCE MINISTRY

An architect who plans a building that will last, will ensure that the foundations are solid. Jesus also advised us at the end of the Sermon on the Mount of the importance of putting down good foundations. He compared a wise man, who listens to his words and puts them into practice, to a builder who built his house on the rock.

The ministry of Jesus included healing and deliverance. The Church cannot ignore these vital elements of the Gospel if it is to be an effective means of bringing hope to the hopeless, healing to the broken, restoration to the sick in body, mind and spirit and freedom to those who are oppressed or held captive by the enemy.

The first part of this book is all about laying solid foundations and ensuring that the reader has a good understanding of the teaching which is at the heart of an effective healing and deliverance ministry. Chapter 3 provides an appreciation of the sort of symptoms that could have a demonic root.

Chapter 1

Introduction

A Balanced Healing Ministry

In his ministry Jesus dealt with every type of healing need and ministered to each individual according to his personal situation. Through the cross Jesus made it possible for the Church to continue his healing ministry. Satan seeks to bring chaos and disorder. Healing is the restoration of God's order to the spirit, soul and body.

The fact that Jesus' first act of healing involved the casting out of a demon (Luke 4:31-36) is an affront to some twentieth century minds, and many would want to dismiss the deliverance aspect of Jesus' ministry as a delusion of first century understanding. But to do that, by necessity, labels Jesus as having been deceived by the limitations of his own culture - hardly an acceptable conclusion about the character and spirituality of the Son of God!

The healing ministry of Jesus was totally balanced - this meant that he ministered healing to the spirit, soul and body of people as well as delivering them from the powers of darkness. A ministry which ignores any of these aspects could be said, therefore, to be unbalanced!

There have been many books in recent years on different aspects of healing, and whilst there has been an outburst of literature on spiritual warfare, there has been relatively little which brings together healing for the spirit, soul and body with a scriptural understanding of the demonic and deliverance ministry. In view of the fact that sickness and disease are consequences of the fall, when man succumbed to Satan's temptations, it seems hard to understand how any form of Christian healing can ignore the possibility of there being a demonic dimension to the healing ministry.

But it was only when I began to pray for the sick myself, and came up against situations that did not respond to more traditional healing prayer, that I became aware of the twentieth century relevance of and the need for the deliverance ministry. In the first volume of *Healing Through Deliverance*, therefore, I explained in detail the scriptural foundations and practical outworking of the ministry of deliverance as practised by Jesus, which was so effective in bringing healing to those who sought out his help.

Neither my upbringing nor my church experience prepared me for this ministry. In some ways this is very surprising. For it is in the scriptures that the instructions to cast out demons are so clearly written down. And both my family upbringing and the churches I have been associated with have underlined the vital importance of knowing and applying the scriptures, so that our lives are lived in harmony with their teaching!

I might have expected, therefore, that such a vital part of the Gospels would have been carefully established in my life from an early age. But in common with most Christians of my generation, it seems as though the whole area of deliverance was a theological blind spot, caused either by the mistaken belief that demons are only found in the 'heathen parts of the world', and therefore we need not worry about them in 'Christian England', or the deception that demons cannot possibly affect Christians, and therefore deliverance ministry is quite irrelevant to the modern church.

If I had been brought up in Malaysia or Nigeria, my perception would have been radically different. For there, and in many other parts of the world as well, the spirit realm is so much a part of the culture that any expression of Christian faith that does not have an answer to this vital area of life would not be very credible to much of the local population.

It is widely believed by rationalistic western man that education and civilisation either get rid of demons or enlighten us to the 'truth' that demons don't exist and so no longer need to be considered when explaining conditions or phenomena which are said to have only perfectly logical scientific explanations. Is it not possible that science is only producing rational explanations for the way the demonic has operated in causing some diseases?

Not only has lack of belief in the supernatural affected the rationalistic world, it has also dominated much religious thinking, especially in the liberal and evangelical sectors of the church. Such rationalistic thinking has no expression in scripture, where a recurring theme is the direct intervention of God in the affairs of man. And if one can so lightly dispense with such a large sector of the ministry of Jesus (one third of the recorded healings of Jesus were deliverance ministries), one has to ask if there is anything in the word of God that is not open to doubt and disbelieving scrutiny.

Thankfully, I was taught that spiritualism and all other forms of occult involvement were dangerous. But I was never told that if I did these things I might become demonised. Nor was I warned of the many other ways in which the demonic could gain a foothold in my life. I knew what sin was, but not that the continued practice of sin could give rights to the demonic in my life. I knew all about confessing sin so that I could be forgiven but never that I might also need cleansing from the consequences of sin, including deliverance, if my sin had led to demonisation.

With the benefit of hindsight I now see that a whole dimension of spiritual understanding was completely missing from my Christian education. Not that anyone had done this deliberately - I had, like so many others, simply been taught out of the limited experience of others.

Early Beginnings

God gave me the vision for the work of Ellel Ministries some ten years before I was led to the building, Ellel Grange, in which the work began. I can see now that during those years of praying, waiting, planning and preparation, I had very occasionally encountered the demonic when praying with people in need, though I had mostly failed to recognise just what was happening!

One girl, I remember, gave a remarkably good imitation of a wild-cat. I have seen this sort of thing on various occasions since then, but at that time it was a frightening experience and I was profoundly relieved that it didn't last too long! On other occasions I became aware that some less obviously demonic symptoms may also have had a supernatural origin. These could not be explained in any other way than by the activity of malevolent supernatural beings, probably called demons, behaving remarkably like the 'creatures' Jesus dealt with and expressly told the disciples to cast out.

Ellel Grange

By the time the doors of Ellel Grange were eventually opened in November 1986 I had come to realise that deliverance ministry was a vital part of healing, and was beginning to teach others that this was the case. I had no doubt that demons were real and that Christians had the power and authority to cast them out, if they could but find any! In practice, however, I think I had cast out one or two demons at the most before the work at Ellel began in earnest!

The first few weeks changed all that! We discovered that many of the people who came for help, especially those with long-term problems, were caught in a demonic web and were in need of deliverance. One young man was brought by his pastor. For two years the pastor had given John and his wife first class counselling. But in spite of such good help, the relationship was getting progressively worse and John was in a pretty bad way.

There seemed little we could do to help that had not already been done by the pastor. So we simply prayed and asked the Lord to show up any darkness in his life. I've since come to realise that when prayed in faith that is quite a 'dangerous' prayer! As the Holy Spirit came upon him there was a strong physical reaction in his body as the demons reacted to the presence of God. His fingers went stiff, his body went nearly rigid, and he slid off the chair onto the carpet and slithered across the floor vomiting. Clearly, John had a problem! We were about to cast out our first demons at Ellel Grange. I remember telephoning another member of the team very late at night and shouting down the phone, *"Help, get here fast!"* as the demons in John began to manifest violently and turn our beautiful lounge into a furniture battlefield.

John was eventually delivered, not just of one but of many demons, and years later John and his wife are still getting along well. I now know that without deliverance there would have been no answers and no hope for John. The relationship would probably have broken up and John himself would be in a very bad way. John was the first of many such people whom God sent along as we entered on a crash course in deliverance ministry.

Another was the very first person to come forward for ministry at the end of our first healing service at Ellel Grange in January 1987. Lawrence stood at the front of the meeting trembling from head to foot. All eyes were on his heavily tattooed figure and violent looking body, wondering what we would do with such an unlikely candidate for Christian healing.

He said, *"I'm filled with fear"*. I touched his shoulder and there was such a violent reaction from deep inside him that he crashed dramatically forwards onto the floor. At that point discretion took over and we decided not to minister to him in front of everyone else. So we asked him to come back later in the week with his pastor.

When he came, we found out more of his story and realised the wisdom of not always dealing with everything that presents at a healing service straight away. Lawrence told us how he had sold himself to Satan when in prison, but how later in solitary confinement he had read a Gideon's New Testament and found Christ. The powers of darkness in him were strong, but such was the grace of God that the Lord took us by the hand and showed us step by step what to do in order to bring him through to deliverance.

Less than twelve months after commencing the work, the Lord led us to conduct our first *Deliverance Ministry Training Course*. We didn't have all the answers – no-one ever has. But as we shared what the Lord had already given to us, we began to see revelation dawn in the eyes of those brave souls who had risked their reputations to be there! Even Anglican vicars went home knowing they now had keys to help people in their churches.

At the time of writing we have now run the *Deliverance Ministry Training Course,* in various forms, on more than forty occasions. It might seem to be a risky course to attend, for there are always people on it who are healed through deliverance, as revelatory knowledge undermines demonic strongholds. People who previously might not have considered that they had any personal demonic problems are set free from the powers that had been at work deep within their lives.

Whilst this book does set out much of the information on the practicalities of deliverance ministry taught on the courses, it is not intended to be a substitute for setting time aside for a period of teaching and training to learn about this ministry first-hand, in fellowship with other Christians. Even if books had been widely available in Jesus' day, I don't think he would have limited his teaching of the disciples to asking them to read a manual!

Scriptural Foundations of Faith

The first volume of *Healing Through Deliverance* was written to establish the biblical basis for the deliverance ministry. Whilst I know that the temptation to get straight into the practicalities of deliverance ministry will be very strong for some people, if you have not already done so, may I encourage you to take time now to read the first volume before continuing with this one.

If you do so, you will find yourself far better equipped to appreciate and apply the contents of this volume and minister healing in the Body of Christ. The scriptures are our primary source of knowledge, and it is vital that we understand from the word of God the reality of what deliverance ministry is all about and the source of our authority over demons.

As well as providing a detailed exposition of all the passages of scripture specifically relevant to deliverance ministry, the first volume also establishes some very important foundational beliefs.

These are all vital to the teaching contained in this volume and are listed below for ease of reference.

1.　　God is a Trinity of Father, Son and Holy Spirit.

2. God created all the supernatural beings in the angelic realms.

3. God created man as a spiritual being, gave him a soul and placed him inside a body for the duration of his life on earth. Man is, therefore, also a trinity – of spirit, soul and body.

4. Lucifer (as he was probably then called), one of the archangels, was expelled from Heaven because he wanted to attract to himself the glory and worship that was rightfully due to God. He then became known as Satan, the adversary. Some of the angelic hosts joined in the rebellion with Satan and were also expelled from heaven.

5. Jesus saw Satan thrown down to earth.

6. On earth Satan continued his rebellion against God by tempting man to disobey God.

7. Man sinned (joined in the rebellion) and became alienated from his Creator.

8. Man then became vulnerable to Satan and the supernatural beings under Satan's control, known as fallen angels, demons or evil spirits.

9. These powers of darkness have no flesh life of their own and seek to occupy the bodies of men and women in order to pursue their rebellion against God and his creation, man, by keeping people in bondage to Satan and away from a restored relationship with God. When an evil spirit is inside a person, the person is said to be demonised.

10. God prepared a way of escape (salvation) for mankind and sent his own Son, Jesus, to earth. Jesus showed us what God the Father is really like and died on the cross for the sins of the world. As many as believe in Jesus for themselves are born again of the Spirit of God and are released from the only wages that Satan pays, death, and receive instead a free gift from God, eternal life.

11. Jesus began his ministry by fulfilling the prophecy of Isaiah 61:1 by preaching the Good News, healing the sick and casting demons out of the demonised. He told the disciples to do the same.

12. In the Great Commission, given by Jesus before he returned to heaven, Jesus told the first disciples to go and make more disciples, then to baptise them and finally to teach them to do the same things that he had taught the first disciples to do. In this way the embryonic church was commissioned to preach the Gospel, heal the sick and cast out demons.

13. In the Acts of the Apostles the early church began to fulfil the Great Commission by preaching the Gospel, healing the sick and delivering the demonised.

14. These commissions have never been rescinded, and therefore today's church is still commissioned to preach the Gospel, heal the sick and cast out demons.

15. When a person becomes a Christian there is a change of ownership. The new Christian is then 'possessed of God' - the word 'possessed' implying ownership. Any demons present before conversion do not necessarily leave at conversion, but they do not possess (own) the Christian. A born again Christian cannot be possessed by demons, but the territory of his life can certainly be occupied or oppressed. Therefore, a Christian person can still be demonised and in need of deliverance.

16. Generally speaking, deliverance ministry is only for Christians. For it is only Christians who can be filled with the Holy Spirit and be protected, therefore, from the dangers of reinfestation.

17. Demons occupy territory through rights they have been given through sin, abuse, generational powers etc. Recognition and removal of the rights that demons have is a vital part of deliverance ministry.

18. Christians have been given Christ's authority over the powers of darkness, so believers are able to deliver people from demons in the same way that Jesus did.

Whilst you may consider that all the above points are obvious, it is sometimes because the obvious is overlooked that the powers of darkness can be in a position of strength in a person's life. For example, if a person is not willing to believe that he could be demonised, then healing that requires deliverance is rarely possible, because the person is giving the demons a right to be there through unbelief.

The main thrust of this volume is to teach those who are involved in Christian healing ministry how to remove the rights that demons have and to cast them out of a person (or place), so that they stay out, leaving the person (or place) free from the consequences of having been demonised. I pray that it will be widely used to bring healing and deliverance to the Body of Christ.

Chapter 2

Preparing the Ground

(Foundational Teaching for Healing and Deliverance)

Jesus Shares his Ministry with the Disciples

There is no doubt that Jesus saw deliverance as a vital part of his ministry and strategic to his mission as the Messiah. Deliverance ministry demonstrated to the world his absolute authority over Satan and the powers of darkness. This simple fact is at the root of all the opposition there is to the practice of deliverance ministry in the Church.

Then, in Luke 9:1-2 it is recorded that he shared this authority with his disciples. They were the first to be given his power and authority both to heal the sick and to cast out demons. But just as the Gospel accounts give no detailed instructions as to how Jesus expected the disciples to heal people from sicknesses and diseases, neither do they give any instructions on how to deliver people from demons!

It is for this reason that in Volume 1 of *Healing Through Deliverance* I spent so much time looking at the lessons we can learn from the deliverance ministries actually recorded in the Gospels. It seems that Jesus' method of teaching healing and deliverance was largely experiential.

31

In practical terms it reduced to something like this:

a)   Listen to what I say
b)   and watch what I do
c)   then have a try yourself while I'm watching
d)   before going off and trying it by yourselves
e)   Then come back, tell me all about it,
      and share your problems.

   then ...

a)   Listen to what I say
b)   And watch what I do

   etc., etc., ... (repeating as many times as are necessary)

   But remember, I'm going back to heaven before long so get lots of practice while I'm still around!

We have found this system of training members of our own ministry team at Ellel Grange to be highly effective. It enables people of all intellects and personalities to explore their calling before God and learn in a safe environment. The disciples had three years of being taught in this way. It must have been an amazing experience for them to watch Jesus at work. They were seeing things that had never before happened in the history of the world!

It must have been a traumatic experience for them to discover that stages 3 and 4 were to be part of their training. In Luke it is carefully recorded that this is exactly what Jesus did with the disciples: *"He called the twelve disciples together and gave them power and authority to drive out all demons and to cure diseases. Then he sent them out to preach the Kingdom of God and to heal the sick."* (Luke 9:1-2 GNB). What an incredible commission!

If the first part of his teaching method was 'Listen to what I say' then surely there should have been detailed instructions in the Gospels about how to heal the sick and cast out demons but, strangely, no such manual can be found - just a command to go and do it! Not much comfort to the educated world which sets great store by the ability to learn a formula or technique and then pass examinations to prove they are qualified!

The Teaching of Jesus

So what do we find when we look at the teaching of Jesus that is recorded in the Gospels? What we actually see is basic teaching about the Kingdom of God - about love, forgiveness, not hating one's brother, and stories which illustrate foundational truths of what we now call the Christian life. Not much, you might think, to help a trainee disciple cast out a demon. But you would be mistaken! There is much vital information here.

It is significant that most of the major healing ministries that Jesus carried out were in the context of his teaching ministry. For example, at the beginning of the discourse on the feeding of the five thousand, Luke comments that *"Jesus welcomed them and spoke to them about the Kingdom of God, and healed those who needed healing."* (Luke 9:11).

Jesus knew that many (but not all) of the things that people suffered from were there as a consequence of sin and relationships that had gone wrong. Sickness, and much suffering, usually has a root cause, and if the healing Jesus ministered was to be of permanent value it was essential that people should know the truths that would help them put the foundational things right in their lives.

Dealing with root causes is vital. The disciples had to learn that foundational teaching, rather than the technique of deliverance, was the way to unlock root problems.

This was a lesson that the Lord taught me in prayer and vision long before Ellel Grange was established and before I had ever had any significant experience of healing or deliverance. The second part of Luke 9:11 was imprinted upon my heart by the Holy Spirit as absolutely foundational for the ministry to which he was calling me. Welcome, Teach, Heal - and in that order.

If a loving welcome did not undergird the reception that people received when they came for help, they would be unlikely to listen to the teaching they needed to hear. And if they had not heard - and understood - the teaching, then ministry to them would be hard and largely ineffective. It was a difficult lesson to learn, for instinctively one wanted to rush out and see miracles begin to happen!

Ploughing patiently through foundational teaching was not what I first envisaged the healing ministry would be all about. I questioned the Lord as to whether or not I had heard right, but he gave me no other keys. It was only when I took God at his word, and accepted that he knew what he was doing, that he opened my eyes to see just what he could and would do with such a simple formula. After all, it was the same formula he had given to his disciples, and that seemed to work pretty well!

In vision the Lord then showed me how people would come, some of them in great need, for what we would later call Healing Retreats. I 'saw' the people arriving full of problems and with various physical conditions. I 'taught' through all the basics of the Gospel which God had shown me were critical to them, and then he showed me what would happen as a result.

Years later I would often weep before the people as time and again I saw just how faithful God had been to the vision he had given. I began to see people being healed and delivered as they received the teaching and allowed it to break down strongholds in their lives.

I saw that even though we did have to take up authority over the powers of darkness to cast out demons, it was the truth that Jesus taught that had the potential to set people free. But that truth had to be taught in such a way that people were not bored by dry theology or left feeling they had been rejected or condemned by a God who was far too distant to be interested in them. They had to be captivated by the love of a God who had made such provision for them, in spite of the rebellion of sin that was in their hearts. And it worked - the teaching struck home and miracles of healing began to take place.

None of us on the team will ever forget Pat, who, at the end of the first night of an early healing retreat, stomped out of the meeting angry at me for saying that she must forgive those who had hurt her. She had hung on to the bitterness for thirty years and no-one was going to tell her to let go of it now!

She went home and that night the Lord would not let her sleep. At one-thirty in the morning she sat up in bed and decided to obey! First she wrote out a list (she called it her 'hate' list) of all those she needed to forgive. Having done that she prayed through the list, forgave them all, and fell into a deep sleep.

The following morning she was woken by the ticking of a clock. Quite a miracle in itself, for she had taken both her hearing aids out the night before. She had been almost totally deaf in one ear and eighty per cent deaf in the other. God had worked a miracle during the night by healing her of deafness without anyone even praying for her hearing. She came running back the next morning to tell us what had happened.

At the end of the retreat she asked for prayer for her back - the real reason why she had come on the retreat - and we watched as the Lord moved upon her by the power of the Holy Spirit. So heavy was the anointing of God on her that she could no longer remain upright and she crashed to the floor!

She felt God working on her spine. After some time she got up, removed the heavy plastic tube she had been wearing to immobilise her spine and protect it from further damage, and started practising physical exercises on the floor. God had worked an amazing miracle in her life. The doctors had previously told her that her spine was so damaged that within twelve months she would probably be in a wheelchair and would never walk again!

God had indeed honoured his word. Here was a classic case of the teaching on forgiveness being absolutely essential. Without it she would definitely not have been healed. It seems that her physical conditions were partly a consequence of the bitterness that had controlled her.

Basic Principles

The basic foundational teaching that the Lord gave to us as a preparation for healing and deliverance has been repeated many times on healing retreats and on church visits. It is not new to Ellel Ministries, for it is all contained within the scriptures. This is not the place to give extended detail on such foundations as forgiveness and acceptance - a separate book would be necessary for that. But I outline here the key parts of the teaching which are implicit in the Gospel accounts and which we have found to be so effective in preparing people for healing and deliverance ministry.

1.   Who and what we are before God

I found, much to my amazement, that many people, even though they had been in churches for years, had little or no real understanding about how God created them and how he desires us to function in the world that he created. So the basic information on our creation by God as body, soul and spirit became an integral part of the teaching.

For many sick people it was a profound revelation to realise that their bodily symptoms might have a root in their emotions and that there might just be a connection, for example, between the cruel way in which their father had related to them as a child and the condition they were then experiencing forty years later.

2.   How we can be sick

We can be sick in any or all of the constituents of our created being: body, soul or spirit. The soul also has three main constituents: the mind, the emotions and the will, and again we can be sick in any or all of these. Then we can be sick because of the presence of an evil spirit (demon) which is operating in some area of our life. There are, therefore, six primary ways in which people can be sick.

i)   In the body

Physical illness and sickness of the body is more obviously identifiable. When some part is malfunctioning or damaged through injury, or when we have an infection which, for some reason, our body is unable to fight, then we are said to be ill.

ii)   In the mind

The mind is different from the brain - it is part of the soul. One could have, for example, cancer of the brain, which is a bodily disease, but at the same time be of sound mind. Conversely, there are many people who are remarkably fit physically, with no diseases of the brain, but whose mind is quite out of control. When the functioning of the mind is no longer under the ordered control of the person we would say that he is mentally ill.

iii) In the emotions

Emotions are our feelings. When we are hurt in our emotions then we can either express our hurt rightfully and receive healing for the pain, or the hurt can be repressed causing short-term pain and sometimes long-term damage.

For example, if a girl is sexually abused by her father, the emotional pain is intense (Why does my daddy do things like this to me?). But because of fear of what might happen to her if she 'tells', the pain is usually repressed and not exposed for healing. Long-term emotional damage and demonisation can occur as a result, and this can be devastating. Sometimes the damage does not surface until years later when, for example, the marriage relationship falls apart because of sexual problems.

iv) In the will

Many people are sick because they do not have the strength of will to make wise decisions. They are victims of the condition described in the well-known scripture *"the spirit is willing, but the flesh is weak"* (Matthew 26:41 NASB). Their will is too weak (sick) to either resist the pressures people put on them or overcome the temptations that are put in front of their flesh.

v) In the spirit

The most important healing people need is to have their spiritual relationship with God restored. Outside of a personal relationship with Jesus, the spirit is dead (very sick!) to God because of sin, and the spirit, therefore, needs to be born again. When a person is born again the Holy Spirit can then fill him. It is the Holy Spirit who brings the gifts of healing and gives us the authority to keep demons out after we have been delivered.

I am constantly astonished at the number of people who come to Ellel Grange for help who, in spite of years of church experience, have never really understood the basics of the Gospel. Some have even gone out to the front at evangelistic meetings, taken part in weekly Bible Studies, been regular attenders at church prayer meetings or even been leaders of the church!

It is sometimes through their problems that people realise the consequences of being out of fellowship with God. When they see the connection between life in the Spirit and the consequences in the flesh, it brings home to them their desperate need of really knowing God. To be healed in the spirit, therefore, is the most important and primary healing that anyone needs. Such healing has both eternal and temporal consequences.

vi) Through the presence of a demon

Another way a person can be sick is through the presence of a demon. When I have explained to people about the powers of darkness and the reality of evil spirits, and what they can do in people's lives, I have found that they have generally accepted and understood this possibility far more readily than the theologians who question the existence of demons! For many it is a great relief to realise that there is another possible reason for their condition.

These six ways of being sick are not mutually exclusive. Long-term physical disability will, for example, cause much emotional pain and damage. It is not unusual to find people who are suffering in most, if not all, of these ways. In cases of longer-term illness there is almost always a demonic dimension that has to be dealt with at some point in the ministry. Failure to realise this when ministering healing will leave some people feeling better initially, but still carrying within them the root cause of more potential symptoms and illness.

Understanding the ways people can be sick helps them to appreciate what critical factors may be operating in their lives. We have found that explaining these things right from the beginning of each healing retreat means that people are then far more open to listen to God, realising that what is being said really matters and is relevant to them.

3. The need to forgive others

In the Lord's prayer it is clear that Jesus made the forgiveness of our own sins conditional upon our willingness to forgive the sins of others! In Matthew 6:15 he re-emphasised this teaching by saying *"If you do not forgive others, then your Father (in heaven) will not forgive the wrongs you have done"* (GNB). These are devastating words to the unforgiving and bitter of heart, for no-one likes to be told that their sins will not be forgiven. But that is exactly what Jesus is telling those who are unwilling to give to others what they so clearly need from God for themselves.

Many people would like to think that it doesn't really matter what you believe, or what you do, because God is so loving that he wouldn't withhold forgiveness from you or not allow you to enter the Kingdom of heaven.

Such beliefs, however, are not consistent with scripture, and whilst some would say it is too hard to tell hurting people such uncompromising truth, I would respond by saying it is more harmful not to tell them the truth in love as Jesus clearly demonstrated in his life and teaching.

In practice we have found that sharing truth with deep love and compassion makes it possible for people to both forgive and receive forgiveness. To know that they are forgiven, sometimes for the very first time in their lives, can be the most significant healing experience they will ever have. The relief is profound as the influence of the powers of darkness is broken down through the application of truth.

Many times we have witnessed enormous battles with the resident demonic powers as they have employed every weapon in their armoury to try to prevent a person speaking out forgiveness of an individual who has, for example, abused them sexually. The demons can try to take away the voice so that they can't speak, make them want to escape and physically run away, attack their breathing, introduce distraction after distraction, bring on sudden bouts of diarrhoea, clamp the jaw together, make the person try to strangle themselves (or a member of the ministry team!), in fact, anything to stop Biblical truth being applied.

Once the words of forgiveness have been spoken out, the power of a demon that has been controlling them through the sin of unforgiveness has been broken, and deliverance can then take place. We have probably seen more healing and deliverance take place through applying the principles of forgiveness than through any other spiritual discipline.

It's not that the church hasn't known these basic truths before; it's simply that often they have not had the courage or conviction to tell people the truth as Jesus said it. Some theologians have tried to modify the teaching of Jesus to make it more palatable to the questioning, rational mind. This will never bring people through to healing or deliverance. It is only as the unchanging truths of Jesus and his teaching are applied in a person's life that *"God (can) transform you inwardly by a complete change of your mind"* (Romans 12:2 GNB)!

Jesus kept on coming back to the theme of forgiveness in his own teaching. I personally doubt if it was ever left out of any teaching that Jesus gave. It certainly seems that the Sermon on the Mount is teaching that Jesus gave time and time again on different occasions to different people. There was no need for new teaching until the people had really understood and lived out what had already been taught.

I believe that Jesus talked in greater depth, and about other subjects, privately with the disciples on many occasions, giving them insights on his teaching that the crowds were not ready to receive. Some of these precious moments are recorded in the Gospels, such as when he explained to them the real meaning of the parable of the sower (Luke 8:11-15).

We have found, for example, that when people have been very hurt they can initially make a choice to forgive through an act of their will. But as the Lord continues to bring healing, layers of pain may surface. Some people may find it necessary to keep on forgiving until there is no longer any residual pain associated with the damage.

When Simon asked Jesus how often he needed to forgive, his response of 'seventy times seven' could just as easily relate to forgiving the same person many times for the same offence (when different levels of pain surface) as forgiving someone for a series of different offences.

4. Confession and forgiveness of one's own sins

After unforgiveness of others, hidden and unconfessed sin is probably the greatest guardian of demonic power and sickness. Many hidden sins, that have left a poisoned thread through peoples' lives, go back years and years, even into childhood. Many people are plagued with guilt, secretly believing that these sins, often of a sexual nature, are so awful that they could never be forgiven. 1 John 1:9 is an important and favourite verse to share with those who know they have sinned. *"If we confess our sins to God, he will keep his promise and do what is right: He will forgive us our sins and purify us from all our wrongdoing"* (GNB). This was a word spoken to Christians, so John expected that Christians would fall into sin. They certainly can and do! Fortunately, God in his mercy made adequate provision for our fallen nature. But there are times when the consequences of our sin can leave us sick, or demonised, or both, as well as in need of forgiveness by God.

The scripture in James 5:16 is harder for many Christians to accept than 1 John 1:9. *"Confess your sins to one another, and pray for another, so that you will be healed"* (GNB). Most people like to think that their sins are personal and private and that any confession will be to God alone, thank you very much! It is not easy to tell anyone else what they have done. The shame or embarrassment of it is more than they can stand. And yet in this chapter James paints a cameo of a sick person who calls the elders together to anoint him with oil. Confession of sin takes place before healing occurs.

The implication is that sickness can sometimes be a consequence of sin, and in these cases, if there is to be healing then the sin factor must be resolved first. God can sometimes allow sickness in our life so that he may get our attention and speak to us clearly. God does not send sickness, but it is on occasions allowed as a consequence of both personal sin and the fallen world in which we live. Persistent sin creates a prime entry point for the demonic, and demons often bring with them sickness and infirmity.

We have found in our counselling ministry that to be straightforward about the sins of the past and to allow them to come to the light, without being judgemental, is a vital step in preparing people for deliverance.

Why would God consider this process to be so important?
I believe there are several factors at work here:

a) Every one of us will be blessed by knowing that there is
    at least one person who knows the worst about us and
    still loves us.

b) One of the best deterrents against future sin is the fact
    that someone already knows about our weakness.

c) Healing and deliverance ministry will be strengthened
    by the scriptural principle of two or three agreeing
    together in prayer (Matt. 18:19).

d) Self-deception is not such a danger when another Godly
    and Spirit-filled person knows about the sin and is
    willing to help the person with accountability if
    necessary.

e) Sin is very often at the root of a demonic stronghold
    that is being tackled, and help to overcome this can
    sometimes be needed for deliverance.

f) Other areas of healing are likely to be necessary,
    such as emotional healing.

Whilst God can heal sovereignly without the intervention of a
third party, Jesus instructed the disciples to go and heal the
sick and it is our experience that incisive ministry by someone
else in these areas is usually effective and direct. It also
introduces an objective third party who is able to hear from
the Lord for the sick person.

For example, the rich young ruler needed to be confronted
with the sin of his own heart, in which the love of his wealth
was clearly stronger than his love for God. Sin needs to be
exposed, confessed, repented of and dealt with. Then one can
minister healing and deliverance with much greater
confidence that the ministry will be effective and long-lasting.

It is a privilege and a responsibility to hear someone else's
confession. It is vital that those who are asked to do this

should always be totally confidential, never gossip about other peoples' sins, be totally non-judgemental in their attitudes and have an attitude of humility.

Those traditions which incorporate confession as a regular part of their Christian practice have no problem with this and will readily understand the importance of dealing with sin in this way. But there needs to be a caution here, for if confession becomes too much a part of tradition, as opposed to being a genuine response in the heart to conviction of sin, then the very practice of confession can become a stumbling block to being forgiven and healed!

That may sound hard but the key lies in one's understanding of the word confession. To confess sin to God (or someone else) does not mean to tell God what we have done wrong. The fact of the situation is that God is omniscient (knows all things) and he already knows about our sin! The word 'confess' means something more than just telling God what we've done wrong.

Where there is sin, it must be owned. People need to recognise what they have done and decide how they are going to put situations right where another person has been involved and there have been consequences.

The primary meaning of 'to confess' is to agree with God's verdict on the sin that has been committed, to recognise that its practice has been an act of rebellion against God and to repent of (turn away from) the sinful behaviour. Far too often confession has been treated as something that is 'said' (and not done) just to try to clear the conscience, without there being any real intention of turning away from the continuing practice of that sin.

Jesus taught that we must continue to forgive our brothers till seventy times seven and while this implies he will continue to forgive us in the same way, his heart is grieved by our continuing in wilful sin. There can come a time when our supposed confession is just a religious practice and carries with it the stink of spiritual death as opposed to the seeds of new life! For confession to be real it has to be from the heart.

5. Forgiveness of oneself

Every one of us has made mistakes and some of these have been serious, leaving us scarred in a variety of ways. I often ask people at a meeting to put their hands up if they have ever said to themselves, 'I will never forgive myself for ....' It is always a revelation to people that more than half of those present have at some time or another held themselves in bondage through making such a statement.

It is even possible to place a curse upon ourselves by being in bondage to an experience of the past for which we are unwilling to forgive ourselves. We can effectively give permission to the enemy to hold us to the guilt of what we did.

It is not surprising, therefore, to discover how often we have to deliver people from a spirit of curse which has come in through having such an attitude. Scripture tells us that when Jesus died on the cross *"he redeemed us from the curse of the law by becoming a curse for us"* (Galatians 3:13). The effects of every single curse that the enemy might place upon us was dealt with at Calvary, and if we refuse to forgive ourselves we spurn the provision Jesus made for us on the cross.

Understanding curses and how they work is vital to the deliverance ministry. In essence, a curse is something that is said or done against us or others which gives rights to the demonic to exercise power over people.

Curses can be applied through the malevolence of someone else. It could be through overt witchcraft or, for example, through the hatred in the heart of one person towards another. The words spoken by religious folk against Mary Magdalene for pouring out that precious ointment on Jesus were, in effect, curses. If it wasn't for Jesus' immediate commendation of her action, and his condemnation of her accusers, these curses could have been arrows of guilt in her heart for evermore.

Alternatively, the curse can be self-applied when we choose not to forgive ourselves for something which, if it has been rightfully confessed, God has forgiven. Satan rejoices when we continue to condemn ourselves because of failures in the past. I am sure Jesus saw this danger in Simon Peter after the resurrection. If Jesus had not gone to him and personally re-commissioned him at that point, I have little doubt that

Simon Peter would have finished his life as a bitter, twisted old fisherman plying the fishing grounds of Galilee and wondering what might have been! He would have placed himself under the curse of never having forgiven himself for denying Christ three times before his crucifixion.

Forgiving oneself for the mistakes of the past is a liberating experience which undermines the roots of much demonic power. The deliverance which follows can bring deep healing in areas of the person's life which seem, superficially, to be totally unrelated to such self-cursing. But in reality Satan is no respecter of persons and will use any opening we provide through sin to gain access for the demonic.

6. 'Forgiveness' of God

I have placed the word forgiveness in inverted commas because there is no way that God can sin, and so, in practice there is nothing for which he needs to be forgiven! However, I have met many people who blame God for things that have gone wrong and live out their lives holding him responsible for what was either a consequence of their own or another's sin. More often God is blamed for things that are a product of Satan's current stranglehold on the world.

Where there has been some disaster or personal tragedy, people are often held in bondage by the event. This can become a curse on their lives. The solution is to repent of blaming God for things that were not his responsibility, forgive the real human culprits (if there were any) and to tell Satan that there is no way we are going to let the consequences of any attacks of his be ground for demonic access! The first few chapters of Job are very revealing in this respect. They are a telling commentary on the source of many alleged 'natural' disasters.

7. Acceptance of God as he is

God is God. And no amount of wish fulfilment on the behalf of man will change his character! He always has been and always will be true to himself, his word and the revelation of his nature as seen in his Son, Jesus.

Unfortunately, there are many people who are not happy with God. They construct their own caricature of how God ought to behave and what he ought to be like, and then they worship the God they have constructed in their own minds. This is simply a form of idolatry, where men construct an idol of wood or stone, endue it with certain characteristics, work out a belief system associated with the idol and then live in fear lest they should offend the god they have made with their own hands.

What happens is that a demon takes up residence over the idol, assumes the characteristics that have been imposed upon it by man, and then rewards and punishes the worshippers according to how they appease the demonic demands of the idol, which has now become their god. The individual worshippers then become demonised with a spirit that is under the control of the ruling spirit of the idol.

The Greeks and the Romans, who had so many idolatrous gods, were intelligent people. They would not have been deceived easily into such wholesale idolatry if the demons behind the idols did not work for and against them in this way. If things were going badly for them, it was assumed that they had offended their god and he would need placating with some form of sacrifice, religious routine or gift.

The whole cycle of idolatrous worship as a form of appeasement is totally dominating and destructive to the living relationship that God desires to have with all his people. The 'demands' of God for a price to be paid for man's sinful disobedience were met at Calvary when Jesus died for you and me. There are no more sacrifices, no appeasements that can or should be made. As Jesus said from the cross, *"It is finished!"* (John 19:30).

So when people become religious, often in an attempt to atone for their own sin, they are telling God the Father that his act of supreme love in giving his only Son to die at Calvary was an inadequate sacrifice.

As I see people making renewed pledges to God as a direct consequence of trying to atone for their own sin, I understand more and more how God must hate religion which is simply a cover for a sinful heart that has not found its rest in the living God. The message of Isaiah Chapter 1 has not changed or become out of date!

The issue is far deeper and more fundamental than *"What can I do to make God accept me?"* The issue is one of resting in what God has already done, being motivated by love, not fear, and by an act of one's will, choosing God for who he is and not because one is afraid not to! It's a question of *"Whom do you really love?"*

A man who remains faithful to his wife, or a wife to her husband, only out of fear of what their partner might say or do if their unfaithfulness were ever exposed, is permanently in danger of committing adultery. But a man or woman who truly loves, and is committed to their partner, will find that to be a sure defence against the possibility of unfaithfulness.

The Old Testament describes the people of God as having committed spiritual adultery when they went after other gods. If a person's spiritual heart is not anchored in and by the love of God, then, like a man who is not secure in his wife, he will be prone to wander and worship at the feet of other gods. That is spiritual adultery - giving one's heart to another, thereby false, god. Ultimately, all spiritual adultery is the substitution of demons in the place of the true and living God.

Service of God which is even partly motivated by fear as opposed to love, will always be found wanting when the evil day comes, as Paul assures us it will (Ephesians 6:13). Whilst there is a necessary place for a holy and rightful fear of the living God, if fear is the only motivating factor in the relationship between God and man, then the relationship is unhealthy.

All this may sound a long way removed from the lives of those who are in need of healing through deliverance. But it is much closer to home than many people realise. For example, there are many who have come to us for help who respond with fear and terror when we start talking about God as our loving Father. For them a father is someone who treats you unfairly, cruelly, may abuse you or even punish you for doing nothing.

I well remember the woman who cried out in anguish, *"Don't ever talk to me about God being a father."* There was real venom in her voice. She hated her father, who had done unspeakable things to her. She assumed that if God was a Father, then he would be just like her human father, but a million times worse. She had blackened the loving character of God by projecting onto him the sinfulness of her parental upbringing. The God she worshipped was not someone to whom she could respond in love, but someone from whom she was recoiling in terror and fear. Repentance over her sin in believing that God was like this, forgiveness of her human father and then deliverance from the spirit of 'fear of God' followed by healing were essential stages in the road towards wholeness.

Jesus told the story of the prodigal son (Luke 15:11-32) not so much to show how a sinner can come back to God, but to demonstrate the real character of his Father. I am sure that the crowd who listened to Jesus on that day would have expected the story to include hard words of condemnation for the son when he returned home after such a wicked and wasteful escapade.

But no, the father's arms were open wide and he ran, threw those arms around the son and welcomed him home. That is a very accurate picture of the nature of God the Father. To see him as he really is and run into his arms is one of the most secure and liberating healing experiences.

Others project a character onto God which is basically spiritual make-believe with Christian overtones! They cannot cope, for example, with what Jesus said when answering Thomas's question about the way ahead, *"I am the way and the truth and the life. No one comes to the Father except through me"* (John 14:6). So they succumb to a demonic deception by inventing a God which allows them to think that any sincere spiritual path will eventually lead to heaven. They preach a brand of universalism which is clear heresy, imposing upon God supposed characteristics which are wholly foreign to the scriptures.

Such people need to have been involved in delivering people from the religious spirits that have been in control of these other alleged alternative paths to God. They will then have a very different perspective on whether or not they are of God or the enemy! The venom that can be expressed by the demons when they are exposed has to be experienced to be believed.

There are as many distortions of the character of God as there are heresies and false religions. Without repentance over these attitudes and beliefs, many people will remain locked into demonic strongholds.

One man I ministered to was quite shocked and upset at the demons that were manifesting in him but would not leave. I knew in my spirit that the demons were being given a right by some false belief. He had already renounced the New Age Movement, of which he had been something of a disciple and it was the spirit of the New Age which was mocking both him and me.

Further conversation exposed that, as part of his New Age commitment, he had become a dedicated vegetarian. With regard to eating, Paul makes it quite clear that *"everything that God has created is good; nothing is to be rejected, but everything is to be received with a prayer of thanks"* (1 Tim. 4:4 GNB). Such vegetarianism is, I believe, a deception of the enemy which can lead people into spiritual bondage.

I asked him to renounce vegetarianism. He refused, saying that he didn't think it really mattered. Once more I tried to deliver him, again unsuccessfully. I asked him again, *"Will you renounce vegetarianism?"* By this time he was desperate to be free and made a choice to bring his life wholly into line with God. It was only with great difficulty that he managed to speak out the words of renunciation. The spirit of the New Age then manifested itself and the man was delivered immediately. It was quite a lesson - both for him and for me.

Acceptance of the truth of God's word and the character and nature of God as revealed in scripture and in the life of Jesus is a primary foundation stone on which to build a ministry of healing and deliverance. We cannot play around with heresy and expect God to bless our lives. People who play with fire are likely to get burnt.

8.   Allowing God to accept us

The converse of accepting God as he is, is allowing God to accept us as we are. Salvation is a gift we can only accept, it cannot be earned. The blood of Jesus was shed so that we may be set free. The price paid for our redemption cost God everything he had. The old hymn, 'Just as I am' expresses the theology of the Gospel perfectly.

Whatever our situation, whatever our state, once we have heard and responded to the Gospel, we come to God through Christ Jesus just as we are. There is absolutely nothing that any of us can do to earn a place in heaven or buy our salvation. One of the wonders of the cross is that no-one is excluded from receiving the free gift of God's grace. Only recognition and confession of sin are necessary.

Unfortunately, there are some people who cannot cope with such free grace. They have been used to buying their way through life (anything free must be second rate) or impressing people with their wealth, looks, clothes or personality! They hear the Gospel, recognise they are sinners, look at themselves, see what a spiritual mess they are in and rush off to try to improve their image for God! Such image-improving activity may range from joining the choir to teaching in the Sunday School.

Commendable though such activities may be, if the motive is to try to impress God, then they will count for precisely nothing in his eyes! None of us can make ourselves good enough for him. Another old hymn, usually sung at Easter, also expresses this aspect of the Gospel perfectly:

> *There was no other good enough*
> *To pay the price of sin.*
> *He only could unlock the gate*
> *Of heaven and let us in.*

When it comes to salvation, there is only one thing that impresses God the Father and that's a robe of righteousness, won for us on the cross through the shed blood of Jesus. When people feel compelled to try to make themselves good enough for God because of the shame they feel when they become aware of their sin, it is usually because there is a demonic stronghold in charge. So often we have seen people being held into the bondage of their past by guilt, shame, self-rejection etc. Demonic bondage results and deliverance and emotional healing are then needed.

9. Accepting oneself

God created us as we are and each and every one of us is special to him. Not to accept the person we are and to dislike, or even hate, the personality he gave us is to imply that God made a mistake when making us! That is sin. There are many people in deep need of healing and deliverance for whom the root of their problems is self-rejection.

Self-rejection becomes a curse with enormous consequences. Its outworking is at the root of many types of sickness and causes much insecurity. It is a wide open entry point for the demonic. To reject oneself is a spiritual act (remember that we are primarily spiritual beings to whom God gave a soul, and we are living temporarily in a body). It makes people very vulnerable to demons which can then enter the person's life and give them ways of coping which lock the person into demonic control.

Self-rejection is the outworking of initial rejection from others. It results in much emotional and spiritual distress. Demonic powers will always try to take advantage of those who are vulnerable to deep emotional distress.

Some children are never wanted from the moment of conception. Their spirits can sense the rejection, even in the womb. When they are born they already know they are a nuisance. They reject themselves because deep down they have ceased to believe they should be here at all. They feel that they should never have been born.

Others are born a boy when the parents wanted a girl, or vice-versa. The child senses the disappointment, and if the parents are not willing or are unable to put this right by repenting over their attitude, such children may subsequently reject their own sexuality. This is one of the possible root causes of homosexuality or lesbianism.

Some children are not endowed with the physical build, or natural good looks, or intelligence, or sporting ability that other children seem to have. They sense comparisons being made and start looking at themselves critically and subjectively. They then realise that what they are experiencing is a result of how they are, so they start to reject those aspects of their being that are causing the problems.

In adult life people can be equally cruel in their reactions to the tall, the thin, the fat, the not-so-pretty, and consequential self-rejection becomes a way of life. Others, at the other end of the physical scale can come to reject their physical beauty or shape because of the unwelcome attentions they get which may lead to unhealthy adulation, sexual molestation or even rape.

Whatever the source of self-rejection and however understandable it may be, it still needs confessing as sin. This will then lead to both deliverance of any demons that have gained access and open the person up to the inner healing that is always necessary alongside the ministry of deliverance.

Some will find it very hard to change a lifetime's self-rejective thought patterns and behaviour. For many there will be a false demonic personality to deal with which has taken advantage of the attitude of the heart, to give the individual an identity and significance wholly at variance with God's plans and purposes. Often, these demonic personalities have so interwoven themselves with the real personality that separating out the person from their demons can require very skilful counselling and spiritual discernment.

To come to the correct spiritual understanding of creation, to see that we are spiritual beings whom God chose before the foundation of the world (Eph 1:4), and to recognise that in a fallen world there will be distortions that the enemy has tried to bring about, is a profound spiritual step. Simply to recognise that God had a plan and purpose when he made us and to start, by faith, accepting the person that we are is a foundation stone for ministry which will release the enemy's hold on the many aspects of life in which the demonic can have a field day.

I sometimes ask people to speak out loud something like this:

"I am special. God created me for himself and I thank him for the spirit, soul and body that he gave me. I accept them as a gift from God and repent over all wrong attitudes I have had towards them. I forgive unconditionally every person who has thought, said or done things to or about me that has made me want to reject myself. I dedicate my life afresh to the one who made me and I rejoice in his goodness."

A prayer of this nature, which is said from the heart, is life-changing and very effectively undermines demonic strongholds. To try to cast out demons, without establishing a right foundation for healing, can be a futile exercise.

10. Accepting others

There is a divine law of human nature which applies to all people. 'If you accept others as they are, they become more acceptable. If you reject them, they become more objectionable.' A rejected person is a hurting person. A hurt person will often behave irrationally and lash out at those who reject and hurt them.

But accepting people as they are is never easy. Because of the way relationships have been with certain people in the past, especially if they have said or done unpleasant things to us, accepting them and ceasing to judge them is sometimes a major hurdle. Learning to accept the person who hurts us but to reject the sin involved in their behaviour is an important step towards remaining whole in the future.

Jesus encouraged us not to judge, criticise or condemn others (Matthew 7:1). This does not mean you have to condone behaviour which is totally unacceptable, but it does mean that you must still act in a loving way towards them in spite of their behaviour! Jesus went on to warn in verse 2 that *"God will judge you in the same way as you judge others, and he will apply to you the same rules you apply to others."* (GNB)

So, what happens in the demonic realm if we start criticising and judging people instead of accepting them?

Firstly, because of our sinful attitude, we open ourselves up to doing the enemy's work of being an accuser, so that in time we will become known as a person with a critical spirit. Our cooperation with the enemy invites a demon to overlay our personality with its particular characteristics and job function!

The presence of a demon must never become an excuse for sin. We all have freewill to choose, and no matter how much pressure a demon may apply there will always be a way out of the temptation if we want to look for it. The key lies in the disposition of our will. But it will be a struggle to be set free without real repentance and deliverance.

Secondly, we become potential agents for Satan and start firing his darts for him. When people are hurt by our cutting remarks, and the hurt is not properly dealt with, then unwittingly we can become the agent of demonic transference and an evil spirit can gain access to the person we have unfairly criticised.

Many marital relationships founder because one partner continuously makes comments, either directly or through looks or innuendoes, which are critical and judgemental of their spouse. This can go on for years until the criticised and judged partner can stand it no longer and appears to leave very suddenly. But in reality the marriage had probably been over for years, dealt hundreds of tiny death blows with the eyes or the tongue. Outsiders are rarely aware of the poisoned arrows which have finally destroyed the relationship.

Unwarranted critical attitudes are a subtle form of manipulation and control - 'If you do what I want then you won't be hurt by my comments'. No-one would actually say that in a relationship, but that is the underlying manipulative threat. Such control is as witchcraft (1 Samuel 15:23), for it is rebellion against God's plan and purpose for mankind and destroys the sense of free will that God has given to each one of us as his precious gift.

Thirdly, a critical and judgemental spirit is like the worst kind of infectious diseases - very catching. Once wrongful comments have been made in the life of a church, gossip often takes over, others join in, and before very long a spirit of criticism becomes a ruling spirit in the fellowship. It is very significant that the scripture says, *"See to it that ... no bitter root grows up to cause trouble and defile many."* (Heb. 12:15). Gossip spreads like a bush fire and is wholly destructive of Spirit-filled Christianity. Resolution of such a situation requires corporate repentance, cleansing and spiritual warfare.

Failure to accept others as they are has devastating long term consequences, both on the perpetrators and the victims. The family relationship in which most harm is done through such wrongful attitudes is that between parents and their children and children and their parents. If lack of acceptance of certain individuals is a real problem, then it is unlikely that the person will be able to receive healing or deliverance.

11. The Lordship of Jesus Christ

There are many, many people who are in desperate need. They want to be healed. They have symptoms that control their lives and they will do anything to get rid of them. It comes as quite a shock to some to discover that, in ministry, we are sometimes more concerned about their personal relationship with Jesus than about their symptoms!

That is not to say that we are not interested in their condition - we are, desperately. But we have learnt from experience that the most important healing that anyone can ever have is healing in the spirit, through having a personal relationship with God. Continued weakness in this area will have consequences in every other part of the being and whilst healing of symptoms is important, spiritual wholeness is an essential step towards remaining healed.

When Jesus said, *"I am the way and the truth and the life. No one comes to the Father except through me"* (John 14:6), he was not arrogantly projecting himself, but in the simplest possible way telling us of God the Father's plans for the restoration of a rightful relationship between the Father and his children.

When it comes to living in fellowship with God day by day, there is only one question that really matters, *"Who is Lord of your life?"* Sadly, there are many Christians who have never grasped the significance of this question. They have no problem in believing that Jesus is the Son of God, that he died and rose again from the dead, that he ascended to glory, sent the Holy Spirit upon the church and one day is coming again as King of Kings and Lord of Lords.

However, the reality of day-to-day living under the Lordship of Jesus Christ is often quite a different story. Anyone can sing the song 'He is Lord', but the key is to mean every word of it, for that is exactly what he is - Lord of all. God has given each of us free will with which to make choices. Whilst Christians know that Jesus **is** Lord of All, they also have to choose to invite Jesus to be Lord of each and every area of their being - body, mind, emotions, will and spirit. For many, failure to let Jesus be Lord is the root of all their problems. An ungodly way of life has led them into situations which have subsequently created havoc in their lives.

So a starting point for much of the counselling and prayer for healing and deliverance which we conduct has to be the very simple question, *"Are you willing to make Jesus Lord?"* For if Jesus truly is Lord, then there is no blockage to the flow of the Holy Spirit, and the way is open for the deliverance of any evil spirits whose rights are undermined by Jesus becoming Lord. Many people are in need of deliverance ministry simply because they have not been willing to give him the rightful place in their lives.

Many people ask me questions such as, *"How can I be filled with the Holy Spirit?"* I usually answer by asking them a question, *"Who is Lord of your life?"* For if Jesus truly is Lord, then the Holy Spirit will rejoice to fill them to overflowing, but if there are areas of their lives where Jesus is not Lord, then they are likely to have problems experiencing the fullness of the Spirit of God. (Remember also that some people who have problems feeling the presence of the Holy Spirit may also be in deep need of emotional healing. For if the emotions have been damaged by the hurts of others, they may have so many walls around their emotions that they cannot feel anything at all, let alone the Holy Spirit!)

Many religious people find that their practice of religion becomes Lord of their life and not the living Lord Jesus Christ; and that they have unknowingly submitted themselves to the control of religious spirits, from which they will need deliverance before they can truly know the indwelling power of God.

The Lordship of Jesus Christ is the single most important issue that those in need have to resolve. That is why in every healing service I conduct I include an opportunity for people to confess their desire for him to be Lord of their lives. There really is no other worthwhile foundation for life! (1 Cor. 3:11).

In Conclusion

The teaching that is helpful to those in need of healing and deliverance is simply the fundamental truth of the Gospel. But it must be presented in a way that helps people to see the significance of what is being said. When these issues are faced and dealt with in peoples' lives, we can expect to see God move in great power on those who come to him through Jesus.

Chapter 3

Some Observable Symptoms of Possible Demonisation

One of the dangers of writing this chapter is that the uninformed will try to use it as a guide to other people's demons. It is not intended for such use! But I do want to share from the extensive experience that the Ellel Ministries team has had over the years in bringing healing through deliverance to many hundreds of people. Real life observations, the accuracy of which have subsequently been demonstrated through effective ministry, will help counsellors confront the demonic and bring healing to those for whom they pray.

In using the information in this chapter, however, please ensure that you do not reach conclusions about any one person just on the basis of the information you read here. It is absolutely vital in counselling a person that you listen both to their story and to the Lord for yourself. God intends you to use the gift of discerning of spirits and not to depend solely on what you read in books! In most cases there will be more to deal with than just the demonic. It is vital to assess deeper healing needs, especially ones that are rooted in the emotions, as well as the effect of demons.

There is some overlap between this chapter and the next. This is deliberate. The two chapters approach similar material from different viewpoints. In this chapter we look at some of the things which can be directly observed in a counsellee and which can be attributed to the presence of the demonic. In the next chapter we look at the different routes through which the demons are able to enter.

This chapter is not intended to be a comprehensive dictionary of all observable symptoms. It is simply a guide to those most commonly seen. The sections have been arranged alphabetically and no significance should be attached to the order in which the material is presented.

1. Addictions

One of the hallmarks of demonic activity is behaviour that is out of control. This is especially true with regard to the intake of addictive substances.

Once a person is unable to modify his behaviour through free will choice it is clear that control is no longer in his own hands. Chemically addictive substances (such as nicotine and drugs) require more of the same in order to maintain the chemical cycles in the body that have been initiated through first taking them. Treating the body in this way is rebellion against the Holy Spirit, whose temple the body is (1 Cor 6:19). Rebellion opens the door for the demonic, which then further holds the person into the addiction.

Freedom from addiction requires repentance over mistreating the body, exercising the will in wanting to be healed, deliverance from any demons that have gained access through the addiction and a disciplined lifestyle from then on.

Similar considerations apply to the excess intake of substances which, in themselves, are not chemically addictive in moderation. Alcohol, chocolate, sugar, sweets, etc. would fall into this category.

For many people who have become addicted, the root cause lies much deeper than the superficial addiction. Their addictive behaviour can be a form of compensation for underlying problems which also need attention. If, for example, the deeper need is to be healed of the rejection that a boy has experienced from his father, it will not be enough just to minister healing for the addiction. Unless the parental problem is dealt with, the boy will be just as vulnerable either to further addictions or to some other form of behaviour which, at its root, is a cry for help.

The underlying needs of the addicted must be carefully assessed in order to bring full healing. Equally, however, if the demonic dimension is ignored in this healing process it is not generally possible for someone to come through the other side of an addictive problem.

2. Appetites out of balance

A healthy diet and appetite are important foundations for healthy living. Failure to look after the body that God has given us is rebellion against the Holy Spirit. The most common eating disorders are anorexia and bulimia - in the former the person eats the bare minimum of food and gradually wastes away. With bulimia the person may appear to be eating normally but then, in private, will frequently induce vomiting to get rid of the food before it can be absorbed into the body's system. Bulimics also commonly binge on food in private before vomiting.

Both of these eating disorders are a form of rebellion - ultimately against the body. There is usually an emotional root, but in order to bring healing, one must also deal with the demonic strongholds that have gained access. The rebellion, which may have given the demonic access, is usually against someone else, such as mother or father, and is often an attempt to punish the parents for some real or perceived ill-treatment. This is distinct from either meanness or greed - both of which can be demonic strongholds leading to either undereating or overeating.

Additionally, people may be very overweight because they eat for comfort. They are not overeating out of greed, but such is their emotional state that they eat to hide the pain they are feeling on the inside.

Another demonic stronghold which can control eating has its roots in sexual abuse of females - especially if a girl has been abused at or about puberty when her physical sexuality was starting to develop. She may then associate an attractive body with vulnerability to being abused. She hates the abuse and makes the decision either to overeat so as to be very overweight, ugly and unattractive to an abuser, or to undereat so that she becomes anorexic, her periods go into remission and her sexual features fail to develop. Such decisions may not be conscious but made just at a subconscious level.

Eating disorders which are allergic reactions to specific substances are of a different nature. The body is unable to absorb certain otherwise normal substances without producing a bodily reaction with unpleasant, and sometimes life-threatening symptoms. Medical treatment focuses on the chemical reactions involved but it is important to question what has caused the condition.

Many allergic conditions are present at birth; therefore these conditions are likely to have been inherited from one of the parents. The question then has to be asked as to whether there is any sin on the generation line which has given rights to the demonic, resulting in spirits of infirmity being able to cause the allergy. We have found, for example, where there has been witchcraft on the generation line, especially with regard to the use of potions and remedies with an occult dimension, that there can be a demonic curse generating the condition which manifests as an allergy.

3. Behaviour extremes

God is a God of variety! One look at creation confirms the enormously varied nature of the created order. There are billions of people on the face of the earth, but no two either look alike or have identical giftings or interests. Within this enormous variety of people there are ranges of behaviour which are acceptable expressions of their differences, but there is also behaviour which is beyond the limits of acceptability.

God made people to co-exist in meaningful relationships. Satan will always try to oppose God's plan and purpose, so it is not surprising that one of Satan's tactics is to try to push people to extremities so that their behaviour is unacceptable to others and they then become isolated from and rejected by society. Or, in the context of the local church, they become fringe members who are not really in fellowship with others.

There are many behaviour patterns of this nature which tend to alienate people from friends and neighbours. In most cases there is a demonic dimension to this behaviour. Where demons are either responsible, or partly responsible, in this way, they will usually have ridden in on either a relationship that has gone wrong, or be a consequence of generational sin.

4. Bitterness and unforgiveness

Jesus highlighted the importance of forgiveness throughout his teaching. He went further than saying it was important - he categorically stated that if we are not willing to forgive others for the things they have done to us, then his Father in heaven would not forgive us for the things we have done (Matthew 6:15). These are some of the most salutary words in the whole of the Bible.

When people realise the importance of forgiveness and understand the significance of Jesus' words, they usually want to forgive even those who may have terribly abused them, realising that the abuser's behaviour is often a result of the way they themselves had been treated. But once the decision to forgive has been made, the battle with the emotions begins. Working through the pain of feelings that have been damaged by the hurts and abuse of others is not easy.

When someone understands the necessity to forgive but then finds it impossible to make the choice, one has to ask whether or not there is a spirit of unforgiveness or bitterness that is holding the person in bondage. Without an understanding of deliverance ministry it would be impossible to release such people into the healing that begins with forgiving those who have hurt us.

5. Compulsive behaviour patterns

By 'compulsive behaviour patterns' I am referring to the compulsive repetition of otherwise normal activities. Hand-washing or checking that the doors are locked or the gas is turned off are typical examples. People who do such things want to be rid of the habit; there is rarely any question of a person thinking that what they are doing is either acceptable or tolerable. They usually feel cursed by the condition, and in practice that is almost always what they are!

One lady wanted to be free of the compulsion to wash her hands up to twenty times a day. Her whole family was affected by her behaviour. She had no idea why she did it. As we prayed and asked the Holy Spirit to expose the root of the problem, she suddenly looked terribly afraid. As we looked at her, we saw the eyes of a child being terrified by the opening of her bedroom door in the middle of the night.

The memories, which had been totally buried through the trauma of that night, came flooding back. She remembered the lodger coming toward her, forcing her out of the bed and masturbating himself into her hands. He then fled, making threats against her if she ever told anyone, and left her with her hands covered in semen.

She went to the bathroom and tried to wash her hands, but she couldn't get rid of the smell, no matter how hard she scrubbed. So she kept on washing and no-one knew why. Forty years later she was still washing, compelled by the demons that had come in during that moment of extreme fear and trauma. Deliverance led to healing of the behaviour pattern, which began the journey towards complete healing from other consequences of the abuse as well. Wherever there are compulsive behaviour patterns such as this, one is coming up against demons. Compulsion is a hall-mark of the demonic.

6. Deceitful personality and behaviour

Deception is a trademark of Satan. People fall into temptation when they have been deceived. We all have freewill, however, and the capacity to make rightful choices. When people learn that by telling lies or being deceitful in their behaviour they can get away with sin and get their own way, they may then make a conscious choice to use deception as a matter of course.

At that point, in effect, they invite a spirit of deception to help them. When that person seeks help later in life, the counsellor will need to be very discerning to separate out truth from lies. For such is the depth of this deception that the person may not even know themselves whether or not they are telling the truth. Until the spirit of deception has been dealt with, healing and deliverance is very unlikely to occur.

One man I ministered to began to tell lies at school to get himself out of trouble. He found it worked and he continued to tell so many lies that he found himself telling lies even when the truth would not have got him into trouble. Years later the process of healing could only begin when he faced up to what he had done as a child and forgave the parents who had put him into such fear of punishment that he looked for a way out. The demon that came in at that point had controlled him for a generation.

7. Depression

Depression is a broad term which covers a wide range of behavioural symptoms. For some it manifests as an all-embracing blackness from which there seems no escape. For others it results in a total lack of motivation to do anything, loss of appetite, erratic sleep patterns or inability to concentrate. And still others are affected by either the seasons or the weather. During the summer they are fine, but in wintertime they might as well not be alive. Some people appear to be more vulnerable to depression, particularly artistic or sensitive people who may not have any way of discharging their creativity.

It may seem as though there is no obvious cause and that the only solution is temporary or permanent medication. But there always is a cause, even though for some the origin may lie in the sins of previous generations or in the attitude of someone else towards them.

It would be wrong to give the impression that depression always has a demonic origin. It doesn't. More often than not the root is in the emotions or in damaged relationships. But I have yet to come across a person who suffers regularly from depression who is not also affected by the demonic. Once the damage has been done to the emotions, the person is very vulnerable to demonisation and then being controlled by demons who will, unknown to him, hold him into the symptoms. Usually there is a network of different spirits affecting the mind as well as the emotions.

When someone is depressed in this way, all relationships become hard, none more so than the relationship with God. Depressed people need to be understood in this respect, for there are many who have been further depressed by the naive 'pull yourself together' and 'take it to the Lord in prayer' camp. What has been said by friends, with a supposedly good motive, has only served to make them feel guilty about not having any desire to read their Bible or spend time praying or about the lack of joy in their lives.

Unfortunately, the standard medical treatment for depression involves varying degrees of medication which have the dual effect of controlling the depressive symptoms and making it very hard to minister to the person when they are so controlled by the effect of the drugs. It is much easier to pray with people for healing when you don't have to battle through a chemical screen.

Seasonal depression is known to be associated with the excess of melatonin, the production of which is suppressed by light. Treatment involves providing additional light to the sufferer during the winter months. However, it is interesting to consider whether or not there might be a demonic curse in operation, which causes the excess melatonin in the body. Certainly there seems to be some evidence that a demonic link has been passed down the generation line through ancestral worship of the sun or some other aspect of the seasons, and that the depression is a curse which has been given rights through the idolatry involved.

Ministering to depressed people requires patience and discernment as the roots of the condition are slowly and lovingly exposed and, step by step, God brings both healing and deliverance.

8. Emotional disturbance

We all have feelings. God gave us emotions so that we can both express those feelings and enjoy every aspect of human living. Emotions can get out of balance and damaged through the relationships and circumstances of life. There are some people whose emotional responses never seem to be right. They may be either excessively expressed, be quite inappropriate for the situation or appear to be completely absent.

For example, a person may sob their heart out over what others consider to be a trivial matter, or, at the other end of the scale, be totally unmoved by something traumatic. Whilst demonic involvement is not usually the primary cause of the emotional condition, it would be unusual for there not to be some powerful demonic hold over the emotions which entered through the distress that caused the original situation.

9. Escapism

When people run away it is not always they themselves that are doing the running! Many times in meetings, where there has been a powerful anointing of the Holy Spirit, individuals have not been able to stay in the meeting. Sometimes they have had to hang on to their chairs to stay as long as possible, but suddenly it becomes too much for them and something snaps inside. They get up and run. Escaping in this way is usually not the will of the person but the will of the demons inside the person who are struggling to stay in control when the person is under such a heavy anointing of God.

The person is not generally aware of what is happening and it is usually quite a relief for them to learn that there is the possibility of an alien will from demonic powers affecting them so that they are unable to stay in the meeting. Sometimes people have said they have struggled for years with this sort of thing without having any understanding as to why. Similar feelings are experienced by some people at communion services. They are physically quite incapable of either going up to the front of the church to receive communion or staying in the seat if they are in a church whose tradition it is for the bread and wine to be brought to them. Such strong reactions to communion usually indicate that somewhere in their own lifetime or on their ancestral lines there has been some involvement in either witchcraft or satanism.

Whilst physical escape from Christian meetings is very real, there is another form of escape which can also have strong demonic power behind it. Individuals may 'escape' into themselves, into a hobby, into watching television, soaps, reading novels - to name but a few! Once absorbed in their chosen escape they become almost immune to the presence of other people.

Such behaviour is frequently evidence of a serious relationship breakdown which has not been acknowledged. The participants cope by so absorbing themselves in their escapist activity that the need to face up to the pain of the relationship is kept well-buried. This is a classic way of coping with marriage problems.

Superficially, one might see this as simply a matter of resolving the relationship issues. But once a married couple have opted for mutual co-existence, as opposed to a Godly marital relationship, they have walked away from God's best for them. Satan rejoices to see marital relationships either being less than God intended or, ultimately, failing.

Once the partners in the relationship have opted for division, Satan has been given rights and the demonic then reinforces the division by driving one or both of the partners into their own escapist activities. If one or other wants to try to sort it out, they not only come up against their own and their partner's pain, but also against the demons that have a vested interest in keeping the couple apart.

It has been interesting to observe from time to time that some people who behave like this within the close confines of a marital relationship can be radically different people in a different environment with different people. The escapist behaviour seems to fly out of the window when opportunities for painless relationships are possible. It is not in Satan's interest to have people working through their own difficulties and receiving healing, so he ensures that they enjoy themselves with other people when they are apart and retreat into their own shells when they are together.

10. Fears and phobias

Fear is a gift of God. It keeps us from doing things that would be harmful to us. Without Godly fear very few people would survive childhood, such are the risks and dangers that we all face day by day. But as with every good gift of God, Satan will seek to distort the truth and hold us into the bondage of error. When we have a frightening experience, Satan will seek to hold us into the trauma of that experience by using it as an entrance gate for the demonic.

When someone is controlled by irrational fear, and there are many hundreds of different fears which Satan uses in this way, there is almost always a demonic stronghold behind the manifesting behaviour. Jesus is described as perfect love, and the scripture tells us that perfect love casts out fear. It is only in the name of Jesus that the fear Satan would want to control our lives with can be broken and cast out.

It is truly amazing to see the difference in people's lives when the fear that has been controlling them (often for most of their lives) has been cast out and they are free to be themselves. I have seen people healed so that they are suddenly able to drive again, fly in an aircraft, face up to someone they were frightened of, eat food which they had previously associated with some frightening experience, have sexual intercourse again with their husband or wife and many, many more similar things. Christians have a tremendous responsibility to minister the healing love of Jesus into people's lives, so that fear is no longer the god which determines their life pattern and behaviour.

11. Guilt and self-condemnation

When sin has been confessed and forgiven then there is no need for the sinner to remain guilty. If a person continues to feel guilty after the sin has been rightfully dealt with, then it is likely that he has been vulnerable to a spirit which is holding him into feelings of guilt and condemnation. Separating out the demonic counterfeit from real feelings is not easy.

Satan does not want Christians to walk in the experience of forgiveness through the work of the cross. If Christians feel forgiven, they will then behave as if they are forgiven, and that makes them powerful witnesses for the Gospel. So Satan will do all he can to hold people into the experiences of sin through the overlay of demonic counterfeit feelings.

It should also be noted that if someone refuses to forgive himself for what he has done, then he opens the door to the demonic in such a way that almost endless feelings of guilt and self-condemnation are inevitable consequences.

12. Hearing voices

Hearing voices is far more common than most people realise. Many who suffer from this have been reluctant to own up to having the symptoms for fear of being labelled mentally ill. I am not referring here to dreams in which people have transitory experiences of someone speaking out in their sleep, but the ongoing experience of having a voice speaking things into their mind very regularly. For some people the voice never seems to stop.

Whenever these symptoms are prevalent there is a spiritual dimension to the condition. In some cases it may be that there is a strong soul-tie to someone who, knowingly or unknowingly, is impressing their thoughts and words on the person who hears the voice. Even when this happens it is only possible through the involvement of demonic power.

Counselling to investigate whose voice it might be that is constantly or regularly heard will help to determine which soul-ties need to be broken before deliverance can take place. Some people hear more than one voice, and for them each voice will probably need to be tackled separately. The peace and silence that people enter into after deliverance is almost unbelievable for them to experience. It's a miracle - the miracle of the work of the Cross in overcoming the power of the enemy.

13. Hereditary illnesses

When a patient experiences major symptoms the doctor will usually ask if any other member of the family has ever suffered in a similar way. They are looking for medical clues in the generation line which will help them with their diagnosis and treatment of the patient. I ask a similar question but with a different objective.

Remembering the scriptures which remind us that the sins of the fathers are visited on the children (Exodus 20:5, Lamentations 5:7) encourages me to realise that when a sickness appears to have passed down the generation line, what is actually being passed down may be the spirit which has induced the symptoms in each generation. We have seen very significant deliverance and healing take place as we have confronted these powers and as the people involved have forgiven their ancestors for whatever it was they did which gave rights to the demonic to come down the line.

Whilst the idea may be foreign and even repugnant to some theologians and medical practitioners, the hard experience of past years lends ample evidence to the belief that spirits of infirmity can come down the generation line and cause sickness in this way. Conditions ranging from rhinitis (an acute form of sinusitis), which a lady had for 25 years, to double kidney failure have been totally healed through deliverance of the spirit of infirmity which had come down from the ancestors and was causing the condition in the present generation. Wherever there is evidence that a condition has been prevailing in a family line, the possibility of such spirits being present must be seriously considered.

When people die, demons don't! They are spiritual beings without a home of their own and they will simply try to occupy another human being to continue their job function. Through sin they are given rights to the children and the children's children so that the most likely recipients of demons, following death, are members of the family involved.

14. Heretical beliefs

Satan is not just behind false religions. He is also at work within Christian denominations to spread false understanding of the Gospel and to encourage divergent views of the truth and ultimately heretical beliefs. Once people have accepted unscriptural beliefs, they are then vulnerable to receive a spirit which will hold them into the false belief and blind their eyes to the truth - just as Satan blinds the minds of unbelievers so that they cannot see the light of the Gospel (2 Cor. 4:4).

In this ministry we have found it of vital importance not to depart from the foundational truths of God's word. It is only through adhering to the truth that we are able to discern where there is deception at work. There are many occasions when we have spoken out truth in a ministry and the demons from inside the person have commented sarcastically with words like, *"We know that's true, but he doesn't believe it, and he is giving us the rights to stay!"*

Demons have a very acute understanding of what is truth and what is error. Equally they have a very precise understanding of the truth of God's word and know that when people don't believe it, they are given rights to lead the person into deception.

Once a person has fallen for deceptive beliefs, especially about the foundational tenets of faith, the authority of the word of God and the work of the Holy Spirit, they are then very vulnerable to further demonisation which will control their mind and their understanding. We have begun to see how hardness of heart towards the Lord in one generation, as a result of deceptive beliefs, can have the effect of producing physical heart conditions in succeeding generations.

Whilst there may be obvious medical reasons why a heart condition has developed, one has to ask the question where those obvious medical conditions came from. This is an area where I believe there is much understanding that God will bring to the church as Christians are obedient to the commission of Jesus to go and heal the sick and cast out demons. We have begun to see how the words of Leviticus have a very real meaning in the present day, where it says that the consequences of breaking the covenant will include experiencing *"sudden terror, wasting diseases and fever that will destroy your sight and drain away your life"* (Lev. 26:16).

15. Involvement in false religions

Satan was thrown out of heaven because he wanted to take for himself the worship which was rightfully due to God. Pride in himself led to his fall from grace and glory. As god of this world, he continues to seek out those who will worship him, but with the exception of overt satanists, who know exactly what they are doing, Satan has worked a major deception on the whole of mankind by initiating a plethora of religions, each with its own belief system and behavioural code.

In spite of the fact that Jesus made it very clear that there is only one way to the Father and that he is the way, the truth and the life (John 14:6), the proponents and followers of other belief systems also think they are right, or else they would not make such deep commitments to the tenets of their faith. The claims of Jesus Christ, however, stand unique above every pretender to the throne of truth, for no other founder of a world religion has ever claimed to be God and then demonstrated the truth of his claim by his words and actions.

Behind every false religion there is a demonic power seeking to enmesh the worshippers in its hold. When people have been involved in deception, even in a passing way, then they have laid themselves open to receiving a demon which will hold them into the deception they have embraced. Whilst a person may be converted to Christianity through the preaching and teaching of the word of God, deliverance following repentance is the only way that a person can be healed of the consequences of the idolatry which every false religion entails.

16. Irrational behaviour

When a person behaves quite normally most of the time, but every now and again breaks out with irrational and unacceptable behaviour, there has to be a reason for the conduct. The husband of one woman I ministered to only behaved in this way once. Early in their marriage, which was of nearly twenty years standing, she had burnt some food and served up a meal which he found unacceptable. Any normal husband would have made light of the matter and had a good laugh about the situation as he encouraged his wife. Not him - he lost his temper in a quite bizarre way, threatening her with all sorts of things if she ever did anything like that again.

She was traumatised by the experience and from that moment on never put a foot wrong. The spirit of fear she had received ensured that she always did everything her husband wanted. The spirit of fear was controlled by the spirit of domination in her husband, so that the husband never needed to display his temper again. The spirit of fear did the job for him. Everyone at the church, all their friends and their neighbours thought he was a model husband, she was a model wife and they had a perfect Christian marriage.

In practice it was a sham of a marriage held together by fear arising out of the one outburst of irrational behaviour from a husband who did not understand anything about love. The husband had his own needs, but there was no way in which he was going to let anyone get near enough to help him. His wife just had to suffer the dreadful consequences of a lifetime that was spent meeting his wants and never daring to step out of line.

Outbursts of irrational behaviour are usually powered by the demonic. But they will also have a root, often long buried, in the hurts and pains of the past, or even in the ancestral line.

17. Lack of mature relationships

Some people find it very hard to maintain mature adult relationships. Frequently they behave in very childish ways and their adult peers tend to be similar people who, to some extent or other, are locked into experiences of childhood.

This book is not the place to discuss in any depth the problems associated with what some people refer to as ministry to the inner child. What is being dealt with is broken-ness of the personality that can occur during the traumas of abusive childhood experiences. Understanding this specialised ministry is beyond the scope of the pages of this book. But it needs to be stated here that what these people experience is real and not imaginary. In our experience there has always been a demonic dimension to such situations, but it would be unwise to launch into deliverance ministry without reaching a deep understanding of what it is that has caused the broken-ness in the first place, otherwise much damage could be caused to already broken people.

A different aspect of immature relationships is typified by the person who never seems to be real. You never quite know who you are talking to, or whether or not you have ever known the real person! They can even have a different voice for different occasions. Usually, where the different aspects of personality are well developed there is quite a complex demonic stronghold behind each deceptive behaviour pattern. At the root of the person's problem will usually be some fairly major reason to enter into deception in order either to cover something up, or to behave according to the expectation of others.

If a child is not acceptable to his parents unless he behaves in a certain kind of way, then the child is under pressure to perform, even though the required behaviour is inconsistent with his God-given giftings and personality. Once the pattern has been established, repeating the trick for a variety of circumstances in adult life is not difficult. Once again, healing is a mixture of healing from the consequences of the past and deliverance in the present.

18. Legalism and spiritual bondage

Jesus reserved some of the harshest words in the Bible for the Pharisees - the religious leaders of his day who knew the law upside down and back-to-front as well as the right way round! He called them whited sepulchres, indicating that for all their religion they might as well be dead. They burdened people with the fine details of the law, but their hearts were a million miles away from having a meaningful relationship with God.

Pharisaism is not dead, only today we call it legalism. The same spirit drives the legalists of today that drove the Pharisees of yesterday. Paul summed it up succinctly when he said *"The letter kills but the Spirit gives life"* (2 Cor. 3:6).

It is a similar spirit which places the dictates of a denomination above the Lordship of Jesus. Whilst none of the denominational leaders would perhaps not see they are doing that, when you place equally sincere leaders from radically different denominations side by side, and realise that they are saying very different things with equal conviction, it is not hard to see that they can't all be right! Satan loves division, and if he can turn Christians against each other through the requirements of a legalistic spirit, he will have succeeded in insulating the church from the dynamic of Holy Spirit life.

Many local churches are locked into tradition, another manifestation of the bondage of legalism. *"This is how we've always done things, and we don't intend to change!"* has been the stone against which many an enterprising young minister has stumbled and lost his vision. The curse of tradition ensures that the spark of real spiritual life, through which God is always doing new things, never gets fanned into a flame.

When dealing with demons we have to remember that they can operate over a group of people just as easily as in and through one person. A local church fellowship needs to question when it is experiencing opposition whether there is some aspect of its history that needs to be repented of and dealt with. It may just be that the battle is with spirits of death (the curse of legalism) which have been given rights through the legalism of previous leaders of the church.

19. Nightmares

When we sleep we slip into the subconscious. During those night-time hours we are not fully in control of all that happens in our minds and it is important for Christians, before they go to sleep, to ask the Lord to guard their mind and keep them from the attacks of the evil one. The Lord's prayer is particularly relevant at this time, *"Lead us not into temptation, but deliver us from the evil one"* (Matthew 6:13).

A nightmare is a dream which brings with it fear, panic or frustration. Frequently people wake up from a nightmare in a state of distress and it can then take some time before they are able to return to sleep. Some nightmares are recurring in nature or subject. Invariably, when there is some regular pattern to the nightmare, the scenes are being gener-ated by demons who, when the defences are down during sleep, push up into the subconscious and cause distress to the person.

The source of the nightmares could be trauma, abuse or some frightening experience of early childhood. The actual incident is often not accessible to the conscious mind, but the demons which gained access through the incident never forget how they got in and whenever they are able will try to distress the person.

Sometimes nightmares are caused by demons that gained access to the mother or the father and have passed down into the children. Sometimes children will tell of nightmares that couldn't possibly relate to anything that has happened in their own lifetime, but the events described are very real, and from an earlier age. Demons don't forget! And when they gain access to the succeeding generations through the sins of the fathers, they will continue to re-live the route through which they gained access, in whoever they happen to be at the time.

Deliverance of the spirit that is causing the nightmare is a necessary part of healing when there is a demonic dimension to dreams and nightmares. Sleeping pills are not the answer!

20. Occultic involvement

The word 'occult' means hidden. What is most hidden in the occult is that Satan is the one being worshipped through all occultic activities. For some people the fascination of occult things draws them towards one form of occultic activity after another. And once the door is open to one practice, it is but a short step to experimenting with whatever may come along next. One of the appendices to this book is a *Glossary of Occult Terms*.

Behind each of these practices is demonic power, despite the conviction of practitioners that they are dealing with a neutral power, or worshipping the living God through their own particular favoured channel. Satan has power, and he does use it to draw people into his control. That is why things definitely happen when people get involved with the occult. The fact that something spiritual happens does not mean that it is of God. Scripture warns us that the days will come when even some of the very elect might be deceived. We have been warned that Satan can come as an 'Angel of light' to make us think that we are in touch with God.

When people have been involved with the occult, it is absolutely essential for them to make a total renunciation of every demonic power that has influenced, controlled or occupied them through their involvement. In Paul's day, those who had books of magic had to burn them (Acts 19:19). Destruction of occult objects, associated with whatever practice people have dabbled in, is an important part of repentance. If someone is not willing to get rid of their occult objects, one has to suspect the reality of their confession.

Deliverance is vital, otherwise people's experience of Christianity will always be coloured by their experiences in the occult. They will slot Jesus and the work of the Holy Spirit into an occult framework, so for them Jesus will be like the manifestation of a demon whom they can use for their own ends. In practice the demons use the people but occultists believe they are controlling and using the power, being mostly unaware of the demonic dimension.

21. Out-of-control tongue

James talked about the tongue as a fire that is in danger of getting out of control! When demons speak during ministry they use the tongue. At times like that it is easy to spot the demonic activity. It is much harder to discern when demons are speaking out through the tongue of a person during normal conversations. Our experience indicates that this is far more common than people realise.

If a demon wants to influence others, it can only do so through the speech or the behaviour of the person it is in. James described the wisdom of this world as being demonic (James 3:15), and when we remember that it is Satan who, for the time being, is god of this world, it is not hard to understand the thrust of James' argument.

I have often heard in Christian meetings, especially church council meetings, a voice which has spoken out with what seems to be wisdom. But, at the same time, I have had a sick feeling in the pit of my stomach. It has been the wisdom of this world trying to divert the people of God away from the plans and purposes of God. We must be on our guard against the voice of the enemy speaking out through the lips of Christians in order to undermine the work of the Spirit.

A tongue that is not under Holy Spirit control is in danger of getting out of control. Most readers of this book will know of at least one, and probably more than one person whose tongue gets out of control from time to time. In order to avoid conflict you find yourself tip-toeing round the individual so as not to cross him and risk the end of his tongue. We should not need to be in such fear - especially of fellow Christians. But it is a fact of experience that many Christians are not free of the demonic power that was controlling them before they became Christians. They have carried over into their Christian life the same ungodly way of dealing with people that they found worked when they were operating fully in the world.

The tongue is capable of speaking out the wonderful truths of God's word, capable of blessing and encouraging people, but it is also *"... a fire, a world of evil among the parts of the body. It corrupts the whole person, sets the whole course of his life on fire ..."* (James 3:6). No wonder demons like to control the tongue: they can do so much harm through its use. And when a person does not allow the Holy Spirit to control his own tongue, you can be pretty sure that what comes out of the mouth will be influenced by the demonic and, on occasions, be the very words of demons.

22. Recurring or long-term sicknesses

Some people seem to get everything. Whatever sickness is going around, they get it! As they have progressed through life their days have been highlighted by one sickness after another. Whilst some people may remember life by the good experiences they have had, these people remember that it was the 'year of the glandular fever' or 'the year they got meningitis'!

Where people are so vulnerable to one sickness after another, there is often a spirit that is inviting spirits of infirmity in at regular intervals. I once tried to pray for a person who was regularly sick. Without telling him in advance what I was going to pray, I took authority over the ruling spirit of infirmity. Up to that point he appeared to be really blessed by the prayer, but as soon as I prayed very quietly against the demon I knew was there, he quickly came to himself, sat up straight and said, *"Don't ever pray for me again like that"*. The demon had risen up and taken charge and the time of prayer was over!

Normally the demon was very happy for anyone to come and spend time praying for the man. It knew that ordinary prayer was no threat to the demonic. But as soon as I exercised God-given authority, the demon was immediately on the defensive and made sure that the man terminated the prayer session immediately!

A spirit of infirmity of this kind has generally been given rights to rule so strongly through some experience in the past, when sickness has been welcomed and used by the person for his own ends, either to gain attention or to get his own way. Using sickness like this is dangerous, for it is making a declaration that sickness, which is a direct consequence of the fall, is good and is to be welcomed.

Satan loves it when people pervert scriptural truth and walk into his camp. Whenever people use sickness to manipulate other people, or for any other reason, they open themselves to demonic control that will only be dislodged through deep repentance.

I have sensed there are many people who come for prayer for physical healing who would love to lose their symptoms, but would never repent over using these or other symptoms to get their own way. Not surprisingly, they don't get healed. I am not saying that all people who are not healed are like this, but that all who are sick need to examine themselves and ask the Lord to show them if there is any situation from their past which the enemy could have taken advantage of.

23. Self-centredness

There are some people who are only capable of sustaining a conversation if they are talking about themselves! Self-idolatry and self-elevation reign supreme. All forms of idolatry are sin and self-idolatry was the foundational sin for which Satan was thrown out of heaven. So where someone is always putting himself forward and expresses interest in other people only as a conversational tactic to turn the conversation back to himself, one has to suspect that there is a powerful demonic stronghold operating on his personality.

Helping such people to see themselves as others see them is not easy. So deep is their arrogance and self-importance that they seem totally impervious to seeing or understanding anything that they haven't first thought of! It would not be unusual with such people to find that there is a generational line of similar characters and that the real battle will be with a familiar spirit that has held the whole family in bondage for generations.

24. Sexual aberrations

All sexual expression is a form of worship, whether the participants are aware of this fact or not! The marriage service contains the vows *"With my body, I thee worship"*.

God designed sexual intercourse to be the means by which mankind would pro-create. Sharing in God's creativity is worship of the creator. The psalmist says that God inhabits the praises of his people (Psalm 22:3). When we get involved in the praise and worship of the creator then we are open to receive blessing from him. Since sex is worship, therefore, we can expect God to bless sexual activity which is Godly in nature as he rejoices in the creativity of his children.

Conversely, however, we cannot expect God to remain on the

throne of a relationship which is ungodly. For he cannot bless that which is contrary to his word and laws. There is another one, however, who will rejoice to 'bless' such activity and to take the throne over the relationship. Wherever ungodly sex is taking place, Satan will be there - not to bless, but to try to take God's place, receive the worship to himself, and curse the participants.

That is why there is so much sexual activity in the rituals of satanism and witchcraft. Satan rejoices to receive the worship that this entails and trap the participants into the demonic bondage that ensues.

It is a fact highlighted by extensive experience that the soul-ties established through ungodly sexual activity are a prime entry point for the demonic. If when counselling someone, it becomes clear that there has been ungodly sexual activity, then it would be reasonable to expect that there is demonic power attached to the sexual sin. Satan uses these soul-ties to hold people in demonic chains throughout their lives. In practice we have found that when people get this area of their lives sorted out and cleansed by God, an enormous amount of healing and deliverance can then take place.

25. Suicidal tendencies

Taking one's own life is the ultimate sin against one's own body - the ultimate rebellion against the Holy Spirit, whose temple the body is. I am not saying that there can never be forgiveness for those who have taken their own life. God is the righteous and merciful judge to whom each of us must answer, both for the things we have done to ourselves and for those things we have done to others. I have no doubt that there will be many people who have committed suicide who, when they stand before the Lord, will be amazed at God's love and mercy as they realise they have been more sinned against than they have sinned themselves.

That is not to say, either, that we can look lightly on suicide or suicidal tendencies. If Satan can persuade someone to take his own life, he has scored a major victory. In our experience there is always a demonic dimension to suicide attempts or desires. In most cases the person has been so hurt by the way he has been abused or treated that the future seems utterly hopeless. And if there is no hope for tomorrow, it is but a small step towards saying, *"I might as well die today"*. In these cases the demonic entry point is invariably the trauma or pain associated with the experiences a person has been through.

There are, however, those who feel suicidal for whom there has been no obvious trauma, abuse or tragedy to make them want to run from this life. There is an inner blackness and compulsion to die. In these cases there may be some deeply hidden abuse which has never come to the light of the conscious memory but has opened the door to demons which have a powerful effect on the person's way of life. Alternatively, the person may have received a spirit of death down the generation line, or from someone else close to him who has died, which will continue to drive and motivate him, even though he himself has no personal reason for wanting to die.

Another possible source of feelings of death could be an attempted abortion by the mother, leaving the growing person with feelings that they are not wanted and shouldn't be there. The overwhelming blackness of such feelings leads almost inevitably to occasional thoughts of suicide.

In all cases of suicidal feelings, one should be aware of the demonic possibility. At recent Christian meetings, in various countries and places, when I have asked how many people at some time of their life have thought about suicide, there have always been about 50% of the people present who raise their hands. Suicidal feelings, even in the Body of Christ, are far more common than one might expect.

26. Undiagnosable symptoms

It is not unusual for people to have aches and pains that on medical investigation do not appear to have any known cause. The symptoms persist, but no matter what treatment, or even surgery is prescribed and actioned the person remains unhealed.

We have found in many cases that such persistent symptoms can be demonic and are caused by a spirit of infirmity which has either come down the generation lines or has entered through shock, trauma or, even, sexual sin.

In experience we have found this to be particularly common where there has been an accident at some time in the distant past. The physical injuries have healed to some extent but there is then a persistent symptom which fails to go away. The trauma of accidents makes people vulnerable to the demonic, and following such incidents people often need deliverance as well as physical healing.

We have found, too, that where there has been heavier involvement in occult activities, and a person is converted and sets out to be healed and delivered, there can be demonic curses which will cause apparent physical symptoms even when there is nothing medically diagnosable.

Another source of physical pain is emotional pain. The body reflects the pain in the soul. Physical treatment has no effect since it is the emotions that need to be released and healed.

27. Violent tendencies

Violence against another person is another form of rebellion. Violence removes free will choice from the victim and is contrary to God's created order. The person who perpetrates violence opens himself up to being used by the demonic, and the trauma associated with being a recipient of violence leaves the victim vulnerable to the demonic at the time of attack.

The demonic can transfer to the victim directly from the perpetrator of violence through the ungodly soul-tie which is created through the attack, or through the fear which is a natural consequence of being attacked in this way. Where a person has regularly demonstrated violent behaviour, it is not unusual to find a lot of buried anger from much earlier in life, often associated with abuse or unreasonable physical punishment.

We have also seen that violence in one area of life can be an uncontrolled outworking of demons which have been given rights through the controlled violence of activities such as the martial arts. Most people are ignorant of the occult foundation of many of the martial arts and of the spiritual danger they are in when participating in such events. Churches which allow martial arts classes to take place in church halls (along with yoga and any other occult based activities) are opening their whole ministry up to the control of demonic power.

28. Withdrawn anti-social behaviour

Man is a social being. God intended people to enjoy relationships with each other and to grow and benefit from the experience. He did not intend people to be forced to withdraw into themselves so that they live out most of their days in the isolation of loneliness. Those who behave in this way have little control over their desires and, whilst they might like to be different, know that their will is not strong enough to rise above their feelings.

Usually that is because there is an alien will which is affecting or controlling their feelings, and there is a battle going on inside for supremacy. If you are fighting a hidden enemy without knowing of its existence, victory is rarely possible!

To bring healing, deliverance is necessary, but it is also essential to explore the reasons why, in the first place, the person may have made a choice to want to be alone. The demonic will usually ride in on the feelings and choices of a person at the time the crisis first became apparent. If the person is not healed, then the doorway for further demonisation will remain open.

Invariably the root will have its origins in a relationship which has caused hurt and pain - usually in childhood. Sometimes, those who have done the 'damage' may not even be aware of the fact that they have done anything to affect the welfare of the child. It could even be that the enemy has taken advantage of experiences in babyhood or, before birth, in the womb. This is especially the case if, for example, an unmarried girl falls pregnant, and she spends the whole of their pregnancy hating the child that is in her womb. The spirit of the child will sense these feelings from the spirit of the mother and come into the world knowing that the person entrusted with his welfare had wished he did not exist. Rejection has been established at the earliest possible moment and the demonic will feed on the emotional damage that has already been done to the child.

In Conclusion: A Note on Medical Practice

I realise that in writing this chapter, many people with medical experience might be saying that these things can't be true, because there are well-known medical reasons for the conditions described, and these have nothing to do with demons! I understand the dilemma which faces those involved in the scientific process, as I myself was, when considering these issues. There is, however, no conflict between scientific observation of what is happening to a person and discernment of the spiritual roots of the condition that has been observed and measured by the scientists. It's largely a matter of whether one is studying the chicken or the egg!

The presence of either an excess or a deficiency of a chemical in the body, for example, is real and measurable. The excess or deficiency of the chemical is known to cause the symptoms which the person experiences. In the case of a deficiency, where there is a synthetic or a natural source of the chemical, then the observable symptoms can be removed, or at least improved, by the patient taking the substance by way of a prescribed medicine from their doctor. The person is said to be healed.

I would, however, disagree with this description of the person at this stage. If the dietary supplement was removed, there is little doubt that the original symptoms would return very quickly. The person is not healed, therefore, but a temporary cure has been effected through applied medication. This is a wholly acceptable and commendable medical practice, and there are many millions of people around the world who are rightfully thankful to God for the medications that keep them healthy and in many cases keep them alive.

However, when it comes to healing, what we are concerned with is not just the removal of symptoms through applied medication, but the restoration of the body's system so that the person is whole without the need for any applied medication. We are taking the investigative process one stage back from the scientific and measurable, to asking why it is that the body's system has been so distorted that medication has become necessary.

At this point we can ask many more questions that are not generally open to scientific investigation. Questions such as the effect of emotional pain and damage on the body's system and, more specifically with reference to this book, the physical symptoms caused by demons who have a specific job function to come against the person they occupy and oppose the work of God in their life.

We are beginning to see some significant breakthroughs in various areas of ministry and believe that as the Body of Christ seeks to be obedient to the commission to heal the sick, God will bring revelation to those who pray for the sick, just as he has brought knowledge and understanding to those who have sought to treat the sick through medical means.

There is no primary conflict between those who minister healing through deliverance and the medical profession. But there is a greater need for medical practitioners to be willing to see that there might just be another dimension to the conditions that they spend their lives seeking to cure. Equally, there is a greater need for those involved in healing and deliverance ministry, who might, somewhat naively, want to undermine or attack the medical profession, to realise that doctors are not their enemy, but people who are fulfilling an essential, difficult and God-given task.

But there is also a need for the medical profession to be more aware of the dangers of some alternative medicines and the alternative spiritualities that can lie behind them. We live in a world which is increasingly dominated by what is broadly termed New Age practices. Many of these, which are increasingly condoned within the medical profession, have their origin in the occult, and doctors need to be aware that some of these will appear to effect a 'cure', without the person actually being healed of the condition.

For those who have been 'cured' through practices whose foundation is demonic, it is possible that their original symptoms are now being controlled by a higher demonic power. Deliverance of any such powers is likely to result in a return to a manifestation of the original symptoms. The person can then be truly healed of the condition, following any deliverance from powers of darkness which may have caused the condition in the first place.

PART B

UNDERSTANDING DEMONIC ENTRY POINTS

Knowing how demons enter is a major key to their eviction. A demon can only enter a person if it has rights to do so. Removing these rights is foundational to effective and long-lasting deliverance ministry.

Jesus introduced the concept of demonic entry points when he commented on the condition of the woman whose back was bent double through having a spirit of infirmity (Luke 13:10-17). He stated categorically that she had been bound for eighteen years, which means that nineteen years ago she had been free. Something must have happened eighteen years previously through which the demon gained access. It may have been that she had been sexually abused, or suffered an accident, or perhaps a member of her family with a similar condition had died.

We may not have been told in the scripture exactly what happened to her, but we are told specifically that the woman in question was a 'daughter of Abraham' - a phrase which is generally understood to have meant a committed believer in God, not just a Jewess. So in one and the same story, Jesus makes it clear that believers can be demonised and that there was a specific time in her life when she was vulnerable and became demonised.

Counselling will expose many facts about an individual, some of which the counsellor will recognise as potential demonic entry points. When the symptoms which the person has are matched by the evidence of potential entry points, it is reasonable to consider the possibility that the person's problems have a demonic origin. Natural observation and spiritual discernment can, and should, go hand in hand. Discernment of spirits is a gift of the Holy Spirit, but God has also gifted us with natural abilities that must be used as we minister the love of Jesus to those in need.

For example, there have been many times when I have had no particular spiritual discernment that a person's problems were demonic, but having observed the symptoms and recognised a possible entry point, I have first dealt with this in the appropriate way (eg. through repentance of sin). Then I have addressed the demon which I believed lay behind the problem and have seen the person healed through deliverance.

Unless the entry point is fully dealt with, any such demon is unlikely to go when commanded to do so, as it will hold on to the rights that it has claimed. The importance of dealing adequately with entry points in the appropriate way cannot be over-emphasised, hence the importance of this part of the book.

Most of the usual entry points can be analysed into the broad categories shown in Chapter 4.

Chapter 4

How Demons Enter

1. The generation line

There are many scriptures which carry with them an unpopular message. The second part of Exodus 20:5 is one of these: *"The sins of the fathers will be visited on the children until the third or fourth generation."* "Why?" people ask. "That's not fair. After all, doesn't Jeremiah tell us that the children's teeth will no longer be set on edge by the sour grapes the parents have eaten?" (Jeremiah 31:29)

The questions and reactions can come thick and fast when it is first suggested that people could be demonised as a result of the sins of their fathers. Yet for many people, as soon as they hear this teaching, light dawns. At long last they are hearing a credible reason for the problems they have had to endure for so long, and, often for the first time, they have heard a message which carries with it the hope of an answer.

Countering the opposition

So let's examine the various reasons people propose as to why this teaching is either wrong, unpalatable or not relevant to the present day.

a) This teaching is contained within the law; We live in days of grace, not of law, and therefore it is not relevant for believers in this Christian era.

It is, however, part of the ten commandments given by God through Moses to his people for the whole of time. Jesus made it clear that none of the law would pass away until the end of all things (Matt. 5:18), which must be after Christ comes again. We are, therefore, still living in the dispensation of time for which the law is relevant.

In saying this, however, we must distinguish between dietary or ceremonial laws, which were only appropriate to Jewish rituals of worship and which were abolished in the New Testament (Mark 7:19, Acts 10:14-15) and the moral laws which were reinforced in the New Testament and which are still applicable today (Matthew 5:27-28, Mark 7:21-23).

We cannot ignore any part of the basic moral and behavioural commandments. If we were to pick and choose which of these instructions are relevant to us today, where would we stop? If we reject the commandment that carries with it consequences to the children if it is broken, should we not also reject the other side of this commandment which promises blessing to children born into a Godly generation line? Or even reject other commandments such as: 'Do not commit adultery'?

If we accept any of these commandments, we must accept them all and then wrestle with the consequences, believing that God included them there for our good. We may live in days of grace, but that doesn't mean that all people born after the coming of Jesus will be saved. The remedy for sin still has to be applied. If people choose not to believe in Jesus, then no amount of protestation about so called 'days of grace' can change their eternal destiny!

However, the fact that we do live in 'days of grace' means that the consequences of the sins of the fathers on the children can be dealt with through the cross. For it was through the punishment he received that we can be healed. But, just as the work of the cross has to be applied personally into each believer's life, so the work of healing and deliverance must be applied to the lives of those who have been damaged by the sins of their fathers. It does not happen automatically.

No wonder Jesus commissioned the church to heal and deliver as well as preach. He knew that only if the church ministered full salvation could the children, whom he loved so much, be liberated into the freedom that had been won for them.

b) **There cannot be any generational demonisation
for it's not fair that people should suffer for the sins
of their parents.**

Unfortunately, the world's concept of fairness is not directly
relevant to the situation! Fair or not, people do suffer because
of the sins of the fathers. It is inconsistent with experience to
pretend that they don't, in order to win a theological
argument! British newspapers are filled every day with stories
of how children have suffered because of what parents have
done to them. If a father chooses to abuse his daughter, that
child has been dreadfully damaged through the sin. It is naive
in the extreme to suggest that this particular child has not
suffered because of the sins of her father.

We live in a fallen world and Satan has been fighting a dirty
game ever since the fall. One could say that it isn't fair that
our earliest ancestors sinned in the first place and gave Satan
rights over the whole of God's creation, including you and me.
But they did, and we have all suffered as a result!

Conversely, one could say also that it wasn't fair that Jesus
should have to die on the cross, being punished for things that
he had not done. That certainly was not fair, but he did, and I
thank God for the fact that he loved us so much that he
allowed his son to die there in your place and mine.

c) **What about the prophecies of Ezekiel & Jeremiah?
Do their prophecies not imply that the children
cannot be harmed as a result of the sins of the
fathers, by saying that the children's teeth will
not be set on edge? (Jeremiah 31:29, Ezekiel 18:1-4)**

No, they don't. What these passages are referring to is the
guilt for the sins of the fathers - not the damage done as a
result of the sin. Ezekiel makes this very clear. He says *"the
son will not share the **guilt** of the father, nor will the father
share the guilt of the son"* (Ezekiel 18:20).

So the child who is abused is not guilty and will not be
punished by God for the father's sin. The father will be judged
for his own sin. Ezekiel 18:4 makes this plain by saying, *"It is
the soul that sins that will die"*. Clearly Ezekiel is not talking

about immediate physical death, or there would have been no-one left alive in Israel within a very short time of Ezekiel speaking these words! He is talking about eternal death as a consequence of sin and the resulting judgement of God.

A careful reading of Ezekiel 18 expands this teaching in unmistakable words, spelling out how judgement will fall on the perpetrators of sin, not on those who have been damaged as a result of the sin. Ezekiel explains that no matter how bad a father has been, if the son chooses to live well before man and God, then he will not come under judgement. What Ezekiel does not explain, however, is how much harder it is for people to be obedient to God when they have been so damaged through the sins of their parents.

The Jeremiah passage has a slightly different emphasis. The whole of this passage is related to the future prosperity of God's people. And it is clear in this case that Jeremiah is referring to a time when Jesus is reigning here on earth. Verse 34 says, *"None of them will have to teach his fellow countryman to know the Lord, because all will know me, from the least to the greatest."* This cannot refer to the time we live in, for very few people know the Lord. It is a clear reference to the millennial reign of Christ (Rev. 20:1-6), when Satan and all the demons will be bound. Then there cannot be any generational demonisation, because at that time there will be no demons! When interpreting prophecy we must be careful to apply the prophecy correctly to the right time of fulfilment.

d) ***The scriptures say that "if any one is in Christ, he is a new creation; the old has passed away" (2 Cor. 5:17 RSV). Doesn't this suggest that once a person is a Christian there cannot be any remaining consequences of the sins of the fathers?***

Yes and *No.*

Yes, in that the old era of alienation from God has passed away because the spirit has been born again of God. But *No* in that the moment a person becomes a Christian they are not given a new flesh-life to replace the old. The consequences of damage that has been done in the past are still there. It is only by the ministry of healing and deliverance, following the receipt of the gift of salvation, that the work of the enemy down the generation line can be undone in a person's life. It is when a person becomes a new creation in Christ that it is then possible for the work of restoration to begin.

One has to look also at the evidence of the counselling room and be honest about the people who walk through the door. Time and time again we have looked at the consequences of the sins of the fathers in people who, as babies, were deserted by their parents, or whose mothers were prostitutes, or whose grandparents were in witchcraft or . . . I could list a hundred or more different possibilities from our counselling files.

We must now ask the much more fundamental question. Having accepted that the sins of the fathers are visited on the children, how does it work?

It is easy to understand the physical consequences to a battered child or the social consequences of being brought up by alcoholic or drug-addicted parents. But when we look again at Exodus 20:5 we see that the sins of the fathers are visited on the children because of the sin of idolatry - the sin of worshipping something or someone other than the true and living God. The consequences of this sin is not so obvious. Superficially one might be tempted to wonder how there can possibly be any consequences at all other than perhaps through the vindictive activity of a malicious God who rejoices to punish people for things they have not done!

But is that really the character of God? If we want to know what the character of God the Father is like we only have to look at Jesus. For Jesus said, *"He who has seen me has seen the Father"* (John 14:9 NASB). We see nothing malicious or vindictive in Jesus. Indeed we see the very opposite. So, clearly, there must be some other means through which the sins of the fathers have an effect on the children.

At this point we have to introduce the possibility of the demonic. For all false worship is ultimately the worship of Satan via the worship of demons. Demons are behind all false religion and every thing that would raise itself up as an idolatrous object, relationship or activity.

Satan is an imitator, not a creator. Just as when a person worships the true and living God, God by the power of the Holy Spirit inhabits the praises of his people (Psalm 22:3 AV), when a person gives his allegiance to a false god he comes under the influence of the evil spirit behind the false god which will seek to indwell the 'worshipper'.

Not all such worship is obviously of idols – there are many objects, activities (especially of a sexual nature), recreations, and even pets, that can become idolatrous through the devotion that they are offered. As Paul says about money, it is the love of it that causes problems, not money itself (1 Timothy 6:10). One might say about sexuality that it is the lusting after wrongful sex that causes problems, not sex itself, which is a rightful and wonderful gift from God.

So idolatry (and most sin is ultimately a form of idolatry) gives the demonic a right of entry. And once the demon is in, it is only through repentance and deliverance that the person can be set free. Furthermore, the demon is not just restricted to the person who has sinned, but it will seek to transfer down the generation lines to future generations. The sin of one generation 'uncovers' the next generation, leaving the children unprotected in the area of that particular sin.

This whole area of transference down the generation line is therefore a major topic in deliverance ministry. Additionally, there is also the possibility of transference to anyone with whom the individual has a soul-tie.

So we have introduced here both the problem of transference and the importance of soul-ties. These are vital keys to understanding how to deliver people from demons so that they can stay free. Much more will be said about them later. ·

With generational demonisation, transference can take place to the next generation at conception, at the death of the parent or at any time in-between these two extremes – although conception and death would appear to be the most commonly encountered moments of transference.

So, in addition to the natural consequences of the sins of the fathers (eg. abuse, poverty, violence, deprivation etc.), we also see that there is a spiritual (demonic) dimension that must be taken into account when ministering healing to those in need. For what we are often dealing with are demons that have come down the family line and are now a curse on the present and succeeding generations.

Even the medical profession asks questions such as, *"Did your father or grandfather have this?"* Doctors know that it is not unusual for a particular medical condition to be dominant within a generation line. What the doctors rarely recognise is that in some of these cases they are looking at the consequences of generational demonisation and not simply a prevailing physical condition or something genetic.

An 18 year old girl came to one of our healing services and told me the doctors had given her less than twelve months to live because of a viral condition affecting both her kidneys. She had already had prayer for the condition, but there had been no improvement. As she stood there I sensed the Holy Spirit telling me to ask her about her mother. She told me that she was adopted. Her mother had been unmarried and, when she became pregnant, had offered the child for adoption. She had no idea who her real parents are.

Recognising that her parents had therefore been in sexual sin, I asked her if she would forgive her natural Mum and Dad for their behaviour and then thank God for her life. After she had done both of these things, I broke the curse that was upon her because of the sin of her parents. I took authority over the spirit that had come into her at conception and ordered it to leave. She immediately felt something happening in her stomach as the spirit began to move and come out. It came up through her chest and she coughed and spluttered for a little while as the demons were cast out of her body.

An 18 year old member of our young people's team was alongside me that night to get ministry experience. She had never prayed for a sick person before. I asked her to lay her hands on the girl's kidneys and pray for healing. The girl felt things happening in her kidneys. A few minutes later she bent down and touched her toes, something that moments earlier would have been impossible for her because of the pain. She wrote to me six weeks later, saying that she had been back to the hospital. The doctors had re-examined her, found nothing wrong and told her to go and live a normal life and forget all about their previous diagnosis.

This was a classic case of generational demonisation, where the demonic power in the child was given access through the sexual sin of the parents. The girl's sickness was a direct consequence of the spirit assigned to curse the next generation. Without deliverance ministry there would have been no healing, and without dealing with the specific entry point there would have been no deliverance!

In this case the generational demonisation was only from one generation to the next, but the scripture talks about the consequences affecting three or four generations. And if any one of those three or four generations enters into further sin of a similar nature, a new cycle of three or four generations is begun. In practice, therefore, the generational consequences can be indefinite as one generation after another compounds the ancestral sin.

We have ministered to many people where it appears that the demons entered the family line of the victim even hundreds of years ago - an experience which is common to all those who are involved seriously in setting the captives free. It is also worth noting that Deuteronomy 23:2 appears to indicate that where sexual sin is involved, the generational consequences could be up to ten generations, for that is the length of time that these people would be excluded from the assembly of God.

In the Gospels the disciples saw a blind man and came to Jesus with a question, *"Who sinned, this man or his parents, that he was born blind?"* (John 9:2). In this case Jesus replied, *"Neither"* but the question itself would not have had any relevance unless, in their discussions with Jesus, it had been accepted that it was possible for someone to suffer as a result of the sins of his parents.

With generational demonisation one often sees a repetition in the next generation of the same sort of demonically induced symptoms as were evident in the previous generations. These can be physical symptoms, emotional conditions, psychological or psychiatric conditions, spiritual blindspots etc.

For example, one may discover that, as long as people can remember, all the women in the family have been asthmatics. Or, as one man said to me, *"My great-grandfather was an adulterer, as was my grandfather. Then also my own father, and now I'm just the same."* What he was describing was the activity of the spirit of adultery which had been passed on from one generation to the next and induced in each one the behaviour pattern of adultery.

Each generation has its own free will to choose and say, *"No, I will not commit adultery"*, but the continuous pressure from a demon within is hard for people to withstand forever, and the time may come when the will is finally broken and the individual gives way to temptation and ends up in the despair of unwanted sin.

It is easy to understand with the hindsight of many ministries how wise some sectors of the early church were to insist that people went through deliverance ministry after conversion and before baptism and church membership. In some parts of the world this is still common practice. They knew that unless the converts were delivered of both the demonic powers that had controlled their own pagan lives and those which had come down the generation lines, they would end up with a demonised church which would quickly assume an attitude of compromise with the world and would decline into patterns of spiritual death and religious routine. I believe there would be a far stronger body of believers if this were normal practice throughout the church today.

Unless the leaders of the church embrace an active and ongoing deliverance ministry, I believe that every move of the Spirit of God will, in time, be quenched from within through demonic pressure. It is small wonder, therefore, that Satan so opposes and seeks to discredit the deliverance ministry, for if the church is being obedient in preaching the Gospel, healing the sick <u>and</u> casting out demons, the Body of Christ will be a force that cannot be stopped from within or without.

The Principle of Covering

God intended children to be covered (protected) by their parents and be brought up 'in the nurture of the Lord'. That means that parents are meant to be 'in loco parentis' for God and bring up their children to know God as Father.

The covering which parents should provide for their children is rather like an umbrella. No matter how hard it rains, if a person remains under the cover of the umbrella they will remain dry. But, if there is a hole in the umbrella those under it will get wet in the area where the hole is but will remain dry everywhere else.

So if a father wilfully enters into sin he is blowing a hole in the cover (puncturing the umbrella) so that those under the umbrella then become vulnerable in the same area. Or, to be more specific, if the father becomes demonised through a particular sin, then the children are made vulnerable to the same demonic power.

When the father, whose preceding four generations had committed adultery, looked at his son and asked, *"What hope is there for him?"*, we could explain to him what had been happening in the demonic realms and assure him that he could make a choice to turn from the sin, forgive his ancestors and be delivered of the spirit which had induced adulterous behaviour from one generation to the next. There was hope, but without the ministry of deliverance one generation after another would be cursed with the sinful behaviour pattern that was originated by the great-grandfather's sin.

No wonder the writer of Lamentations said, *"Our ancestors sinned, but now they are gone, and we are suffering for their sins"* (Lamentations 5:7 GNB) and in Leviticus we read *"your descendants will confess their sins and the sins of their ancestors, who resisted me and rebelled against me"* (Leviticus 26:40 GNB).

It is important to remember, also, that a Godly covering provides secure protection under which children can grow up in the nurture of the Lord. No wonder Satan does everything he can to lead the parents into sin so as to try and claim the children for himself through the holes blown in the generational umbrella! The other side of this is also expressed within the ten commandments, *"I show my love to thousands of generations of those who love me and obey my laws"* (Exodus 20:6 GNB).

2.   Personal sin

Satan and his demons are in the business of promoting sin! But that is not to say that every time one commits a sin a new demon enters. It doesn't. However, the ongoing practice of sin, which remains unconfessed and unforgiven, will inevitably give rights to the demonic to enter and control a person in specific areas of his life. And it is not unusual for an apparently isolated instance of a particular sin to have opened the way for demonisation. Satan is no respecter of persons and he will take advantage of every opportunity that is presented to him to dominate and control people - especially those who are seeking to live for Jesus!

There is a remedy for sin. It is detailed in 1 John 1:9. These are words to Christians. Confession – Forgiveness – Cleansing, and in that order. If we confess our sins to God, he is faithful to his promises. He is also just, in that the price which has already been paid by Jesus is sufficient to cover every sin. So he will forgive - he has to be true to his own word. But the promise goes on to say that not only will he forgive us, but he will cleanse us from all unrighteousness. Where the demonic has entered through sin, then the cleansing process must also include deliverance.

Why should sin be an entry point for demons? The answer is both simple and profound. Sin is rebellion against God. Satan began that rebellion in heaven when he sought to take for himself the glory that was the Father's alone. Satan continued that rebellion on earth by tempting man to join with him in it by committing sins. Sins are things that we do which are contrary to the will, plans and purposes of God. We commit sins because we have a sinful heritage.

When we sin we are not only rebelling against the living God, but we are also offering worship to Satan. All sin can be considered as idolatry, for through it we place Satan ahead of God in our lives. Once we have understood the nature of sin in this way, it is not hard to take the next step towards understanding that when we worship Satan we are making ourselves vulnerable to being occupied by one of Satan's agents, an evil spirit.

Once such a spirit has gained access through sin, it will then create pressure from within us to continue sinning. There has been a shift of ground. Previously we would experience temptation from the outside, as Jesus did in the wilderness when he consistently refuted the attacks of Satan. But if we open up doors to the demonic through our sin, the attacks come from the inside, and are far harder to refute. Because the demons then have access to our thoughts, they will seek to deceive us into thinking that their thoughts are our thoughts and make us think that we want to do the things they want us to do.

Having gained access, demons will seek to strengthen their position. Each time we succumb to further similar temptations it is as if the demons are able to increase their hold by putting down fresh roots. The more well-worn the pathway of sin, the harder it is to get a particular demon out. More will be said later about the processes of deliverance, but I would not want people who, even now, are sensing a demonic grip around some area of their life, to think that there is no hope of deliverance. There is.

The primary keys to deliverance from demons that have entered and established themselves through personal sin will always be confession and repentance. Confession is not just telling God that we have done wrong when, once again, we are caught out in some sin. It is seeing the sin for what it really is and agreeing with God's verdict on both sin in general and our sins in particular.

To agree with God over something means to say that God's perspective on the matter is now more important than our own and we are willing to lay down our own will in favour of his. That is part of true worship. As Jesus said to the woman at the well. *"God is spirit, and those who worship him must worship in spirit and truth."* (John 4:24 NASB). We cannot worship God in truth if we are allowing sinful deception to determine our relationship with him.

Repentance is the positive act of turning from the sin now and on future occasions. We always have a choice over whether or not we sin, no matter how demonised we might be. Satan is not able to take away our free will. But the more we have sinned, the more power the demons have to influence our decision-making and the harder it is for us to say 'No'. Holy Spirit-inspired determination to say 'No' is one of the most powerful and effective deliverance tactics! Without the power of the Holy Spirit, however, we are beaten before we even start!

Each time we resist demonic pressure to sin we force the demonic more out into the open and it has to loosen its grip. The old hymn 'Yield not to temptation' contains in one of its lines a very powerful truth of enormous significance in the battle against the demonic:

'Each victory will help you, some other to win'

Full confession and heart-felt repentance will always undermine the rights of the demonic. Without such, however, no amount of commanding the demonic to come out will have any effect. This is probably why Jesus tackled the sin in the paralysed man's life (Luke 5) before attempting to heal him of the paralysis. Failure to confess and repent is probably the greatest single reason why some attempts at deliverance ministry are unsuccessful.

The best defence against demonisation through personal sin is immediate confession and repentance. When we have been caught out in sin our natural reaction is to hide (see Genesis 3 for example!) in an attempt to conceal the sin either from God, the people we have sinned against or both. But if when we have sinned we immediately come to the Father in true confession and repentance, and ask for his forgiveness, then we continuously remove the ground on which the demonic would want to stand. The longer we wait before coming to God, the deeper rooted the demonic will get, and the harder it will be to gain one's freedom from the clutches of the enemy.

One problem some people have with personal sin is that the sinful lifestyle or characteristic has become so much a part of them that they are not even aware that they are committing sin, let alone aware of the fact that they may have been demonised through the sin!

An important prayer, which should be part of the devotions of every one of us who would seek to be obedient to the Lord, was expressed by David in the last two verses of Psalm 139 when he cried out to God to test him and expose anything evil there was within him. For, the heart is desperately wicked (Jer. 17:9) and left to our own understanding we will never be able to accurately discern what is truth and error in ourselves. It is only God who knows us that well. It is only he who can be trusted to expose all that is bad (so that it can be dealt with appropriately) and bless that which is good.

In recent years I have ministered to many elderly Christians, some of them with well-known and established ministries. In the confidence of the counselling room they have shared their inner problems and some have been broken-hearted over the way they have had continuous struggles with temptations, often of a sexual nature, that they have been powerless to fight off. In many cases, such people have never understood that they are not just fighting temptation from without, or their own fallen flesh nature, but are struggling with demons within which have never been recognised. It is impossible to fight an enemy whose identity is never recognised!

How Satan must rejoice when Christians are taught that they cannot be demonised. No other teaching gives such rights to the enemy to walk all over the saints of God unrecognised and unchallenged. What a relief it is for people to realise that the thoughts and temptations they have battled with for years have an origin which can be dealt with through deliverance.

Usually with such people, when their whole life's story is laid out, one will find some sexual sin earlier in life which has been dealt with in terms of confession and repentance (*"it's all under the blood"*, they'll say!) but which has never been dealt with in terms of cleansing and deliverance. There are few people I counsel who do not have some sort of sexual skeleton in the cupboard. Opening the door can be painful, and requires much humility and honesty, but without such radical ministry the person will have to live with demonic pressure from within for the rest of their days.

Jesus commissioned the church to cast out demons. How it must grieve the Lord when he sees the saints of God still struggling with unrecognised demons, when the blood of Jesus was shed so that both the guilt and power of sin could be broken. It has also been a fact of common experience to see that much of the physical infirmity people have is a long-term consequence of the demonic which entered through sin early in life and which, unrecognised, has eaten away at the very foundations of their existence.

All sin needs to be dealt with in the same way, but we have found certain areas of sinful activity to be so significant as far as demonisation is concerned that we have given several of these separate headings.

3. Occult sin

'The Occult' is the broad term which is given to practices, often of a religious nature, whose power source is most definitely not of God. Occult practitioners range from those who clearly know that their particular brand of occultism relies upon the power of demons (eg. witchcraft) to those who would not even recognise the existence of demons but have been duped into the fringes of a demonic power system that has them under its control (eg. casual attenders at a yoga class).

The word 'Occult' simply means hidden, and as such is a very accurate description of the way Satan tries to operate in this world - secretly - and in such a way that people are deceived into offering worship to him, sometimes without realising that he even exists. For in offering Satan worship they are saying 'Yes' to the demonic, and once occultic demonic power is operating in people's lives, then Satan has a handle on them which is not easy to remove. Without deliverance ministry they are stuck with this for their own lifetime, and, according to the word of God, their children could suffer for three or four succeeding generations (Exodus 20:5).

The warnings in the scriptures are many and varied. In Deuteronomy 18:9-14 the Lord, through Moses, warns the people of Israel before entering the promised land not to use divination, consult the spirits of the dead or do any of these disgusting things which are detestable in the eyes of the Lord.

In 2 Kings 21:6 Manasseh, the King of Judah, reintroduces a number of evil practices including divination, magic, and consultation with mediums and fortune-tellers. This disobedience led to the eventual downfall of Jerusalem in 598 BC. For ease of reference all the scriptures referring to occult practices are collected together in Appendix 2.

What we have found in experience is that Satan does not often wait for a second invitation to invade a person's life through involvement in the occult. Many of the people we have counselled have been demonised through just one encounter with a fortune-teller or a gypsy palm-reader, a ouija-board session in a nurses' home, the 'prophecies' of an astrologer, or any of a hundred other possibilities.

Involvement in the occult is serious and dangerous and is the root of many people's problems. I am constantly surprised at how many people who come to us in need have dabbled in some aspect of the occult, or have had parents, aunts, grandparents etc. who took them, even as young children, to an occultist of one brand or another.

There is only one way out and that is through the power of the Name of Jesus.

The steps to freedom are as follows:

a) Willingness to recognise the nature of the sin - idolatry, which is ultimately the worship of Satan.

b) Full confession of all known involvements.
    (As ministry proceeds the Lord may expose deeper involvements that had previously been hidden from memory.)

c) Repentance from the heart and with the will.
    (Being sorry is not enough, the will must be consciously involved in choosing to turn away from all such practices in the future.)

d) Deliverance from the demons that have entered (or controlled from the outside) through the occult activity.

e) Healing of the spirit, soul and body from the damage that has resulted from the demonic activity in the person.

The treatment has to be radical and determined. Half-measures are not enough. Satan knows whether or not we are serious about repentance, and if there is any doubt in our heart then the demons have a right to remain there by our own decision, and no amount of shouting at them will have any effect. James put it very clearly, *"When you pray, you must believe and not doubt at all. Whoever doubts is like a wave in the sea that is driven and blown about by the wind. A person like that, unable to make up his mind and undecided in all he does, must not think that he will receive anything from the Lord"* (James 1:6-8 GNB).

If there is full repentance then all Satan's rights are removed and the demons, when challenged, will have to leave. (Normally they do not leave of their own free will, without being ordered to do so. Remember that they, too, are under orders from Satan to hang in there and fulfil their job function!)

Many people are in total ignorance of the dangers of the occult, or of the fact that some of the things they thought were harmless were occult activities. A check-list and descriptive glossary of the more commonly encountered occult activities is listed in Appendix 3. I would strongly recommend that all readers of this book prayerfully go through the list, asking God to show them anything they have been involved in personally (knowingly or unknowingly) or anything in their generation line which has been affecting them without their knowledge.

One person we counselled could not get beyond the word Kabbala in the occult check list. She had no understanding of what Kabbala was or of anyone in her family that had been involved. But the Holy Spirit told her that she must renounce the sins of her ancestors in this respect. She did so and immediately spirits that had entered the family line through the practices of Kabbala manifested violently in front of us. God is a revealer of secrets, for *"everything in all creation is exposed and lies open before his eyes"* (Hebrews 4:13 GNB) and *"He reveals things that are deep and secret; he knows what is hidden in darkness, and he himself is surrounded by light ... there is a God in heaven, who reveals mysteries"* (Daniel 2:22,28 GNB).

4.   Some alternative medical practices

When people are ill they will try anything that seems to offer them hope. Often when people come for help through prayer, we find that it is only after having tried everything else that they have eventually resorted to the possibility that God may be able to help them! The first place they look is almost always the conventional medical profession, but after exhausting the medical possibilities without healing or relief of the symptoms, people begin to search farther afield and wonder if there are any other avenues that they ought to be trying.

When they start looking at alternative medicine, they find many differing options. All sorts of practitioners are willing to offer the earth and charge expensively for the privilege. Alternative medicine is big business. Some of it is completely above board and genuine. But there is much more that is either plain quackery (at best) or dependent on demonic power (at worst). Much harm can be done by trusting oneself to practitioners whose framework of operation could more accurately be classified as of the occult than as a branch of medicine. I have separated these alternative medical practices out from the occult in order to draw attention to their dangers, which might otherwise be lost in a much larger occult check list, and so get overlooked by people who would feel sure they have never been involved in any occult activity.

Appendix 4 lists some of the suspect alternative medical practices which we would advise Christians not to be associated with. I fully recognise that the practitioners of some of these alternative medical or pseudo-medical procedures may be completely ignorant of the powers that lie behind the treatments they are offering. Listing these practices in the Appendix is in no way meant to be a personal criticism of individuals, whose integrity is not in question. But it would be wrong not to warn readers of the potential demonic dangers.

For those who have been involved in any of these alternative medical practices, there is the possibility that, as a result, demons will have been given rights in their body and they will be in need of deliverance. We have ministered to many people who have had to be delivered in this way, a number of whom had experienced significant healing of symptoms through the suspect alternative medical practices they had tried.

There is no doubt that many of the demonically empowered healing practices do in fact work. Indeed, if they did not work to some degree, they would not draw people's attention and interest. The scripture makes it clear that the enemy is a great deceiver, and he is quite capable of using demonic power to bring a measure of healing in order to fulfil his wider objectives. But what we have observed is that a subtle exchange often takes place. A symptom may be removed but a far deeper spiritual bondage is entered into.

For example, one person who went to a spiritualist healer for his condition was healed quite dramatically of the obvious symptoms of his illness, but shortly afterwards he began to develop other symptoms. For many years he endured the trauma of one operation after another for a developing series of problems, but still had the strange symptoms that had only commenced following his visit to the spiritualist.

What he then needed, after confession and repentance, was deliverance from the spirit of infirmity which had come into him through the medium and tormented his life ever since. It is common at this stage for the original symptom, which is no longer demonically subdued, to return. Further ministry is then possible so that the person is genuinely healed of the original condition.

Similarly, on numerous occasions we have had to deliver people of spirits that have entered through acupuncture. Sometimes, as the Holy Spirit has exposed the darkness, they have experienced intense pain at just the points where the acupuncture needles had originally been inserted, identifying the specific locations where demons had entered.

Many of the healings that people have experienced through demonically empowered alternative medicines can seem to be permanent healings whilst the individual remains an unbeliever. But when a person becomes a Christian, the Holy Spirit will gradually bring light into the darkness so that the demonic has to be exposed and deliverance and true healing can then take place.

Often we see that demonic medicine will also lead people into a spiritual wilderness. After using occultic methods, the individual seems to lose a sense of trust and dependence on God and assumes an attitude of independence from the Lord. The simplicity of the Gospel is no longer attractive to them. We have also seen people who have followed the alternative medicine way of life then go on to adopt superstitious behaviour, typical of people with an occultic background.

5. Religious sin

A friend of mine commented, *"It seems that Christian demons are some of the hardest to get out!!"* What a statement! How could there possibly be such things as Christian demons? My friend was not actually suggesting that demons can be converted, but that religious spirits, which have taken on the character of Christian behaviour in order to deceive, are the hardest to positively identify and the most difficult for the host to admit having!

Both Isaiah, in his message from the Lord to the leaders of his day (Isaiah 1), and Jesus, in his words to the Pharisees, were utterly contemptuous of those who were religious but whose hearts were a long way from being in fellowship with God.

"Listen to what the Lord is saying to you. Pay attention to what our God is teaching you. He says, 'Do you think I want all these sacrifices you keep offering to me? I have had more than enough of the sheep you burn as sacrifices and of the fat of your fine animals. I am tired of the blood of bulls and sheep and goats. Who asked you to bring me all this when you come to worship me? Who asked you to do all this tramping about in my Temple?

It's useless to bring your offerings. I am disgusted with the smell of the incense you burn. I cannot stand your New Moon Festivals, your Sabbaths and your religious gatherings; they are all corrupted by your sins .... No matter how much you pray, I will not listen, for your hands are covered with blood. Wash yourselves clean.

Stop all this evil that I see you doing. Yes, stop doing evil and learn to do right. See that justice is done - help those who are oppressed, give orphans their rights and defend widows.' The Lord says, 'Now let's settle the matter. You are stained red with sin, but I will wash you as clean as snow. Although your stains are deep red, you will be as white as wool. If you will only obey me, you will eat the good things the land produces. But if you defy me, you are doomed to die. I, the Lord, have spoken'." (Isaiah 1:10-20 GNB)

What the Lord was telling Isaiah to say was that religious routines, without the heart being in harmony with God, were sheer hypocrisy and such a burden to the Lord that he could not stand it. But nevertheless the Lord still promised the people good things if they would only get themselves right with God and live lives in obedience to him. That message has not changed. God still patiently waits for us to turn to him in spirit and in truth. When Jesus spoke those words to the woman at the well they cut right to the heart of all relationships that God longs to have with his people.

God is a spiritual being and if we try to relate to him only through the flesh of our body and our soul, then no matter how hard we try, our religious expression will always fall short of what God desires and intends for us. Satan does all he can to occupy that spiritual dimension, so that in the spirit we are not relating with God but with powers of darkness under Satan's control. In order to do that successfully, Satan will often send a religious spirit whose job function is to simulate a form of Christian life that is soulish rather than spiritual.

So in his guidance to the woman at the well, Jesus not only said that you must worship God in spirit, but also in truth. There must be no hypocrisy. What we say to God must be a rightful expression of our true desire and not what we think God would like to hear. Isaiah summed all this up very accurately.

This is why Jesus was able to look at the tax collector, whose heart was right before God as he confessed his sins, and commend him for his honesty. He then made a stark contrast between this man and the religious leader who in his hypocrisy could only thank God that he wasn't like other men while in reality he was far worse! (Luke 18:9-14). He may have got all the rituals and words of the religious routines correct, but his heart was not right before God. In contrast to him, we have seen people who are still quite highly demonised and struggling to overcome their problems, but have hearts towards God that are utterly pure in desire and intention.

The religious person, who is controlled by religious spirits that 'dot the I's and cross the T's' of religious practice, is as much in need of deliverance as the person who is repenting of a lifetime of occult practice. For in reality, there is not much difference between the effects of occultic spirits that control the spirituality of man and religious spirits that also control the spirituality, but through having learned Christian behaviour patterns!

I am not saying that either of these categories of people cannot be born again at the same time as having such demons - many of them are. But equally, there must be a large number of people who think they are born again because they are adept at using the right sort of Christian language and doing the right sort of Christian things but who do not have a personal relationship with Jesus.

Satan is a very religious being. When in heaven, he sought to gain for himself the worship that was due to the Father, and it was for this rebellion that he was expelled by Michael and his angels. So it should not be considered surprising that some of the most effective demonic powers in Satan's armoury are the ranks of religious spirits who subtly try to divert people from worshipping God and lead them into giving homage to a substitute.

In ministering to people who have been demonised through involvement in some of the heavier occultic practices, or through being deeply committed to a false religion, or who are descendants of people who have been involved in this way, it has been a matter of relatively common experience to find that there have even been demons with specific job functions of imitating God the Father, God the Son and God the Holy Spirit.

This has meant, for example, that the demons have been quite happy for the person to sing songs which refer to the Lordship of Jesus. For when there is a demon present who has taken the name of Jesus, and the person does not know the real Jesus for themselves, then the deception is complete.

i) Religious practices

Any religious practice which becomes more important to a person than God himself and the relationship they have with God is a potential target for demonic deception. For the religious practice becomes an idol and the person is involved in idolatry. We have seen that within the life of the church there are many things that can become idolatrous.

Some examples are: The choir, the music group, the organ, the pews, the previous pastor, the stained glass windows, the graves in the graveyard, the tradition of the church, the founders of the church, the routine, the prayer book, the hymn book, the chalice, the pulpit, the sacrament, the sermon, the mid-week meeting and even the Bible! Bibliolatry is just another subtle form of idolatry. We have had to deliver people of religious spirits attached to a wide variety of religious objects, traditions or practices.

Then there is the whole range of churchmanships. Demons are adept at being liberal, high church, evangelical, conserv-ative, left-wing, right-wing, charismatic, non-charismatic,

charismatic evangelical, charismatic catholic and a wealth of other combinations too numerous to mention!

When one begins to explore this whole area it becomes increasingly obvious how critical the gift of discerning of spirits is to the Body of Christ. For without the exercise of that gift we have no chance whatsoever of discerning between the real and the unreal, or the religious and the genuinely Spirit-filled. We are then vulnerable to electing people to key church positions on the strength of their personality (very dangerous) or as a means of appeasing people (in reality appeasing their demons) to avoid the backlash there may be if these people do not get the jobs they want.

One of the ways in which Satan uses religious spirits most effectively is in the election of officers to key positions in the Body of Christ. If Satan can ensure that people who look right, but who at heart are not (even though they believe they are), have the decision-making positions in a fellowship, then he has a strategic fifth column neatly in place which will block every genuine move of the Holy Spirit. They may also try to obstruct the appointment of every person whom the Lord sends to put his foot down for God in that particular local church.

The election of Stephen and the other six men to serving roles within the emergent New Testament church is a highly significant passage of scripture. Even though the jobs in question were not, primarily, up-front spiritual positions, the injunction was not to get just anyone who might be willing to help, but to *"choose seven men from among you who are known to be full of the Holy Spirit and wisdom"!* (Acts 6:3 GNB)

We overlook this caution at our peril. It is better to have no-one in a particular office than to have a person occupying a key role who is not filled with the Holy Spirit. For if we elect people who are not filled with the Holy Spirit to any office within our churches we are in danger of handing over the spiritual life of the fellowship into Satan's hands! That is why so many of our churches are moribund, just pottering along at the lowest level of spiritual life with no apparent hope of climbing out of the trough of mediocrity.

ii) **Denominationalism**

Once a denomination becomes more important than the relationship each member of the denomination has with the Lord, then denominationalism has taken over. Those who are members of that local church are then in danger of being occupied by a religious spirit whose job function is to perpetuate the character of the denomination, as opposed to encouraging believers to live lives which demonstrate the character of Jesus.

A classic case is to be found in the early history of Methodism. John Wesley died an Anglican priest. He never had any desire to leave the Church of England, but the Church of England could not cope with the fire of God within him, his love for Jesus or his discipling of believers. His followers so adopted his lead that they instituted a denominational structure which took upon itself the name of Methodism, following the gibe that was thrown at John in his earlier Oxford days of being methodical in the practice of his faith. It is interesting to observe that the methodist gibe came from the years before he was baptised in the Holy Spirit, when he was very religious but was not truly born again of the Spirit of God. (This latter experience took place some years later at Aldersgate Street, at a Moravian meeting in London, after his return from the new colonies of America as a failed missionary.)

Many of the early Methodists were truly filled with the Holy Spirit, but it was not long after John Wesley's death that the new denomination settled down to perpetuating Methodism and its particular emphases. Although much good was, and is, done through those within Methodism who are on fire for God, the seeds of denominationalism gradually became a stranglehold from which the denomination has never recovered. It seems as though it was a masterstroke of the enemy to get the new grouping labelled by a name which had its roots in religiosity rather than Holy Spirit anointing.

I would caution any who think their own denomination must be alright because I am using the Methodists by way of illustration. For not only have I cast out religious spirits of Methodism, I have also delivered people from spirits that have been tied to the name of many different denominations. In the UK I have also delivered people from spirits of the Anglican,

Catholic, Baptist, Brethren and Congregationalist churches and just about every other denomination you can think of, including some of the modern-day new churches!

It is not unusual for people who are being delivered of religious spirits to experience severe head pain or the feeling of tight bands around their head as the demons manifest and are expelled. We have seen that these spirits can also be the source of mental and physical infirmity. Satan will use any door he possibly can to invade people and attack them in body, soul or spirit.

iii) Heretical beliefs

The borderline between heretical beliefs and false religions is very thin, though it is recognisable. For example, I have no difficulty in including Freemasonry amongst false religions (Freemasons worship a god whose very name, Jahbulon, incorporates the names of Baal and the fertility goddess of Egypt!), along with Jehovah's Witnesses, Mormons and many others. But I would have more difficulty in classifying Christian organisations who do not accept the authority of scripture as false religions, when they also subscribe to the majority of main-stream Christian beliefs.

Much of the first volume of *Healing Through Deliverance* was spent in substantiating the position that Christians can have demons and that deliverance ministry is for them. It was seen that the belief that Christians cannot be demonised is a demonically inspired deception designed to keep people in bondage to the enemy without hope of any healing through deliverance. Ignorance of the enemy's ways makes it impossible to counter his attacks. However, there are other false beliefs, some of major significance, which also need highlighting in this respect.

For the purposes of this exercise I am defining a heretical Christian belief as an aspect of belief which we have found in ministry gives rights to demonic religious spirits and from which people have subsequently needed deliverance. As such, I admit that it is an experiential definition, but it is one of very considerable significance, especially when it is understood that we are talking about a wealth of experiential information from a number of different people operating in different areas of Christian ministry across the world.

If a belief has given rights to an evil spirit (become a demonic entry point), instead of opening the door for an anointing of the Holy Spirit, then one is standing on pretty strong ground in questioning the origin and nature of that particular tenet of a person's faith. Of course one has to be on one's guard against deception, for Satan will certainly want to confuse the body of Christ on these issues. That is why I emphasise that what I write here is not just the experience of one person operating in a spiritual vacuum, who could be in danger of being deceived. This is the condensed experience gained from ministering to many people and gathering information from many different sources and ministries.

In the following pages I will look in detail at beliefs concerning the scriptures, the Gifts of the Spirit, Baptism and Universalism. There are many others which could have been picked out for attention, but once readers have learnt to understand the principles, they will be able to recognise other possibilities for themselves. For example, beliefs about the second coming, creation, heaven and hell, the sacraments, ordination, etc., which run contrary to the collective teaching of scripture, will inevitably prove to be demonic entry points for those who hold them. We need to be very much on our guard against regarding any of our beliefs and practices as more important than either our relationship with Jesus or the authority of the word of God.

After swallowing an unscriptural view as if it is truth, the way is open for a spirit of deception to enter the mind and lead the person away from the truth into further deception.

iv) Wrong attitude to the scriptures

Satan and demons hate the scriptures, for they know them to be the inspired and authoritative word of God, written by the Holy Spirit through men. They know that the word of God is truth, and that inside every believer is an innate recognition of this fact. That is why Satan will sometimes even try to use scripture (suitably distorted to achieve his objectives) to tempt people, as he did with Jesus in the wilderness. For Christians are more likely to respond to a temptation that is dressed up in scriptural clothing than one which is a blatant lie from the enemy.

We have seen in many ministries that demons know scripture extremely well and are well-versed in how to counter the arguments of scripture. The ultimate example of this is the demons of satanism, which have so distorted the word of God that they have convinced satanists that the satanic bible is the one which is total truth and Christians are the ones who have twisted the truth for their own ends. One demon even tried to persuade us to believe that it is Christians who will one day have to face Satan, and not Satan who will have to face Jesus!

People can be deceived by the arguments (lies) that demons speak, but the demons themselves know the reality of God's word and need no convincing of its truth.

Satan's kingdom is a kingdom of fear. It is fear of punishment that holds the demonic powers in a hierarchy of satanic control in this dispensation. The fallen angels were expelled from heaven, along with Satan, and all that waits in eternity for the powers that joined Satan's cause is the lake of fire described in Revelation.

The idea of the second-coming is utterly horrific to the demonic powers, for they know that the coming of Jesus into the world for a second time will herald the beginning of eternal torment for them. Through fear of Satan the demonic powers are, in this age, held into the workings of the satanic web, which has been carefully constructed down the ages to enmesh as many human beings as possible and take them with the demons into eternal punishment. The very name of Jesus spells freedom to those who believe.

Those who would question the truth of the word of God need to see the horror on the faces of demonised people when the demons have been exposed and, as part of the process of deliverance, we have read from Revelation 20 and 21 or the words of Jesus about the *"eternal fire that has been prepared for the devil and his angels"* (Matthew 25:41). There is no doubt that the demons (supernatural spiritual beings who know the real truth about Jesus and the word of God) know that every word of scripture is true and that those who trust in the truth of God's word are a real threat to them!

It is interesting to observe that a less faithful attitude towards the scripture usually goes hand-in-hand with the brands of Christian belief which are either religious (without any emphasis being placed on the need for a personal relationship with God in Christ) or liberal (without any recognition of the personal nature of evil, and probably with a rampant disbelief in the actual existence of Satan or any of his demons).

The only attitude towards the scriptures which puts the fear of God into the demonic is one of absolute trust in the inspiration of the Bible by the Holy Spirit. We have seen armies of demons put to flight by those without theological training but with a trust in the word of God, which Paul described as the very sword of the Spirit (Ephesians 6:17). Equally, I have seen people with a string of theological qualifications powerless to wage war against the enemy!

One cannot be involved in this ministry of healing and deliverance without being challenged to the core about one's attitude to the word of God. Disbelief in the truth, authority or authorship of the scriptures is a major demonic entry point.

v) Abuse of the gifts of the Spirit

Even in circles which believe in the inerrancy of scripture, there are those who have such a distorted view of the New Testament church and the gifts of the Spirit that they deny the reality of those gifts for today. They propose, for example, that God intended the gifts of the Spirit to die out once the first generation of Christians had used them to demonstrate the truth about Jesus. All Christians from that point onwards needed to have only faith (not sight) in the fact that these sort of things did happen once. They would probably argue that to seek for the gifts today is evidence of lack of faith!

This sort of belief generates a somewhat surprising marriage of the traditional conservative evangelical and the liberal positions - two strands of Christian tradition which rarely have anything in common. One might be tempted to say that if there is anything which draws such widely diverging traditions together in unity it has to be either God or the devil! As the belief is, in fact, a denial of part of the word of God (written by the Holy Spirit) one has little difficulty in recognising the source of the deception.

One major difference between the rigid conservative evangelical viewpoint and the liberal position, however, is that the conservatives sometimes say that those who use the gifts of the Spirit (especially speaking in tongues), are using demons themselves or operating in the occult. The liberal, who does not believe in the existence of demons would not make such an accusation and would probably refer to simple delusion.

C. Fred Dickason, writing from the conservative viewpoint in his otherwise excellent treatise on *Demon Possession and the Christian*, unfortunately concludes (p.189) that *"spiritual gifts and tongues in the early church were (only) evidence to the Jews that Jesus had replaced Moses and that his Gospel was the truth"*. He goes on to say that he doubts if *"there are any tongues from God today in the New Testament sense"*. (Kurt Koch, in his books on healing and deliverance, makes a similar mistake.)

As evidence to support his viewpoint, Dickason states that he has delivered people of tongue-speaking demons that came in through the laying-on of hands. In one instance of ministry to a lady, he says that the demon admitted it had come in *"to give her what she desired and lead her astray"*. I believe the key to understanding what was going on in this case lies in the sentence quoted above. She was seeking the gift and not the giver. This simply emphasises how vital it is for all aspects of our faith to be Jesus-centred; otherwise the dangers of deception are immense. In cases such as this Satan will always be on hand to deceive people into receiving a demonic imitation of the real thing.

The evidence of such a deception does not deny the possibility of tongue-speaking being real; the very reverse is the truth. Satan only tries to imitate what is real, or else the deception would not be a temptation, for it would have no significance! I, too, have delivered people of demonic tongues, but that doesn't mean that all tongue-speaking is demonic.

In a body of people either speaking or singing in the spirit, it is not difficult to discern a tongue that is not of God. Often it seems spiritually harsh or strident, and one has an inner witness in the spirit about the source of the tongue. The gift of discernment is given to us by God to distinguish between those things that are from him and those things that are not (1 Corinthians 12:10). One would not need this particular gift if the need to distinguish between the true and the false was not going to occur.

To declare that all must be false is to deny the reality of a precious gift that God has given to bless his people. Whilst such a belief system may be convenient, non-threatening, non-demanding and risk-free, it does not have any scriptural warrant or experiential support from church history.

One could present similar arguments about the use of other gifts of the Spirit as listed by Paul in 1 Corinthians 12, Ephesians 4 and Romans 12 etc. But the conclusion in each case would be the same. Failure to accept that it is God's desire to bless his people through the use of these gifts and that as believers we should use them in all Christian ministries and spiritual warfare, is a demonic entry point that will hold the local church into the dictates of religious routine as opposed to the liberating dynamic of Holy Spirit life.

One senses that some church fellowships are like strong fighting men who are restrained by chains which are held in position by a massive padlock called unbelief. Often it is fear in the leadership which keeps their eyes so closed that they cannot even see the chains or the padlock, let alone put the key of faith into the padlock and liberate the congregation into actually being the Body of Christ!

vi) Universalism

The universalist ultimately believes that all people will be saved and that it does not really matter what you believe. They say that God is a loving God and he would not want to see any one of his children suffer the judgement of eternal punishment described in the scriptures. Rather than accept that Jesus is Truth, they invent a character for God which is more compatible with their own sensibilities and more tolerant of their own unbelief in the scriptures and the character and claims of Jesus as revealed in them.

God is indeed a God of love. He is also a righteous and holy God of judgement and mercy. The scriptures say that it is not the Father's will that any should perish. But the universalist takes this scripture in isolation and quietly glosses over the wealth of teaching, from most books of the Bible, which reveals the Father's heart for his children and the plan of salvation which was completed in the coming of Jesus, so that those who believe on him should not perish but have eternal life.

There is a ruling spirit behind universalism which is totally at variance with the work of the Holy Spirit and the teaching of the word of God. It is a spirit that blinds the eyes and the understanding of people to the real truth about Jesus and plays on their emotions in an effort to convince them that God cannot also be a God of judgement. The demons know only too well that judgement awaits them and that the resurrection of Jesus was ample evidence for them that what Jesus said about the judgement would certainly come true. During a recent ministry, an angry demon that was being cast out cried, *"If all Christians believed in the Bible as much as you and I do, we wouldn't have a chance!"*

Universalism is a heresy and a deception. Those who have been brought up in churches that have preached a universalist Gospel need to repent and turn from such beliefs, place their belief wholeheartedly in the Jesus of the scriptures, ask God for forgiveness and receive eternal life. They will also need deliverance from the demons that have tried to cloud their minds and hide them from the truth.

Where a minister of a church knows that previous ministries have had a universalist (or other heretical belief system) emphasis, it will be necessary for the minister to repent on behalf of his predecessors and to take authority over the demonic powers that will have been given rights over his church. Without such action he will be continuously fighting unseen demonic powers which are hanging on to the rights given to them by previous leaders of the church.

vii) False religions

I have given some considerable space to helping readers understand some of the ways in which the demonic can be operating in churches, as this area is generally much less understood than the more obvious demonic power behind religions which are clearly heretical in their attitudes to the person of Jesus Christ (eg. Mormonism, Jehovah's Witnesses and Christadelphians,) or which are specifically non- or anti-Christian in their belief system (Buddhism, Sikhism, Islam, Hinduism etc).

All of these are deceptions. Many of them are hundreds or, in some cases, thousands of years old. They were devised by Satan as a means of attracting worship to himself via the deceptions of religious demons. There seem to be as many forms of religious expression in the world as there are races or cultures. Each of them holds their own religion up as the truth, but clearly this cannot be so, for one person's truth conflicts with that proclaimed by another equally convinced worshipper of a different God.

When people have been converted to Christ from these other religions they not only need to proclaim their faith in Jesus, but they also have to turn their back on the beliefs and powers behind their former religion. Churches operating in eastern cultures know this only too well, and it is quite normal in East Asia, for example, for new converts to be taken through a course of deliverance ministry as part of their Christian initiation.

Would that the western church might begin to realise that when people are converted in their countries it is from just as pagan a cultural or religious background as is found in other parts of the world. The only difference is that the nature of the demonic power controlling their previous lives may not have the character of a known false religion, but may be of atheism, materialism, agnosticism etc. If we were to recognise the amount of work there is to do in the lives of new Christians, so that they can be cleansed and made whole, then the church itself would have far fewer problems in the future having to battle, usually unknowingly, against the resident demonic powers that lie hidden in its members!

For ease of reference an outline of the belief systems of the better known non-Christian religions is provided in Appendix 5, along with details of the more commonly encountered wrong beliefs which are regularly found within the church.

For those who have been actively involved in the practice of one of these religions, there is likely to be a whole nest of demons attached to each aspect of demonic deception.

Deliverance, therefore, is not necessarily of just one demon, but may require systematic repentance and deliverance from each demonic stronghold in turn.

6. Ungodly soul-ties

This and the next section (on sex and sexuality) need to be read side-by-side. Sexual relationships which are outside God's plan and purpose will always introduce ungodly soul-ties into a person's life and make that person vulnerable to the demonic.

A soul-tie is a relationship in which we are either rightfully bonded or subject to bondage. I am using the word bond (bonded and bonding) to indicate a rightful and healthy relationship and the word bondage to indicate a relationship which is unhealthy and has in it an element of being tied against both the free will of the victim in the relationship and against God's plan for healthy relationships between human beings.

In the Old Testament we have a description of the relationship between David and Jonathan, and it was said that their souls were knit together in love (1 Samuel 18:1 AV). This was a healthy and Godly relationship which clearly brought great blessing to them both. In contrast, there was an obviously ungodly relationship between Saul and David, in which Saul tried to dominate, control and eventually kill David. These two extremes of relationship typify the differences between bonding and bondage, between Godly and ungodly soul-ties.

There are many basically Godly relationships which can also have an ungodly dimension to them. For example, a father has a Godly relationship with his daughter, but if that father chooses to sexually abuse his daughter, he would introduce another soul-tie into the relationship - one of bondage as opposed to healthy bonding.

As a general rule, Godly soul-ties are God's provision for healthy nurturing and for relationships throughout life, whereas ungodly soul-ties will lead to sickness, and more often than not, the danger of being demonised.

i) In family life

We cannot choose our parents or the family into which we are born, yet the first people we have soul-ties with are our family, as a direct consequence of our conception and birth. If parents have a Godly relationship with each other, and in turn establish a Godly relationship with each child, providing each one with a healthy parental bonding and adequate discipline without unnecessary domination or control, then the child will grow up in the security of a soul-tie that will be liberating for life.

Children will learn from their parenting how to develop healthy relationships with other children, and as the children grow up the soul-tie with the parents will steadily mature and change so that the parents will be able to release their adult children into the world, free to be men and women in their own right. With parental soul-ties like these, maturing adults are free to relate to God without the imposition of unhealthy parental pressures and free to choose a mate with whom a Godly soul-tie can be established without claustrophobic parental control.

Such ungodly controls can lead both to wrong choice of a marital partner and the eventual destruction of the marriage relationship. Mother-in-law jokes have a deep root in the reality of life's experiences!

An upbringing with ungodly soul-ties can produce a harvest of problems and pain. For example, if the parents themselves have a selfish, body-centred, sinful and immature relationship, children born to them will not be equipped to relate rightly in their own lives.

The children will not be able to relate well with their peers at school, as they will be reflecting the inadequacies of their own parenting in these relationships. Many teachers see the relationships between the parents lived out in the playground! The boy who gets his own way by hitting the girls has probably learnt the technique from a father (or possibly a grandfather) for whom it is an effective means of dominating his wife.

An ungodly marriage relationship will inevitably lead to parent-child ties which have an ungodly element within them, and there is likely to be more bondage than bonding between the parents and the child. Bondage leads to rebellion. This is sometimes known as bitter-root judgement where the sinful attitudes of one generation become reflected in the pressures and pain experienced by the next. It is a cycle from which the only way of escape is through the saving, healing and delivering power of Jesus.

The natural reaction of a child to parental soul-ties born out of bondage is to escape. Deep down such a child is suffering from rejection. There are a number of well-worn paths that children follow when they are seeking to break free from the chains that rejection has placed upon them.

The extremes are total retreat into an externally passive personality (but inside there will usually be a cauldron of pain, ready to erupt like a dormant volcano without prior warning) and at the other end of the scale is the rebellion of teenage years which can manifest itself in drugs, violence, promiscuity, crime, running away and a host of other rebellious activities. The range of potential behaviour patterns is almost limitless, as is evidenced by the heartbreak of many parents of teenage children.

Within all this hurt and pain the demonic can have a field day. The entry points created by ungodly family soul-ties are enormous, many of them having a root in rejection. But once the reaction to ungodly parental soul-ties has set in, be it one of rebellion, passive sullenness or a mixture of both, the demonic will then further ride in on all the sinful behaviour patterns which are then established.

ii) Abuse of freewill

All abusive relationships result in the formation of ungodly soul-ties, whether the abuse is that of parents who simply reject their child for any of a variety of reasons or the more overt abuse of sexual handling or manipulation. The key to understanding whether or not a soul-tie is Godly or ungodly lies within the scriptural understanding of what it means to live in the free will that God intended each of his children to exercise.

God intended free will to be exercised within the secure framework of parental discipline, which is gradually enlarged and relaxed as the child prepares for adulthood, and the even more secure framework for living provided by a direct relationship with God, as the child finds personal faith in Jesus and is equipped for life in spirit, soul and body.

Free will is perhaps the most precious gift that God has given to mankind. The fact that man used his free will to sin by turning his back on the God who had made him, did not cause God either to turn away from his creation or to take away man's freedom to choose. God does not want to have relationships with people who are compelled to relate to him whether they like it or not. He gave us free will to choose who we should relate with and how we should spend our lives. His desire is that, through faith in Jesus Christ, we should choose to re-enter the covenant relationship with him that was destroyed by sin.

We are made in the image of God (Genesis 1:26) and, among other things, that must mean we should have the same attitude towards others that God has towards us. We must respect the free will of others and choose not to dominate or control them against their will. To do so runs contrary to God's creation ordinance and is in direct rebellion against God's plans and purposes for mankind. But take note, Godly discipline of those for whom we have responsible care is not the same as domination and control. Without discipline, children (and adults!) will not learn how to use their free will in such a way that they will avoid further problems!

The scripture describes rebellion as being *"as bad as witchcraft"* (1 Samuel 15:23 GNB). It is not insignificant, therefore, that domination and control of others (often through fear or direct demonic intervention) are hallmarks of witchcraft practice. These are the methods and tactics of Satan. When domination and manipulation are used to control people with whom we have soul-ties, the effects can be as devastating as the direct actions of witchcraft.

This is graphically illustrated when at a public meeting I ask all those who sense in their spirits that they have been dominated and controlled in an ungodly way by their parents to stand. Often as many as 30% to 40% respond. I ask them all to forgive and honour their parents (for however bad the parents may have been, they were the vehicle for God's creativity, and we are commanded to honour them) and then I break the ungodly soul-ties that have existed between them and their parents.

I am usually cautious only to do this when I have a significant ministry team available in the meeting with me, for the reaction can be instantaneous. The moment the soul-ties are cut, both the demonic power that has been held in by them is free to go and the emotional pain that has been created by the domination and control, often over decades, is free to be expressed.

The healing that flows from times like this is quite extraordinary. The letters which follow such meetings, describing physical as well as emotional and psychological healing and healing of relationships, have to be read to be fully appreciated. It is only when one sees the extent of demonic bondage that is controlled by ungodly parental soul-ties that one realises how vital the deliverance ministry is for bringing people through to wholeness.

Those that seek to heal parental relationships using an inner healing model only, will often come up against the demonic without recognising it. Clearly some demonic is dealt with, almost by accident, in this way. But sadly, it has not been unusual for inner healing ministries to go on for weeks, months and even years trying to cope with what is believed to be just emotional pain. In practice what is being encountered is an unrecognised demon which is both enjoying the attention of continuous ministry and delighting to occupy the time of both the counsellor and the counsellee in totally unfruitful ministries!

Demons cannot be 'inner healed'! If that lesson alone could be learned and appreciated by those who practice inner healing, but don't either believe in or have an understanding of the need for deliverance, many otherwise extensive ministries could be concluded almost immediately. I am not saying that inner healing is not necessary and important - it is. For almost as big a problem can be caused by those who only want to cast out demons and have no appreciation of the need for inner healing - especially of damaged emotions! Both ministries have to go hand-in-hand in a balanced way for maximum benefit.

All ungodly soul-ties, whatever their origin, seem to be a direct channel for the demonic to use as an entry point. In ministry to people with complex problems and complicated personal histories we have found that systematically dealing with any necessary repentance or forgiveness associated with particular relationships, and then breaking the soul-ties, has been a very effective foundation for healing and deliverance ministry. Sometimes, the demonic has been so undermined by this procedure that deliverance has happened spontaneously as soon as the soul-tie has been cut with a word of command. But most times we have found that commanding the demons that came in through that entry point to leave has resulted in extensive deliverance ministry taking place.

iii) Potentially dangerous relationships

The following are the principal ungodly soul-ties which we have found to be regularly used by the demonic as powerful channels for demonisation to take place.

a) Sexual partners other than one's husband or wife

It is rare to find that a person has not picked up demons through having immoral sexual relationships. Sex is primarily spiritual and so when people enter into sexual relationships that are sinful they should not be surprised that the demonic will take advantage of the channel that has been opened up through sin. (Whether they are aware of the spiritual dimension or not is irrelevant, as far as the demons are concerned).

We live in an age when it is relatively rare not to be ministering to people who have had more than one sexual partner, and it is not unusual for people to talk about ten or more sexual partners that they have had over the years. In addition to the demonic factor, which is so powerful in all such cases, there is also the fragmentation of the spirit and soul that takes place every time a person has sex with a new partner.

When two people are joined together in sex, it is not just a bodily (flesh) union. It is also a spiritual one. A husband and a wife are spiritually aware of each other at all times because there is rightfully something of each other's spirit in each of them - that is part of the mystery of marriage. But this spiritual transaction is not only a consequence of sexual relationships which take place inside marriage, it is a consequence of all sexual relationships whether they take place inside marriage or not. So, when a person has had sex with many partners it is as if their spirit (and soul) is spread out all over the place. Often people will describe it in words such as, *"I sometimes wonder who or where I am"*.

When people have truly repented of their sinful sexual behaviour and the ungodly soul-ties have been broken, we have then found it to be a important part of the ministry to ask God to bring back to the individual every part of them which has been attached to the different partners involved. Very often people will describe what happens in words such as: *"I felt myself coming back together - for the first time that I can remember, I feel whole"*.

The dissipation of the spirit and the demonisation of the person that happens through sexual sin helps one to understand why Satan pushes this particular temptation so relentlessly. Sexual sin leaves people very vulnerable to the enemy, often labouring under overwhelming guilt, and in bondage to the demonic in a wide variety of ways.

Sex was designed by God as his way of allowing mankind to express his creativity. Satan cannot create, he can only distort. To distort what God planned and purposed in sexual relationships for mankind is a major achievement for the master deceiver. The voice of the tempter, *"Has God really said that it's wrong?"* has trapped countless millions of people into relationships through which people have, as it were, sold their birthright for a few minutes of pleasurable acceptance.

For many, the dangers of disease from a promiscuous lifestyle have proved to be insignificant when compared with the spiritual dangers and spiritual blindness which have resulted from an undisciplined sexual life.

Having said all the above, I realise that many people reading this may suddenly be feeling uncomfortable as they review both the potential and the real consequences of their previous indiscretions and wonder if there is any way back for them. There is, so be encouraged!

We have seen countless people set free, some very dramatically, from their past and liberated into being the people God intended them to be. But there is no short cut to restoration that does not go via the cross. The scripture says, *"Confess your sins one to another, that you may be healed"* (James 5:16). We have found, especially in the area of sexuality, that confession of sin to someone else, followed by the necessary prayer ministry has had enormous healing consequences in the person's life, sometimes, even, of a dramatic physical nature.

We have usually found that the first sexual partner is the most significant. The moment a person loses their virginity is a spiritually traumatic occasion, usually surrounded with extremes of emotional feelings ranging from elation to disappointment. If this moment does not occur within the spiritual security of a Godly marriage, it can be accompanied by heavy doses of guilt and fear as well. That is a moment when the participants are especially prone to the demonic.

Another time of intense demonic activity is when a person betrays their marital partner and commits adultery by having sex outside of marriage. At that moment the marriage vows are broken, and spiritually an act of divorce has taken place. In the spiritual realms it is as if the innocent partner has already been divorced by the intent of the guilty one, because a new spiritual union has been established in addition to the original one. Divorce and remarriage have taken place simultaneously!

No wonder the consequential spiritual pain associated with adultery is so great that there are very few relationships that fully survive the experience of adultery, irrespective of whether or not it is ever found out. If it is never found out the marriage relationship will suffer in many intangible ways, with the other partner often left wondering what they have to do to please the one they married.

There are many couples who carry on living together in a married relationship in spite of one of the partners having committed adultery. But one has to ask questions about the quality of the marriage from that moment on. To come through the experience with both partners fully healed requires full confession and repentance, followed by total forgiveness. Then, because a divorce has already taken place, there should be a renewal of one's vows to each other before God and witnesses (a remarriage).

At that point the relationship has a chance of being even better than it was at its best before the adultery took place. But if the adultery remains a secret sin, the marriage will be so impaired spiritually that there will be consequences at every level.

Whilst this section on soul-ties is not a treatise on divorce and remarriage, it does need to be said in passing that there are occasions when the person who goes off and commits adultery is not, before God, the initially 'guilty party' in the breakdown of the relationship, even though he or she has been the one caught in the act. There are many marriages in which the superficially 'innocent party' has so subjected his or her partner, often with deep rejection and belittling behaviour, that the 'guilty party' has already been divorced by their partner and, literally, been driven away from the marriage.

I do not say this to excuse the sin involved in adultery, but as a caution to counsellors to tread gently when trying to help people who have suffered the pain of such marital problems. It just may be that the superficially innocent party is the more guilty! It is too easy to tread heavily on the toes of the hurting. Jesus' attitude to the woman caught in the act of adultery was one of compassion and forgiveness. Let us not go beyond the attitude which Jesus had. But remember, also, he said, *"Go, but do not sin again"!* (John 8:11 GNB).

b) Sex before marriage

A sinful sexual relationship can also take place between those who are intending to get married! Those who anticipate marriage and commence a sexual relationship outside the security of the marriage bond are just as vulnerable to the demonic as those who are promiscuous without any intention of getting married to each other, or who commit adultery outside of marriage.

One person who confessed that she and her husband had commenced sexual relations together three months before they got married (neither of them had ever had sex with any other partner either before or after marriage) had become an epileptic shortly after they married. We did not know this when we first ministered to her. But she heard and understood the teaching and wanted to put it right before God. Immediately she confessed the sin and the ungodly dimension to the soul-tie with her husband had been broken, the powers of darkness were commanded to leave. As they did, she collapsed and manifested all the symptoms of having a grand mal epileptic fit on our meeting room floor.

Ten minutes later she had a second fit, but then got up off the floor claiming to have been completely healed. We asked her why she said that. She told us that she was on the highest possible safe dosage of anti-epileptic drugs allowed and still she had many fits. Every time she had a fit it would normally take two to three days in a darkened room to recover from the pain, the trauma and the flashing lights. But after two fits in the course of her prayer ministry, she got up immediately and felt great!

Three years later she wrote, telling us how she had come off all her anti-epileptic drugs (in cooperation with her local doctor) within a matter of weeks. Since then, she has had no further fits and has not been on any medication either! In her case the sexual sin had opened up a demonic doorway for two spirits of infirmity, causing epilepsy, to come into her and as soon as her relationship (which had become ungodly) was consecrated before God in marriage, the curse of epilepsy that had been placed upon her began to manifest itself.

I doubt if the spirits of epilepsy would have manifested at all if she had decided to continue in a promiscuous lifestyle with other people. In that case they would have then been passed down the generation line to her children who would have been wondering where the epilepsy had come from. Many people are suffering from the effects of demons which have gained access through the sins of their fathers without ever realising it. There is only one answer: forgiveness of those in the ancestral line, repentance for any known sin, cutting the soul-ties and deliverance, leading to healing.

One must not conclude from this story that all epileptics have committed sexual sin – they haven't. Nor should one conclude that all those who commit sexual sin are likely to become epileptics! But in her case that was the outcome. The potential nature of the demonic which invades a person through sin can vary from straightforward spirits of lust to spirits of infirmity bringing a specific disease - sometimes the consequences are related to whatever demons were in the person one had sexual relations with.

As I ministered to one man, who had established many soul-ties with a variety of sexual partners, I systematically broke the ties and took him through deliverance for the first four of the partners. But when I came to the fifth, a demon roared from inside the man, *"You are not having her!!"* It transpired that this particular partner had been into active witchcraft, and through sex with her the man had picked up some powerful witchcraft controls. Whilst the kingdom of darkness that ruled in the man was not too concerned about losing the demons associated with the first four partners, the demons that came from the fifth were very important in the demonic kingdom. A real power struggle ensued until the rights of the demons to stay had been fully dealt with through repentance and deliverance had taken place.

c) Inside marriage

As was hinted above, all may not be well within a marriage relationship, even if the partners appear to be living happily together and neither of them has tried to escape into an adulterous relationship. There are many marriages, even Christian ones, which are often very well camouflaged for public observance, but which fall a long way short of the relationship that God intended them to have – a joyful love-filled union of spirit, soul and body with:

i)   Complete trust on both sides of the relationship

ii) Mutual respect for each other as people

iii) Appreciation and encouragement of each other's gifts and abilities

iv) An uninhibited sexual relationship which is the fruit of harmony in spirit, soul and body

v)   Physical care of each other and the children that God gives

vi)   Joint desire that God's will for their relationship should come first at all times, and

vii) No domination or manipulation from either partner!

I realise that in describing a marriage in the above terms I am describing a relationship which is probably of a standard rather above the average marriage, be it Christian or otherwise. But what I can say is that the further from the ideal that a couple go, the more likely it is that the ungodly dimensions to their relationship will provide entry points for the demonic. Too often we have counselled people who have behaved within a relationship as if they have absolute liberty to treat their husband or wife without respect, using and abusing them and then complaining when he or she cannot stand it any longer and goes off with someone else!

Manipulation and domination within the marriage relationship is responsible for a huge amount of marital unhappiness and is nothing but sin! Marriage does not entitle either partner to use the cover of a marriage bond to tie the partner into being the victim of what has become an ungodly soul-tie. Sadly, there has been very little training within the church as to how marital partners should behave towards each other without resorting to manipulation or domination. This whole area has been given scant attention. Most people are ignorant of the huge amount of damage that is caused, and the extent of demonic power that is liberated, when marital relationships become ungodly in this way.

For example, some of the classic tactics used by partners against each other are as follows:

Early in the marriage the husband will lose his temper violently. Then such is the wife's fear of it ever happening again that for the rest of the marriage she tiptoes round her husband so as never again to awaken the 'sleeping giant'. Thus the husband has his wife totally controlled through fear. That aspect of the marriage is ungodly and demonic.

Should she ever be allowed to receive help, the wife will eventually need to have the ungodly tie cut and be set free from the spirits of domination and fear which formerly held her in bondage. And the husband will need to be in deep repentance over what he has done. He will also need to seek the Lord over his own personal needs which have made him behave in such a way. When a man behaves like that, and such behaviour is very common, it is indicative of his own deep needs, possibly arising out of childhood rejection and fear.

On the other side of the relationship a wife will often belittle her husband, especially in the sexual area, and use sex as a system of reward and punishment in order to keep her husband exactly where she wants him. Usually, neither party can fully understand what is happening, but at heart the husband will know that his manhood is belittled and she will know that if she does not control this area of the marriage that she will lose the power she needs to stay secure.

These are just examples. There are many other ways in which ungodly distortion of the marriage can take place, but at root they are usually variations on the theme of manipulation, domination and control. In all such cases the ungodly soul-ties need to be cut so that people can be set free from the demonic dimensions involved and hold up rightful spiritual authority within the marriage that can then become Godly. The process may be painful, but without such courageous action the only future for the marriage is more of the same, with the prospect of things getting steadily worse until old age, when the remaining fruits on the tree of marriage will be unhealthy and bitter.

Finally, before moving on to other soul-ties, it needs to be said that even though two people are married, they are not allowed to use each other sexually in acts which would otherwise be categorised as abusive or perverted. We have counselled many couples, one of whom feels the victim of sexual abuse. This is usually the result of the husband wanting the wife to do things (such as anal or oral sex) that she does not want to participate in. We have found in ministry that perverted sex, even inside marriage, is a direct demonic entry point, and that even married couples who have practised sexual perversions have needed deliverance as a result.

Equally, it needs to be said that sexual intercourse is a normal, rightful and necessary part of married life. Paul makes it very clear (1 Corinthians 7:5) that there is only one reason why intercourse should be discontinued within marriage, and that is for prayer, and only for a short season, because of the dangers of temptation arising through the consequential frustration.

The husband or wife who denies his or her partner regular and willing sexual relations is abusing the other partner. I have counselled many a man who is made to feel like a 'dirty old man' for desiring sex with his wife. But we have also counselled many women whose husbands in middle life have allegedly lost interest in sex with their wives.

Sometimes I have felt that the wife's attitude to her own body has been a definite discouragement to the husband, but on other occasions I have wondered if the reason why the husband has lost interest in his wife is because he is getting his sexual fulfilment elsewhere, either through another relationship, or, more commonly in a Christian marriage, through pornography and masturbation.

The opportunity for ungodliness in the soul-ties between husband and wife are many and varied. Wherever there is ungodliness there is also the potential for demonisation. It is a fact that the greatest potential pain and joy is found in relationships with those who are closest to us. Breaking the ungodly ties and delivering from the demonic are necessary foundations for healing between marital partners.

d) Parents and children

Most parents rejoice in the gift of children. They enter fully into the fun (and frustrations!) of raising a family. However, for some parents, their whole identity can get wrapped up in the role of being a parent. This can especially be the case for the mother. If the marriage relationship itself is insecure, or if she does not have a career to take up again after the children have matured, then definite precautions need to be taken against potential problems. For God did not intend our whole identity as people to be tied up in our children's dependency on us.

For some women the presence of dependent children gives them their security. They provide affirmation and cherishing, and if these essential ingredients to marital life are not provided by the husband then Mum feels like a spare part without a future once the children grow up and leave home.

So, a woman in this situation will do all she can to continue the years of dependency for her children well beyond the age of growing up into adulthood (individuation) so as to extend the years of the mother's usefulness. However this is dressed up it is ultimately sin, for it is an attempt to deprive the children of their free will and independence, without which they will never make it successfully into the maturity of adulthood. They are especially unlikely to make successful marriages because the ties to mother will be too strong for the offspring to relate rightfully with his or her new partner.

The scriptural formula for a successful marriage in this respect is to leave and cleave. The leaving of the parental home and security must be clear and definite. The specific meaning of cleave in this context is to join together in a marital relationship independent of all other human relationships. The word used for leave implies a severing, not just a waving goodbye till next time we meet!

That does not mean to say that parents will never see their children again. It means that the children will be free to relate with their parents in a mature and adult way and will not be afraid to establish adult relationships with their parents, for they know that they will not be dominated by them. It is only when parents are willing to 'lose' their children in this way that they 'gain' them for the rest of their lives.

I have always been astonished at the amount of demonic power that is exercised over children by parents in order to hold them in bondage. When the ties are cut the release of emotional pain and subsequent deliverance is often quite astonishing. What is also of great significance when praying for physical healing is that sickness and infirmities that have been passed down the generation line are often transferred through a dominating parental relationship. When that ungodly soul-tie is cut, illness which has resisted every other form of prayer previously is suddenly free to be healed through deliverance.

Would that in every marriage service both mother and father of the bride (and not just the father as is our tradition) 'gave away' their daughter, and both parents of the bridegroom would equally release their son. Much heart-ache and many mother-in-law problems would be instantly resolved!

7.   Sexual sin

I have already touched on many different aspects of sexuality, sexual sin and sexual relationships in the above sections on the demonic dangers of ungodly soul-ties. Sexuality has implications across many frontiers of life and in this section I want to draw together the different ways in which sexuality can be distorted by the enemy, so creating a wealth of demonic entry points which he delights to use.

Part of the advantage in this area has been handed to the enemy by the church through their failure to teach sexual ethics in a positive and helpful way to the succeeding generations of young people who have passed through their hands. The Bible does not adopt this coy and prudish attitude to sexuality. In many places it is very explicit in its descriptions. By way of contrast with the scriptures, casual observers of the church's teaching might be tempted to think that sexual reproduction was not the way Christians are born into the world, for they must have their own special sanitised and sexless way of creating children!

The mode of reproduction for mankind was a supreme part of God's creative act in making men and women. In it he chose not only to share with mankind his creative power, but to give to mankind something unknown to the whole of the rest of creation. For only man, and not dogs, monkeys or any other creature, are described as having been made in the image of God. They have the ability to know each other in the spirit as well as experience each other with the emotions and be connected, via the sexual organs, in the flesh.

Intercourse which does not reflect this divine and spiritual knowing is less than God intended for mankind. Strange though it may seem, especially to those who only associate prudishness with Christian belief, it is only believers who truly know God, who as a result are able to truly know each other (spiritually, as well as in the flesh) and for whom sex has the potential of being the very best that it can possibly be!

To propound a theory that a good sexual relationship in marriage and Christian belief go hand in hand may be considered, by some, to be going beyond the bounds of propriety, and for others, with traumatic and painful experiences in the sexual area both inside and outside of marriage, to be beyond the bounds of possibility! All people come into marriage with a range of hurts and difficulties. If these remain unhealed then they will affect, to one degree or another, the sexual relations of the respective partners.

However, I believe that where there has not been an irretrievable breakdown of the relationship through undealt-with sin or hidden sexual abuse to one or both of the partners, and both partners are willing, restoration of a joyful sexual relationship is not only possible but highly desirable. And make no mistake, this is one area of Christian healing which Satan will fight tooth and nail to oppose. He cannot stand the joy that marital partners will experience together, and he fears the consequence of two people who are rightfully married fulfilling their full potential before God. Two who are fully joined together and who are totally fulfilled in every aspect of their relationship are a very powerful combination in which the enemy will have to struggle to gain a foothold.

By placing emphasis in the above comments on sex inside marriage, I am only emphasising the fact that God intended sex to be restricted to within the marital state. I am not saying that single people do not have sexuality, or that they do not have sexual problems. The sexual problems of the single state are often far greater, especially living as we do in an era where the social climate is one that encourages a very lax attitude towards sex outside of marriage.

The demonic problems created by sexual sin clearly affect both the single and the married, but often in very different ways. A spirit that entered a girl through sexual abuse may so work within the girl as to prevent her from ever wanting a married relationship, because of the sexual content. But as a person she is desperate for love and companionship. So she is held in the painful cleft stick of longing for a relationship which, by an act of her own will, she has chosen to deny herself. All the signals that go out to men are that she wants friends but no intimacy. But there are not many men who would willingly choose to enter a marriage on these terms, and so many potential marriage relationships never get off the ground. If the demonic root is unrecognised then there is no hope for the victim.

Since sex is such a spiritual matter, it is clearly very important that people should understand the ways in which Satan will pervert sexuality so as to destroy the spiritual dimension which gives Christian sex inside marriage such wonderful potential, and which will cause frustrations, and even desperation, in the single person.

Our experience in the counselling room would indicate that, for many Christians, their sexual relationships fall a long way short of God's intention. It is important that people should understand the ways in which the enemy creates problems so that they can be overcome.

The following are the major ways through which the demonic invades the life of man and affects the sexuality:

i) Generational sexual sin

As referred to earlier, the sins of the ancestors can result in demonic power affecting subsequent generations. For example, a family history of adultery will not only make the succeeding generations more accepting of adulterous relationships, but a spirit of adultery is likely to be in operation forcing members of the family down this particular track.

ii) Sexual abuse

Wherever there has been sexual abuse, however light or heavy it may have been, there is a likelihood of demonisation which will always seek to distort and damage Godly relationships.

For example, a girl may have been sexually abused only once in early childhood. Traumatic though the event may have been at the time, it is likely to have been well buried amongst the other events of the past. However, the demon which came in through the incident has not forgotten, so when the girl marries a Christian man, the demon (often a spirit of fear) will do all it can to interfere with their sexual relationship.

For distress in this area will create maximum havoc in the relationship and destroy much of the potential before God that the couple have as man and wife. It is not unusual, therefore, to find that spirits that came in with the abuse surface shortly after marriage, although they are usually not recognised for what they are. Unless the woman is delivered, the couple are likely to experience a lot of pain together before being forced to settle for a very inadequate sexual relationship, or abandoning the relationship altogether.

Along the way they may have been encouraged by a range of marriage counsellors, usually not Christians, to try all sort of different ways of improving things, even including the use of pornography or varieties of perverted sex. With such methods there may seem to be some temporary improvements in some aspects of sexual function, but always, the end result is that the couple have given access to more demons through these practices and the eventual result is yet greater problems from which they will have to recover. It sometimes seems as though the couple have been handed a spade with which to dig their own grave. You cannot improve sexual relations which are in a state of dysfunction due to spiritual problems by conduct which is aimed at improving only the fleshly area of the relationship through the soul and the body.

In saying the above I am not saying that there isn't a place for advice and counselling to help with the emotions and medical advice to help with any actual physical problem that either the man or the woman has, for clearly there is. What I am saying is that unless the spiritual (demonic) problems are resolved, no amount of help or counselling will offer more than short-term hope, and when this is dashed the result is yet greater pain and despair.

iii) Dominating soul-ties

Dominating parental soul-ties spell disaster for healthy sexual relationships inside marriage. A dominant soul-tie with mother, for example, will often result in the child having a spirit that has gained access through the mother. Such an evil spirit can even mimic the character and dominance of the mother, so that even if mother is many miles away, the person feels the pressure inside of mother's influence.

Marriage is a rightful breaking away from the parental cover. A dominating maternal spirit will always oppose such attempts at liberty. This is experienced most obviously in the bedroom. Some men, for example, have recounted to me how when they are having sex with their wife it seems as though their wife's mother is around, and sometimes, worse than this, as if at those times the wife is indeed the mother! In practice what these men have been coming up against is the spirit of their wife's mother manifesting in order to oppose the liberty which the wife has set her heart on by getting married.

For illustration I have used an example of a man coming up against the spirit of the mother in his wife. In experience the reverse is just as common! A woman will come up against the spirit of her husband's mother, which so dominated him that he is not free to relate to his wife as a wife, but only as a mother substitute! Many is the marriage, Christian or otherwise, that has foundered on this particular rock!

It is easy to see, with this understanding, how important it is to break the ungodly soul-ties to parents and deliver people of all controlling and dominating spirits which have come down the generation line. Indeed, without such freedom the scope for healthy and liberating sexual relationships inside marriage, and a healthy and controllable sexuality for singles, is considerably limited, with the result that sexual temptation, of varying types from pornography to having a lover, becomes ever more difficult to resist.

iv) Pre-marital intercourse and trial marriages

All forms of sexual relations which are not within the secure bounds of a marriage relationship are sin. Sadly, sexual sin is not often openly confessed and dealt with fully before God. Unconfessed and, therefore, unforgiven sin gives clear ground to the enemy for demons to enter and stay.

Every time a person has sex outside of marriage an ungodly soul-tie is established and the demons are given rights of entry. The deeper a person enters into such immoral relationships the stronger becomes the hold of the demonic on the participants and this can then become a gateway for further, and sometimes extensive, demonisation. In counselling we have found it necessary to explore (gently) this whole area of previous sexual relationships, especially with people who appear to have been suffering for some long time with problems (medical or otherwise) that have persisted without apparent reason or which have been undiagnosable.

For example, it is not unusual to find that spirits of infirmity or of the occult have taken advantage of an ungodly soul-tie and transferred across from one sexual partner to the other. God's standards for sexual relationships as set out in the Bible may seem, to some, to be out-of-date. It does not take much experience in this area of ministry to underline that it is the participants in sexual sin who are out-of-date!

v) Oral and anal sex

God designed man and woman to be able to have intercourse by the insertion of the male sexual organ into the female one. Subsequent orgasm is then a source of intense pleasure for both partners and the ejaculation of the sperm into the female is the means of fertilising the eggs so that reproduction may occur. Ejaculation of the sperm into any other orifice is a perversion of what God planned and purposed for mankind.

We have found that when people, married or not, have indulged in such perverted sex, demons with a similarly perverted character have also entered. The consequences have been everything from physical infirmities in and around the organs involved, often of a medically undiagnosable nature, to an increasingly lustful desire for more and more perverted sex. It is a pathway that the demonic will always encourage people to walk down, once having entered through the gateway of perversion.

There are no grounds for encouraging oral or anal sex, even in the case of people who for other physical reasons find normal sexual intercourse a human impossibility. Oral and anal sex are major demonic entry points.

vi) Homosexuality and lesbianism

The homosexual lifestyle is expressly forbidden in scripture. There are several references underlining this in both the Old and the New Testaments (eg. Lev. 18:22, Rom. 1:26-32). No amount of reinterpretation of the scripture in the light of social or cultural considerations can so moderate the implications of the word of God on these issues as to convince even the most liberal of theologians that the scripture says anything else but that in the eyes of God homosexuality and lesbianism is wrong.

What I have observed, however, is that amongst those who advocate such things as the 'gay Christian movement' (there never really can be such a thing, just as there never can be such a thing as Christian yoga!) there is a marked aversion to respecting the authority of scripture on anything. Once having declared that homosexual relationships are acceptable, one can do nothing else but adopt an equally liberal view of the rest of scripture. There is then no longer any standard, which can reasonably be upheld, which is based on scriptural truth.

Indulgence in homosexual relationships of any type provides such clear grounds for the demonic that it is rare to find someone who has either been the victim of homosexual abuse, or someone who has willingly, even in ignorance, had such contact with people, who is not demonised and in need of deliverance. For example, there are many men who as young boys were wrongfully touched by older men in homosexual abuse. This victimisation, as well as intentional homosexual involvement, can sometimes lead to demonically induced impotence inside an otherwise Godly marriage.

The worldwide scourge of AIDS is a disease which has been spread extensively through homosexual immorality. Even medics of no Christian belief spell out clearly that if there had not been homosexual relationships between men, AIDS would not have spread in the way that it has. But now the disease has spread and many people who have had no homosexual relationships have become victims. The sins of the fathers have been dramatically visited on the children in the case of babies born to those who have been infected by the HIV virus.

There are many potential causes of homosexuality, but I believe that in all cases the option of condoning homosexual sin, on the grounds that the homosexual person did not choose to be homosexual and therefore has no personal discretion in the matter, avoids the issue of a spiritual source being at the root of the homosexual tendency. I believe that following confession and repentance, homosexuals can be delivered and healed and that this should be the normal Christian response to a homosexual who seeks help. It does not help the person to condone the sin attached to the lifestyle when he knows in his spirit that God has made it very clear that homosexual sin is contrary to his plans and purposes for man.

The basic possible causes of homosexual tendencies, as seen from the deliverance viewpoint, are as follows:

a) **A generational spirit of homosexuality** being passed down through either the mother or the father. This could come from the parents themselves, or much further back in the generation line. The curse of sexual sin in the line would appear to go much further back than the curses of three or four generations for idolatry. Deuteronomy talks about ten generations (Deut. 23:2).

   The generational sin could be anal sex between a married man and a woman. Their son could then receive a spirit which will induce anal sexual behaviour, which can be with either a man or a woman. Once the behaviour is repeated with a man, the door is wide open to receive a spirit of homosexuality on top of the spirit of anal sex.

b) **Rejection of the sexuality** of a baby so that deep down it receives the message in its spirit that it is of the wrong sex. (Remember sex is spiritual, and sexual expectations of the parents will inevitably affect the spirit of the baby). The child will then, probably subconsciously, try to live up to the sexual expectations of the parents and perform as the opposite of what they actually are. Rejection by parents is fertile ground for the demonic and will form an effective gateway for a spirit of homosexuality to enter the developing child.

c) **Rebellion against parents** who only love the child because of their sexuality. For example, a boy who is specially loved by his father because he is male may feel rejection in every other area of his life and rebel against his parent's preference for boys.

d) **Homosexual sexual abuse**. This is perhaps the most common source of homosexual demonisation. Not uncommonly, it can even enter through children abusing each other, especially if there is a generational spirit of homosexuality in one of the children which will push the child into a behaviour which it has not been trained in by the parents.

141

e) **Maternal or paternal domination** leading to homosexuality or lesbianism respectively. The man who is so dominated by his mother that to look for a wife would be seen by his mother as rejection of her, will often look to other men for sexual fulfilment and enter a homosexual lifestyle as a result. The reverse happens with women who have been wrongfully controlled by their fathers.

f) **Willing homosexual relationships**. Some people, who have no previous background of homosexual relationships, either personally or generationally, are willing to try anything. Male or female homosexual relationships are just one of the world's deviant possibilities that the demons suggest to the potential libertine.

Demons will use any of the above routes to enter a person and distort their sexuality. There is a way back, but it requires a determination to bring one's life into harmony with God's will. The gateway is full confession and repentance. Unless the homosexual is willing to see that homosexual or lesbian behaviour is sin there cannot be any deliverance, and the Christian homosexual is condemned, therefore, to a lifetime of sexual pain.

vii) Fantasy and pornography
The use of pornography for obtaining illegitimate sexual pleasure, and inducing sexual lust leading to the orgasmic relief of masturbation, can be the source of extensive demonisation. But using pornography in that deliberate way is very different from noticing images of nudity, which are indeed hard to ignore totally.

We live in an age when pictures of the naked body, especially of women, are pushed daily in front of men and women on news and magazine stands, especially in the western world. This is the world in which Christians have to live without being trapped into the lustful consequences of pornography.

The scriptures encourage us to be in the world but not of the world (John 15:19, 17:1-26), so there must be a way through the overt sexual jungle of the western world, enabling people to live in the midst of such things without so entering into personal sin that the demonic is given a direct right of entry.

I know that in writing on this subject I will be saying some things that will be very good news for those who feel cursed by the problem and will be the cause of much repentance (and highlight the need for deliverance) for those who are willingly caught up in the demonic web of pornography. I have discussed at length the whole subject of nudity in the earlier book and would encourage you at this stage to read pages 168-172 of *Healing Through Deliverance - Volume 1.*

The key to this whole area lies in Jesus' words in the sermon on the mount about looking at a woman to lust after her. Jesus said that this is equivalent to adultery. The borderline of danger will vary enormously from person to person. For some men just seeing the fully clothed figure of a particularly shaped woman can begin a mental train of thought, that, if left unchecked, will lead to lustful sin. For others, the point of danger may be when something much more overtly sexual is seen. But in all instances the entrance gate is the eyes. No wonder the scriptures say, *"if your eyes are sound, then your whole body will be full of light"* (Matthew 6:22).

Every one of us must be on our guard against the deliberate seeking out of pornographic material and using it wrongfully. At that point the danger of demonisation is great. The key to a holy life is Holy Spirit control of the thought life. But the Holy Spirit will not force God's way of life upon us against our free will. There has to be an act of our will to walk away from pornographic material before the Holy Spirit will empower us in the fight.

But there are many people, men especially, who are so drawn by pornographic material that no matter how hard they try, the compulsion to look at or think about sexually stimulating material, often to the point of masturbation, is so great that it seems beyond their power of control. Then, when it is all over the guilt clicks into place bringing with it condemnation and the sense of yet another failure. In such cases the demonic is usually at work. Spirits of lust that entered through the eyes induce the cycle and then, to complete the victim's misery, leave the person with the burden of guilt.

The beginnings of demonisation in this area are usually early in life when children accidentally come across an adult magazine and feast upon it in amazement. They can hardly avoid the front page offerings on full display in most newsagents, and these alone can be sufficient to lead to the demonisation of a vulnerable child. Others may see some pornography which is secretly passed round at school, inadvertently come across a naked person or see a couple making love.

Early in life it can all seem very exciting, but gradually the need for more and more explicit material gives way to greater lust and sin. Many people have entered a promiscuous lifestyle which began with becoming demonised through looking at pornographic pictures and from then on the demonically empowered downward spiral became a pattern for life.

They justify it by thinking of it as a form of secret sexual sin which, they feel, borders on the acceptable because it does not involve anyone else. They feel their secret is secure because no-one else can find out about what is really happening beneath the surface. This is a situation which affects many Christians, even leaders who may even hold a key position in Christian ministry. Many is the man, often much later in life, who has battled with the problem in isolation for upwards of twenty years and has shared his heart with a member of our team, sometimes even with the belief that because of this particular sin he could not possibly be accepted into the Kingdom of God when he dies. What a relief it is for them to know that there is hope, there is deliverance and there can be a new beginning, even though the disciplined way forward is not easy. For the devil does not give up lightly those whom he has controlled through pornography.

In this day and age, the television is the purveyor of pornography which Christian men need to guard against the most. With the advent of satellite television, bringing pictures at the flick of a switch from a dozen different countries, sexual images can be viewed almost throughout the night in total secrecy. No-one else will ever know what they are looking at, not even the 'man at the video shop'. But what is lusted over in secret will have its outworkings in life. It is what happens in the secret place which determines the power and spiritual authority of the life God has given us to live. Just as the secret place of prayer is the source of tremendous strength, the secret place of pornographic indulgence will be the source of weakness, defeat and failure.

There can even be a secret dependence on pornography inside marriage. In such cases it is usually seen as compensation for the disappointment of a marital sexual relationship which falls a long way short of God's best, and from which there seems no legitimate way of escape. A poor sexual relationship, therefore, can be in itself a demonic entry point for pornographic spirits of lust.

Without deliverance and healing for the marital problems, such men are condemned to a steady decline in the marital situation until the marriage reaches a low level of mutual tolerance with no apparent hope of any improvement. Paul certainly saw the marital relationship as a legitimate and Godly means of dealing with sexual desire. In 1 Corinthians 7:9 he expressed this directly and succinctly by saying *"it is better to marry than burn with passion"*! How important it is, therefore, for both husband and wife to work at their sexual relationship so that it becomes the fulfilling union that God intended.

All viewing of pornography is a potential entry point for the demonic, whatever reason is put forward for its use. Sadly, there are some marital counsellors, even Christian ones, who are clearly not aware of the dangers of demonisation, who advise couples having a rough time sexually to indulge in a bit of pornography to get them sexually excited! Whatever short-term gains there may be from such 'therapy' the long term pains are not worth it.

viii) Bestiality

Along with homosexuality and other sexual perversions, the scripture is quite specific in forbidding sexual relations with animals. Under the law, both human and animal participants were to be put to death for taking part in such ungodly practices. (Leviticus 20:15-16). Death was the normal remedy for perverted sexual behaviour. Some say that bestiality might have been the original source of AIDS.

It is interesting to speculate that in those days, before Jesus had come and given the ministry of deliverance to the church, the ultimate sanction of death followed by the ritual provisions of the law for being cleansed after being in contact with the dead (Numbers 19), was the only way of preventing the demons that were given rights through the practice of sexual perversion from gaining access to the generation lines of God's people. Certainly, without such radical action, it seems that there would be no way of preventing the demonic from cursing the succeeding generations.

It only takes a moment's contemplation of this for the spiritually sensitive to realise and appreciate the wonder and miracle of Jesus' coming to earth and his sacrifice upon the cross. At Calvary the price was paid for all our sins, so that instead of us having to die to pay the price that must be paid for our sin, we look to the one who was sacrificed on our behalf and praise God for the forgiveness that is ours because he died in our place.

We have ministered to many people, who, in the privacy of the counselling room, have confessed to having indulged in bestial sexual relations. In the case of willing participants it is usually men who have experimented by having sexual relations with a wide range of animals from cats to cows.

Very often, however, bestial sexual activity is forced upon someone against their will. Women are made to submit to dogs or, in some perverted rituals, have snakes inserted inside their sexual organs. It sounds bizarre and extreme, but we have ceased to be surprised at the extent of sexual sin or the things that people have to confess when God challenges them to make a fresh and clean start with him.

Bestial sex always results in demonisation. It is one of the extremes of sexual behaviour and it so perverts the nature and character of the wonderful plan that God had for men and women together, that demonisation is inevitable in the case of willing participants, and almost inevitable for those who may have such horrors forced upon them. It would take a woman of unusual fortitude and spirituality not to be so traumatised by the experience that demons could not take advantage of the situation.

ix) **Transvestism and trans-sexuality**

A transvestite is someone who dresses up in women's clothes as part of the expression of their sexuality. A trans-sexual person is someone who not only dresses up in the clothes of the opposite sex, but actually wants to be a member of the opposite sex. Such people have drug treatment and physical operations to change their external appearance and sexual organs so as to make them effectively the opposite of the way they were at birth.

The possible roots of such behaviour are similar to the roots of homosexuality. In many cases, childhood rejection of their God-given sexuality gives the impetus to dress up in the clothing of the opposite sex. In other cases a generational spirit with this particular character is passed down the generation line.

Young boys have often been caught out trying on their mother's underwear. One man I counselled was so fascinated by ladies underwear hanging in front of the fire to dry on wash day, that he was taken over by a compulsion to wear it. The compulsion controlled his life. We now know that it was not a compulsion that took him over at that point, but a demon. It then controlled his sexuality from that moment on.

As with homosexuals, there is no root to wholeness which does not include deliverance, but there is much emotional healing that is necessary as well. The biggest problem, however, is the will. If the person who is seeking help does not, in their heart, want to give up the lifestyle, then no amount of counselling will ever bring the person to the point of being delivered. There has to be a ready acceptance that the practice, which is condemned in the scripture (Deuteronomy 22:5) is contrary to God's desire for them.

x) **Sexual abuse**

All sexual abuse leaves people vulnerable to demonisation. For a full discussion of sexual abuse as a demonic entry point, please refer to Section 8(iv).

Summary

The consequences of all wrongful sex, whether willingly or unwillingly entered into, are more extensive than just demonisation. All aspects of the damage need to be ministered to in order to bring healing. This is not a book on the whole range of healing ministries, but it is important to mention the other areas of healing that may be needed, so that no reader of this book will think that healing of the severely damaged is just a matter of casting out a few demons.

Casting out the demons is essential, but our job as ministers of healing is to heal people - not only to cast out the demons. The havoc caused in a person's life through many years of being demonised requires careful, thorough and loving ministry.

The principal areas that may need to be addressed are:

a)   Damage done to the relationship between God and the person involved.

b)   Establishment of ungodly soul-ties with other participants, whether willing or unwilling.

c)   Guilt and condemnation experienced.

d)   Rejection - that is so often involved, either as a prime cause of sexual sin, or as a consequence of one's body being accepted for sexual purposes, but the person not being wanted by the other sexual participant.

e)   Emotional disturbance and distress (short and long-term)

f)   Any breakdown there has been in the unity of the spirit, soul and body, leading, especially in the case of the traumatised and the abused, to a separation of the spirit and soul from the body as a means of protecting oneself from the consequential pain. A variety of possible out-of-body experiences are often indicators of such breakdown.

8. Hurts, abuse and rejection

Jesus was devastatingly direct in his comments about anyone who should offend against a little child. He said that it would be better for them to have a millstone tied round their neck and be cast into the depths of the sea (Matthew 18:6) Why was Jesus so severe in his comments? I believe that part of the answer lies in the understanding Jesus had about the demonic consequences to the child of the damage caused in this way.

I have not yet ministered to anyone who was seriously abused (sexually or otherwise) who did not also need deliverance ministry. The trauma of abuse opens wide the door for the demonic to take advantage of the pain. The consequences of abusive behaviour would be awful enough if one only had to consider the emotional or physical consequences, but the demonic controls that are put upon children through abuse leave a person dominated by demons for the rest of their days and without full deliverance there can be no true healing.

In the section on soul-ties we looked at the whole area of Godly and ungodly relationships between people. A soul-tie is a bonding (good or bad) which holds people into a relationship whether they like it or not. When people are abused an ungodly soul-tie is established between the abuser and the abused. This acts rather like a demonic tube along which the demonic may transfer from one person to the other. This is especially the case if there has been an emotional or sexual bonding between the abuser and the abused.

In these days when there has been so much publicity about sexual abuse we tend to think that this is the only kind of abuse that can cause serious harm to people. But when we seek to look at people as God sees them we gain a much wider understanding of the significance of abuse and rejection. We can see how there is the potential for creating opportunities for demonic entry from the moment of conception onwards, certainly long before any act of sexual abuse could ever be physically possible.

It is important to appreciate that a person is a person from the very moment when the sperm and the egg join together to form an embryonic human being. The arguments by the pro-abortionists about whether life begins at twelve, fourteen, twenty-eight weeks or birth are all built on the dictates of secular convenience as opposed to the reality of spiritual truth and understanding. In that minute assemblage of living material is all that is needed to determine the sex, character, personality, body-shape and looks of the person, but more important than the flesh potential (soul and body characteristics), is the fact that the spirit of the child already resides there.

The spirit, whom God knew as a spiritual being before the moment of sexual union created the right physical environment for the person's creation as a human being, is sensitive to the spiritual powers (both good and bad) from those earliest seconds of life. We have, for example, delivered people of a spirit of rejection which entered during the very act of sex which resulted in the embryonic child. I think, especially, of a woman who was conceived in rape, where neither father nor mother had any sense of wanting or owning the product of intercourse. Rejection is a particularly powerful and dangerous form of abuse.

The whole dynamics of acceptance and rejection are very powerful. A loved and accepted child grows up in the security of relationships which are non-abusive and safe. But a child who is the victim of rejection is vulnerable to being accepted and 'owned' by the demonic, causing much pain and anguish throughout life.

The spirit of rejection that rides in on the pain and trauma of rejection by those who should be in a position of loving care and responsibility can sometimes have a root so deep in a person's life that to separate it out from the true God-given character of the individual requires very deep discernment and a major anointing of the Holy Spirit.

People often ask how it is that such strong demonic power can enter into a person through hurts, abuse and rejection. The answer would seem to lie in the effect that such behaviour has on the spiritual unity and integrity of the victim. The three-stranded structure of man as a spirit, soul and body is a powerful defence against the enemy. (*"A cord of three strands is not quickly broken."* Ecclesiastes 4:12). But when, for any reason, there is a breakdown in the defensive wall that keeps the person whole, then demonisation is an almost inevitable consequence.

Any behaviour which makes the victim want to 'run away from him or her self' is potentially dangerous. A clinical psychologist recently told me that one of the common threads that goes through the case notes of those women he counsels who have been sexually abused is that almost all of them have had 'out-of-body' experiences. By this he meant that they could describe leaving their body and looking back at themselves from a distance, or going 'walk-abouts' in the garden, or going off with an imaginary friend. They had taught themselves that to be out of their body when unpleasant things were happening to it enabled them to cope better with the pain.

Such behaviour is the beginning of what the occultists call astral projection. Astral projection is a demonically executed occultic technique by which a person learns how to leave their body deliberately. Demonisation as a result is inevitable. Children who are brought up in witchcraft or satanism are taught how to astrally project at the earliest of ages, for it is a prime way of ensuring that the demonic is able to enter and control the young child. Once the integral unity of the spirit-soul-body entity is broken down, demonisation is easy.

When through abusive behaviour a child (or an adult) learns to cope with the pain by running away from themselves and into a fantasy world of projected living, demonisation readily follows. A gateway is opened up between the body and the spirit-soul part of their being and the demonic is able to ride straight in and set up a control base. Rejection, a spirit from the abuser, a demonic fantasy friend, fear and confusion are but some of the possible evil spirits that will take up residence, and which, when the Lord opens up a way for personal ministry, must be dealt with through deliverance.

All forms of abuse are rejective in their nature. But care must be taken to distinguish between Godly discipline and physical abuse - they are very different. Excessive and unfair physical punishment will initiate a reactive cycle in the victim, but failure to discipline a child who knows he has overstepped the mark will also induce a rejective cycle! For unless the child receives the discipline he needs and deserves in a measure appropriate to the misdemeanour, then the spirit of the child will sense that the parent does not really care for the child and rejection will take root.

The modern movement away from physical discipline of children (in some countries it is now illegal to physically discipline even your own children!) is a demonic deception designed by the enemy to induce rejection and then premature independence in the children. As a result, when the children grow up, they will not be responsive to those who could lead them wisely through the temptations and testings of life. Children do need to become independent of parents, at the right age. But if independence has been entered into prematurely, as a consequence of rejection, then the damage caused will produce a wall which the parents (and others) will come up against time and time again.

The following list of potential demonisation routes through hurts, abuse and rejection is not meant to be all-embracing and complete. Whilst it does cover the primary types of problem encountered, it should be treated as a guide to problem areas as opposed to a comprehensive check-list.

i) At conception

The act of intercourse may be loving, but any resulting conception may be unwanted. If the mother, especially (though not exclusively), reacts negatively when she realises she is pregnant and persists in her rejection of the child within her womb, then the spirit of the child will sense what is going on in the mother and begin to feel rejected. This then creates the spiritual environment for a demon to start claiming the child, and there is then a danger that a spirit of rejection will enter the hurting child and take over spiritual responsibility for the emergent human being.

Many mothers may go into a state of shock on finding out they are pregnant, but within forty-eight hours they have come right round to the idea and even started knitting! What I am saying here is that if the mother (and father preferably) change their heart attitude to the initially unwanted child then no long-term harm will have been done and rightful acceptance will have overcome any danger of a spirit of rejection gaining a stronghold on the child.

Sadly, many of the totally rejected babies are aborted and are never given a chance in life. In common with most people who have been working in this area of spiritual ministry, I believe that all aborted babies are treated by God as children who have died before the age of accountability and will reach their spiritual maturity in heaven. These children's teeth will certainly not be set on edge by the sins of their fathers (Jeremiah 31:29). They will not come under judgement or suffer eternal death because of the sins of their parents.

ii) Single-parenting and unwanted pregnancies

God intended babies to be brought up in families, and that means under the loving nurture and care of both a mother and a father. Many mothers conceive children outside the security of a stable permanent relationship and are forced to go through their pregnancies alone with their developing child. In these circumstances a loving mother and a supportive family background can help enormously to minimise the spiritual damage of an absentee father during those early months.

But children need fathers as well as mothers, and mothers need husbands (as well as parental support) to provide them with the spiritual, emotional and physical cover that is so necessary to their security during this sensitive time of their lives. The developing child experiences a sense of rejection by the father he has never even known, and in many cases a spirit of rejection will gain entrance as a result. The consequences of a spirit of rejection entering in these circumstances can be many and varied. One of the commonest problem areas is sexual development into one of the extremes of sexual behaviour (heterosexual promiscuity or homosexual lifestyle).

It is not unusual for the period of pregnancy in these circumstances to be one of great trauma and even violence for both the mother and the father of the child. The father, who only wanted a sexual encounter with the mother, feels trapped by the situation into a relationship he never wanted. He goes along with it for so long, but inside the resentment and anger come to boiling point, there is a violent row and the relationship is over.

There are times when we have delivered people of spirits that have come in at such critical times in the pregnancy. The Holy Spirit has sometimes shown the person (many years later) exactly what was happening whilst they were in their mother's womb. Later when they have checked out the details with the mother, they have found that the circumstances were precisely as God had revealed through the ministry.

When parents are going through stormy passages at any time, the children often suffer. This can even be the case during pregnancy. The child cannot assess the situation and account rationally for the difficulties the parents must be going through. So often the child looks at what is going on and assumes that he is the source of the problem. In some cases the presence of the child may, indeed, be the problem, but whether or not the child is the source of the problem is largely irrelevant - what matters is that the child believes he is the source of the problem and, therefore, not only feels rejected but begins to reject himself as well. So that rejection is followed by self-rejection and, ultimately, the child grows up to be afraid of further rejection. One can then have three spirits working together against the child's welfare: rejection, self-rejection and fear of rejection.

An unwanted pregnancy need not be when the parents are unmarried. A child may come along at a very inconvenient time for the mother's career, and she may be angry at having to interrupt a successful development of her business life. The family budget may already be overstretched and another mouth to feed may be a financial disaster. Or the mother may be well over forty, with her other children already teenagers, and suddenly along comes another.

The reasons for rejecting a child in the womb are many and varied, but, whatever the reason, the demonic will try to take advantage of the parents' sin in rejecting the child whom God has created. Failure to accept people as they are leaves them vulnerable to the enemy's attacks, especially with unborn children whose right to Godly parenting has been shattered by the pain of rejection.

iii) Rejection of sexuality

Rejection of the sexuality of a child can have long-lasting and permanent consequences. Each child that is conceived is given his or her own sexual identity, and there is nothing that man can do to change what God has created. During pregnancy, however, some parents begin to build up an expectation that the child is going to fulfil their heart's desire and be the boy or girl that they long for.

If, when the child is born, he or she is indeed what the parents long for, all may be well, but there is a danger at that point of the child only being loved because he or she has fulfilled the wishes of the parents with regard to his or her sexuality. There are two extremes of danger in bringing up such a child.

Firstly, the child can then do no wrong throughout his or her childhood and is, therefore, thoroughly spoiled. The consequences of this can be devastating, especially to any future children who do not come up to the sexual expectation of the parents and feel rejected as a result of the preferential treatment that the first child has received!

Secondly, at the other extreme, the child may start to feel that he or she is only acceptable because of their sexuality, and not because of who they are as a person. Ultimately, to accept a child only because of his or her sexuality may have fulfilled the expectations of the parents, but such acceptance is at the cost of rejecting the child for who he or she is. At this point the child is very vulnerable to demonisation.

It is clear, therefore, that the only safe reaction to the sex of children is to rejoice in whatever sexuality God has given them and not to either prefer one child because of his or her sex or reject another child because he or she does not have the 'right' sex. In this way the children who are conceived will not only travel through pregnancy secure in the knowledge that they are acceptable, irrespective of their sexuality, but when they are born they will not have to endure the extremes of either adulation (for being the right sex) or despair (for being the wrong sex).

There is no doubt whatsoever that when children are born they sense things spiritually that they cannot articulate or understand, especially if there is something about them sexually which is not up to expectation. They may not be able to express the feelings of rejection, but deep down I believe children know that there is something about them which is not up to expectation. Many times we have delivered people of demons which have entered at this precise stage of the person's life, given rights by the wrongful attitudes of the parents towards the sexuality of the child who has just been born into the family.

Rejection of the sexuality can, and often does, have long-term sexual and emotional consequences. It is one of the commonest root causes of homosexuality in both men and women. One homosexual man I counselled had been dressed in pink clothes for the first five years of his life so that his mother could live out the fantasy of having the daughter she longed for instead of the son she got.

As such a child grows in maturity, subconsciously he or she will start living up to the sexual orientation that was desired for him or her by one or both parents, and the demonic homosexual or lesbian spirit becomes deeply ingrained in the whole personality. The demonic root is rejection (of the sexuality of the child) which can become a platform for homosexual or lesbian spirits to then enter and develop the deviant sexual lifestyle.

iv) Sexual abuse

Sexual abuse is a specific form of rejection. It would require a whole book to explain the consequences of being abused in this personal and very intimate way. To understand why sexual abuse is a form of rejection, we need to remember that mankind is more than a body, for we have a spirit and a soul as well.

When a person is being sexually abused it is the body which is the focus of attention by the abuser. The spirit and the soul of the victim is, therefore, rejected. It is almost as if the abuser tries to erect a barrier between the body of the victim and the personality of the victim in order to pretend that the person is not being harmed by the act and so minimise the guilt consequences of what he or she is actually doing.

However, sexual relationships are spiritual in nature and no sexual contact, of any sort, can be experienced without there being a spiritual consequence. The Hebrew word for sexual intercourse is the same word that is used for 'knowing' God. It is the deep and intimate knowing of another person which God planned and purposed for men and women when he created their sexuality – a knowing that transcends all three facets of man's creation as spirit, soul and body.

So, no matter how hard an abuser may try to insulate his sin from the person inside the victim's body, he will never be able to do it. An ungodly soul-tie is always established between the victim and the abuser, creating a spiritual channel through which demonic transference can easily take place.

Once the abusive spirit has entered the victim it is never content to lie low and do nothing; it will always try to encourage activity of a similar perverted character in the victim. Many abused children, in their turn, have to wrestle with desires to abuse, and some give way and become abusers themselves. I haven't yet ministered to a sexual abuser who wasn't first abused as a child.

What then is sexual abuse?

Sexual abuse is usually thought of as the abuse of a young girl by a man. Whilst this is, perhaps, the most common form of sexual abuse, abuse of young boys by women is not unknown, and the abuse of young boys by older men in homosexual abuse is very common indeed. The abuser can follow a sequence of abusive behaviour which can include any or all of the following:

a) Visual abuse and voyeurism

b) Uninvited caressing

c) Handling of the sexual areas

d) Anal handling

e) Masturbation in front of the victim

f) Enforced oral sex

g) Mutual masturbation

h) Intercourse/rape

i) Anal intercourse/rape

j) Bestiality

k) Ritualistic sex

l) Incest - sexual contact of any degree with a member of one's own family

m)   Marital abuse - where sexual demands and practices
     go beyond the rightful physical relationship which
     God planned and purposed for men and women.

All sexual abuse has spiritual consequences, leaving the
victim wide open to the danger of demonisation. The demonic
can enter directly from the abuser (and usually does), but in
addition there is the danger of specific demonisation through
fear, confusion, deception, pain and other emotional traumas.

Consequences of sexual abuse

However, I would not want those who are reading this book in
isolation from our wider teaching on sexual abuse and sexual
relationships to think that I believe demonisation is the only
consequence of abusive behaviour. It isn't. The consequences
are far wider and can include any or all of the following:

a)   Confusion   -   of identity
                     -    of sexuality
                     -    of physical identity
                     -    of emotions

b)   Regression   -   to childhood experiences of abuse
                     -    to childhood emotional behaviour
                     -    to childhood physical conduct

c)   Repression   -   of memories
                     -    denial that anything happened
                          when it obviously did

d)   Fantasy   -   living in a fantasy world of unreal
                     memories
                -    relationships with fantasy friends
                -    living in fear of fantasy enemies

e)   Fracture of trust   -   inability to trust people,
     even those who are obviously trustworthy

f)   Rejective behaviour   -   leading to self-rejection
     and fear of rejection

g)   Rebellion   -   refusal to conform or cooperate
                     -    irrational anger

h) Secretive lifestyle

i) Loss of personal pride in appearance

j) Masking of sexual characteristics through the
    extremes of anorexia or over-eating

k) Guilt

l) Fearful demeanour

m) Inability to respond to love - sometimes does
    not become obvious until after marriage when the
    sexual side of the relationship disintegrates through
    apparent frigidity

n) Promiscuity - some abused people respond to
    their premature sexual maturity by giving it license
    in a promiscuous lifestyle

o) Wanting to die

p) Physical illness - often as a long-term disability or
    infirmity which becomes camouflage for the real
    underlying problem

q) Damage to the spirit - internal anger becomes focused
    on God and relationships with him become impossible.

And there are many more. But the above should be sufficient
to indicate that when ministering to the sexually abused we
are dealing with a complex web of pain and damage which has
been built on the initial platform of rejection and the abuser's
intentions. Sadly, each time a person responds to the pain of
the past with a new ungodly behaviour pattern in the present,
the demonic grip can tighten as further demons are given
rights in the person's life. For example, a teenage response of
promiscuity to a childhood pattern of abuse introduces fresh
demonic power with every promiscuous relationship.

Whilst I thank God for all the secular agencies that have
sprung up in recent years to help people who have been
abused, ultimately, they can do little more than show people
how to live with the consequences of the abuse. It is only

Christian ministry that can bring real healing, so that the victim can walk away from the abuse with a purpose for the future which is not tied to the pain of the past. For no other form of ministry has the authority to deal with the powers of darkness that have entered the life of the victim through sexual abuse.

v) Physical abuse

Physical violence hurts much more than the body of the victim. Violence against the body of a person is an offence against the person in the body. The physical pain may be great but it is inconsequential when compared with the long term emotional and spiritual damage that is done as a result. A child instinctively knows if he is being fairly punished for things he has done wrong and deep down he will accept the punishment as acceptance and loving care, even though there may be a superficial reaction which would seem to indicate otherwise!

But when a child is violated physically, the very opposite occurs. The child knows that the punishment is a form of rejection, and the gateway between the body and the soul-spirit is in danger of being opened up to the demonic in much the same way as happens when a person is sexually abused. An ungodly soul-tie between the abuser and the abused is established and a spirit from the abuser will commonly enter the child along with a spirit of rejection.

Demonic imaginary friends (sometimes mistaken for 'angels') are also a very common manifestation of the presence of demons with the physically abused. They become a listening ear which always understands. What the child can never understand, however, is that the demonic friend is working hand-in-hand with the demons in the abuser, in order to increase the demonic stranglehold on the victim. Unknown to the victim, the demons that have already entered will encourage a behaviour pattern calculated to induce violence from the abuser. Having achieved this objective, the same demons (or other demons working in partnership with them) will then turn comforter so that the victim is encased in a demonic web of punishment and comfort. It's as if the higher demonic powers have to be appeased by a regular cycle of such behaviour.

Satan is a deceiver who will even send a demon dressed as an angel of light if such a garb would suit his purposes, so we should not be surprised at any of his tactics. He is no respecter of persons and will seek to demonise a child at the earliest possible age. He knows that the younger a child is when the demonic strongholds are established, the more difficult it will be for that child to come to personal faith in Christ and, should the child be converted, the harder it will be for the new Christian to be set free from the powers of darkness.

The more one ministers to people who have been demonised through abusive behaviour, the more one understands how important it is for Christian parents to be the Godly cover for their children that he intended them to be. Satan will exploit every possible weakness in the parents to infiltrate the children. Through ministering to the abused, one sees, almost by default, the things that really matter in bringing up children. For in this ministry one sees the things that close the door to the enemy and make it impossible for the demonic to enter. One also sees the things that do open the door, resulting in demonised children. A very brief summary of the requirements of 'Good Christian Parents' arising from the above could be written down as follows:

a)   Parental unity in spirit, soul and body relationships

b)   Parental acceptance of the child, irrespective of its
     sex, personality and gifting

c)   Godly discipline, so that the child will grow up in a secure
     framework and, above all

d)   Sacrificial and unconditional love, so that the child really
     knows that he or she matters to the people to whom God
     has entrusted the child's welfare

I can see now, with the benefits of both experience and ministry hindsight, that any failure in any of these departments will be taken advantage of by the enemy, resulting in the danger of the demonic having access to our children.

vi) **Emotional and psychological abuse**

Sexual and physical abuse are readily identifiable and recognised. However, the emotional and psychological abuse that a large number of parents or substitute parents subject their children to is far more difficult to resolve. This type of abuse is also a common experience of many adults.

Domination and manipulation are sin, irrespective of whether the victim is a young child or an old man, one's husband, wife, son or daughter, friend, associate, colleague, fellow church member etc., etc. Any behaviour which seeks to take away the Godly free will of another is abusive behaviour and will lead to problems of varying degrees. The abuser already has the problem, and the victim often responds to the abuse in such a way that the door is opened to the demonic. Again, all such abusive behaviour is a form of rejection in which the free will of an individual to be the person God intended them to be is overlooked and the person is therefore is rejected.

At this point a few things need to be stated to avoid any confusion. I am not saying that parents should always allow children to have their own way because God has given them their free will. That is a recipe for disaster. The child has to learn that the overall happiness of a Christian family is achieved when we willingly submit one to another, and that the parents hold everything in balance by seeing that no one member of the family dominates unfairly to the detriment of others.

Neither am I saying that there are not times when the head of the family has to take major decisions which would seem, on the surface, to over-ride the interests of the wife and/or the children. But in a Godly ordered relationship such decisions will be taken with the wife's support, and the children will take their behavioural cue from the attitude of their mother towards their father.

Nor am I saying that there will not be times when the wife will seek to influence her husband over issues that at first he may not be willing to consider, either on her own behalf, or on behalf of her children. None of these things is either domination or manipulation if they are carried out with full respect for the various positions held in the family by the different members.

But I am saying this: Violation of the free will of an individual, to be the person that God has planned and purposed, is rebellion against God. Manipulation, domination and control are the tools of witchcraft and it is not surprising, therefore, that the victims of manipulation, domination and control can be demonised as a result.

No-one would doubt the fact that those who dabble in witchcraft are likely to be demonised, and therefore no-one should be unduly surprised to learn that those who use the tools of witchcraft (even though they may not be overtly involved in what is generally understood to be witchcraft) are using demons, albeit unknowingly, to get their own way and are running the risk of their victims being demonised as a result.

One of the commonest problem areas in this respect lies in the relationship between parents and their children. God's intention for children was that there should be a steadily changing relationship between the child and the parents from day one of the child's life. Gradually the protective barriers are meant to be dropped as the child grows in age and maturity, until age 18, 19 or thereabouts when the child is then mature enough to go his own way and start to live life as an emergent adult. Of course the child can come back of his own free will time and time again to seek care, help, love and advice from the parents. That is fine, provided the child is totally free to come and go as and when necessary. Some will need to return in this way more than others.

But problems arise when the identity of the parents is so wrapped up in their children that they do not have a mature identity of their own in order to cope with 'life after the children have left'. For many parents the impending crisis of the children no longer needing them is something that they try to stave off with ever increasing intensity as the children get older. Emotional blackmail, control and domination ensure that the child is never mature enough to totally flee the nest and remains forevermore under the domination of mother, father or both.

The greatest danger is maternal domination, especially in a family where the mother has never been out to work and has been treated by the father as an unpaid housekeeper and child-rearer instead of an equal partner in a dynamic and loving relationship. Once the children no longer need their mother, the rejection felt is so intense that the mother will do everything she possibly can to make herself vital to the son or daughter who is desperate to leave home. The mother-in-law jokes are all founded on the factual experience of many people who have not been able to escape what they see as the emotional and psychological clutches of a tyrant who tries to control the marriage (and the marriage partner) of their offspring.

These are very choppy waters indeed to sail through. For on the one hand there is the command to honour one's parents and on the other hand the scriptural injunction to leave home and cleave to your new partner (for those who leave home to get married). The conflict can be very great and the guilt that is loaded on by some mothers who try every emotional trick in the book (from a cheque book to waterfalls of tears) can weigh heavy on the conscience.

Unless one stands up to the dominating parent and holds up a rightful spiritual authority, one is not truly honouring the parent (who needs help to come to maturity and whose job it should be to let the child go). Not to stand strong on this issue could then create a crisis in one's own marriage that is likely to cause intense pain and possibly precipitate separation and divorce, unless nipped in the bud very early in the marriage and resolved accordingly.

In ministry we have had to break the soul-ties to mothers (and fathers) on too many occasions to count. The demonic power that has been locked into the victim through such domination and control is sometimes awesome to behold. It comes as a major and traumatic shock to some people to realise how much power has been exercised in this way. For others, who have felt the chains wrapped tightly around them, it is no shock at all - just a relief to be rid of the bondage! Many have experienced significant physical healing through deliverance from spirits of infirmity that have been given a right to transfer down the generation line as a result of the sinful abuse there has been of the children!

There are many other relationships which can be dominating, manipulative and, therefore, abusive. The effects are much the same as the above, so I will simply list some of them here for ease of reference:

a) Husband by wife

b) Wife by husband

c) Parents by children

d) Child by older or younger brother or sister

e) Child by aunt, uncle or grandparent

f) Employee by employer

g) Minister by members of the congregation

h) Congregation by the minister

vii) Separation and Divorce

How we respond to things which happen around us can, in large part, determine whether or not the demonic is able to take advantage of the pain we experience. None more so is this the case than with regard to marital separation and divorce.

Separated and divorced people have, for a very long time, felt like second or even third class members of the church. The rejection that can be heaped on them by some members of the Body of Christ can sometimes be far greater and more painful than the rejection experienced in the break-up of the marriage itself. We have had a number of letters from divorcees pleading for help in this area.

I can understand a church fellowship which does not want to give the impression of condoning or encouraging divorce. That is right and good, but it is very different from holding the divorced in a state of suspended judgement so that they never feel accepted as part of the fellowship.

This is not the place to go into the whole ethics of divorce and remarriage, but I would say that on the basis of the many people we have counselled in recent years, there is a lot of hypocrisy in the church on the issue and an unwillingness to face up to the real issues involved.

Not all parties in divorces are acting sinfully, but this is a message that many people who have suffered the intense pain of divorce have not often been told by the church. It has sometimes been the failure of the church to understand and support those who are going through marital break-up, that has given additional ground to the demonic to take advantage of the situation.

All separations involve rejection. Even in the case of one partner leaving to establish a relationship with another person, the one leaving may be doing so because of the rejection they have gone through. And the one who is left behind finds it hard to see, in the midst of his or her own rejection, that their behaviour may have contributed to the break-up.

Counselling those going through separation and divorce is a skilled and necessary operation. Those suffering the pain of being the participants need to guard against bitterness, and those who are alongside the individuals involved need to minister in love with unconditional acceptance - the best antidotes to the attacks of the demonic.

Ministry to the divorced must include, at an appropriate moment, the cutting of the soul-ties to the previous partner. But counsellors need to be especially sensitive here to choose the moment for this wisely. There won't always be demons that are then free to leave, but more often than not there are. When a relationship has reached the point of no return, it is usually only after many years of trauma, and during this time there are many points at which the demonic could have entered.

It also needs to be remembered in ministering to the divorced that the reason why the divorce occurred at all may well lie in the dim and distant past, long pre-dating the marriage. It is always helpful to seek to bring healing to these areas at an appropriate time so that in the event of a second marriage the same mistakes are not repeated.

A further demonic entry point in divorce situations can be in the lives of the children - especially if the behaviour of the parents is such that the children are made to suffer the pain of marital dispute. The trauma the children experience can itself be a demonic entry point creating the possible need for careful ministry at a later date.

viii) Death

Death can seem to be the ultimate rejection for the person left behind. Facing up to the reality of life's partings and learning to accept them is a vital part of being a mature man or woman. Some people, however, have never accepted the death of a loved one, and this in itself has given opportunity to the demonic to control a person.

It has not been unusual to find that a demonic spirit has taken on the character of the person who has died, and this then acts as a controlling influence on the living. It is always necessary in cases such as this to break the ungodly dimension of the soul-tie to the dead person as a pre-cursor to deliverance ministry.

The release experienced when this is done is sometimes very dramatic as the living person, who has become demonised through the pain and trauma of separation, is set free from demonic control through which they can also be held in bondage to grief.

9. Traumas and accidents

Trauma and accident are part of life's experiences. Even when we are Christians we are not exempt from occasional crises and problems. We live in a fallen world of which Satan is the god (2 Cor. 4:4). There are many things that happen in this world as a consequence of the fall, and it is wrong to blame God when things appear to go wrong. It is only when Jesus returns as King of Kings that Satan's reign will come to an end and the Kingdom reign of God will be ushered in on that great and wonderful day.

In the meantime God has promised to be with us always (Matthew 28:20), right until the end of the age in which we live. But that promise is not unconditional. It is related to our willingness to be obedient to the commission that Jesus gave to the church - to make disciples and teach them to do all the things that Jesus taught the first disciples to do (see pages 266-270 of *Healing Through Deliverance - Volume 1*).

We have found through extensive experience that moments of great trauma or major accident are also times of great spiritual sensitivity. We are then vulnerable to the supernatural in a way that perhaps we are not at other times, and if we are not secure in God's love and care when the evil day comes (as Paul assured us it would in Ephesians 6:13), then we are vulnerable to the enemy's attacks.

The enemy is no respecter of persons and he does not think that because someone is going through a traumatic experience he will leave them alone out of the kindness of his heart! There is nothing kind about the heart of Satan and he will choose just these moments to try to gain a spiritual advantage and place one of his 'arrows' (demons) inside those who are suffering. No wonder Paul encouraged us to wear our armour at all times!

The sort of traumas that people have gone through which, in our counselling experience, have proved to be common entry points for the demonic are such things as:

i) Major illness

Sudden illness affecting the individual concerned or a close member of the family is always a traumatic experience. Perfect health on one day can be replaced by fear of death on the next. The trauma experienced by a parent when a child is suddenly taken ill is often far greater than that of the child! The very word 'cancer' strikes fear into the heart of an individual and I know of cases where the fear of getting cancer has been the doorway through which a spirit of infirmity causing cancer has walked right into a person's life.

This can frequently be the case when a close member of the family is dying from cancer. The fear of someone else getting it gives a right to the infirmity to transfer and induce similar symptoms. We have ministered to many people who have developed cancer symptoms subsequent to another member of the family dying of the disease. The symptoms frequently appear in the same organs and in a similar way to the previous victim.

For those who live alone the trauma of sickness can induce fears such as *"Who is going to look after me now? How am I going to cope?"*, with the result that some will conclude they cannot cope, and fear of the future will induce further demonic sickness and possible eventual death.

ii) Unemployment

Unemployment is always difficult to handle but especially when it comes suddenly. Someone may go out to work one day, full of expectation, but return later that same day devastated by the news of being made redundant. The trauma of such an experience can open wide the gateway to rejection, leaving the person unable to cope with life, believing that he is unwanted. The spirit of rejection makes him turn in on himself and lose heart and hope.

If approached in the right way redundancy can become a wonderful opportunity for a man or a woman to put their life back on a new footing before God and establish themselves, perhaps for the first time in their lives, in the place that he intended them to be. Many is the person who can look back on redundancy as the greatest moment of opportunity that God ever gave them! Hope is always the antidote to fear, and with hope, all that the enemy might want to do through the trauma of unemployment can be refused, because our security is not in earthly support and fulfilment but through being in the place of God's appointment.

iii) Accidents

Incidents such as car crashes are high on the list of potential demonic entry points. Often, in ministering to people with long-term accident injuries that refuse to heal, we have found that a spirit of fear or a curse of accidents has been at the root of the condition.

Sometimes the accident itself was demonically induced in order to fulfil the terms of a particular curse. This is especially found to be the case when people experience repeated accidents for no apparent reason. They may also have been generationally affected by a spirit causing accidents that has come down the family line. A curse of accidents such as this can be placed upon a person or their ancestors knowingly through witchcraft or unknowingly through hatred, bitterness or motives of revenge. We have sometimes seen that when the spirit of curse of accidents is challenged, the person suddenly experiences pain in areas where there had been no pain before. The demon often manifests itself in the place where it first affected either the person or one of his ancestors!

iv) Abuse (See Section 7: Hurts, Abuse and Rejection)

v) Fear

Fear is invariably an entry point for demons when people are going through a traumatic experience. Fear of the unknown, fear of what's going to happen next, fear of dying, fear of a hundred and one different things that can grip the heart of man from time to time can be used by Satan to control people. Fear controls vast areas of some people's lives, and the demonic thrives on the opportunities that fear gives to the enemy.

During moments of great trauma people are spiritually vulnerable. A road accident, for example, can give the demonic a prime opportunity to take advantage of the traumatised state that accident victims often experience. It is only much later, often years later, when the person is still suffering the effects of the accident that we have been able to piece together what actually happened as the demons have been forced to identify themselves and then be cast out.

In some cases the demon that entered made the person afraid of cars, or travelling, or that particular stretch of road, or that particular driver. In all cases the effect was long-lasting and demonic, but curable through deliverance, provided that the person was willing to forgive anyone responsible and to deal rightfully with any other basics that had not been resolved in the person's life.

10. Death (including miscarriages and abortions)

i) The transition of death

The moment of death is a moment of transition - a transition from the limitations of the body, which we were given by God in embryo at our conception, to all that lies ahead of each individual. The Christian who trusts in Jesus knows from the scriptures that after death there is a time of separation (of the sheep from the goats) and then a time of judgement.

Jesus talked at some length about 'the age that is to come'. Matthew's gospel records that he told several stories to illustrate the eternal consequences of our earthly actions and behaviour, including the story of the wise and foolish virgins (Matthew 25:1-13). The implication of this parable is that none of us can know when either our time to die will come or when the Lord himself will return again the second time in glory. It is incumbent upon us to be ready so that when that moment comes we will be part of the Bride of Christ, the Church.

At death, the body becomes an empty shell - the person that was in the body has gone. For them, the end of life on earth has come and their future rests in the love and mercy of Jesus their Saviour and God their heavenly Father. From that moment they are outside the limitations of earthly time, but for those who are left behind there is a range of consequences which the demonic will do every possible to take advantage of.

Demons do not have bodies of their own. They seek to fulfil their master's (Satan's) wishes through occupying the bodies of human beings and diverting the person away from the Lord Jesus Christ so that they do not become Christian believers. Inside Christians they will try to minimise the effectiveness of their Christian walk and their influence in the church to which they belong.

For this reason it is not unusual to find demons more obviously at work in believers than in unbelievers! Within them there is work to be done. Within unbelievers, however, who have set their will to serve themselves and turn their backs on God, the demons will normally maintain a very low profile, knowing that they can always increase their level of activity if there is a change in the spirituality of their host!

The moment of death is of great significance. A dead body is generally useless to demons. Therefore death is not only a time of transition for the person who died but a time of redistribution for any demons that were present. However, demons cannot just move from one person to another without having rights, so during the person's lifetime, the demons inside one person will encourage a person to establish ungodly soul-ties with a variety of other people, so that at death, transfer can be effected relatively easily.

At death it seems that the demons will use these ungodly soul-ties as one of the ways of entering someone who is still living. The demons will also use any spiritual weakness in our own being as a point of transference. For example, if someone is very afraid and has a spirit of fear, then this may be used to give further demons a right of entry from the person who has just died. I realise that, in opening up this whole discussion, I am touching on a sensitive and potentially controversial issue.

In the Old Testament law there are detailed provisions laid down on how to protect oneself from the dangers of coming into contact with someone who has recently died. Numbers 19:11 states quite unequivocally that a person who *"touches a corpse is ritually unclean for seven days" (GNB)* and in verse 14 this is extended to anyone who is in the same tent (building) at the time of death of the deceased. The words used to describe the uncleanness always seem to imply 'ritual uncleanness'.

Careful reading of the scriptures demonstrates that ritual uncleanness is always associated with something spiritual that is making the person, place or object unclean. Hezekiah became King of Judah after a period when the temple had been used wrongfully in forms of occult worship. The temple was described as being ritually unclean as a result, and the priests were instructed to make themselves ritually clean and then to make the temple ritually clean according to the law of the Lord (2 Chronicles 29).

Ritual uncleanness is always associated with something of a spiritual nature which is actually defiling people, places or objects, or in other words, spiritual beings and powers which have been given rights there as a result of what has previously happened to the people, places or objects.

So, in Numbers 19 it is made very clear that those who have been in contact with the dead are in danger of being ritually unclean. Why? Some commentators have tried to sidestep the issue by saying that this was God's way of ensuring that if you came into contact with someone who had died from a contagious disease, then washing would minimise the risk of infection, for the means of cleansing that is prescribed in the law involves being washed in the water of purification.

However, if that really were the case, it would not make sense to prepare such cleansing water by sprinkling the ashes of a sacrificed red heifer on the water as part of its preparation. Running water from a stream would be the only sensible medical advice to give to someone who wanted to wash away any traces of disease from his body.

Therefore, the only possible way of interpreting Numbers 19 is that the water of purification had been specially prepared and consecrated (see Numbers 19:1-11 for the procedure) and that the water so prepared was endued with a spiritual power which could deal with the defiling spiritual powers that may have transferred from the person who had just died.

We have found in many hundreds of ministries that to break the all ties between a person and someone who has died, and then to deliver the person of all the unclean spirits that have transferred following the death of the individual, has been a very effective way of dealing with the powers of darkness and removing their rights to be in their new host. So often we have seen how the demons have induced exactly the same symptoms in the new person as were prevalent in the person who had died. The spirits of infirmity that transferred just continued their same job function, unchecked, after transfer.

The use of the water of purification, as prescribed in the law, is definitely an Old Testament procedure for dealing with such spiritual powers. It is interesting to note, however, that the water required the sacrifice of a perfect red cow that had never been put to work. When Jesus died on the cross he became that perfect, all-sufficient, sacrifice. Just as in the wilderness the people were to look in faith to the lifted up bronze serpent for their healing from the poison of snake bites, so we are to look to the Son of God, who was lifted up on Calvary, so that we may be healed from the poison that the enemy has injected into us spiritually and be set free from the consequences.

When Jesus gave the Great Commission to his disciples (Matthew 28:19-20), he stressed that they were to baptise believers in the name of the Father, the Son and the Holy Spirit. We have found in ministry that when in baptism we recognise the power of the name of Jesus to save, heal and deliver, on many occasions people have come up out of the waters to be immediately delivered of the powers of darkness who could not stand the consequences of their obedience and the cleansing powers of the consecrated waters into which the person was baptised. It is interesting that Paul comments on the cleansing of the Church by water in Ephesians 5:26, saying that God made the church clean by washing it in water.

We have found, also, in some very deep deliverance ministries that if we give the person receiving ministry water to drink that has been consecrated, the effect on the demonic can be dramatic and immediate. By 'consecrated water' I mean water that has been prayed over so that it may be filled with the Holy Spirit. There is a power impartation when that is done, similar to the power impartation which takes place when a person receives the laying on of hands.

We first discovered this when a person we were praying with asked for a glass of water. I went to the kitchen to get one, but on the way back the Lord spoke to me very clearly and told me to bless the water by the laying on of hands. I did so, took it to the room and gave it to the person to drink. She took one sip, spat it out and the demon speaking out through her said, *"Get me some proper water!"* We did, and got some water which we did not pray over. She was then able to drink the whole glass without any problem.

She said that the water actually tasted different, and because it was unconsecrated the demons had no problem with allowing the water to enter her stomach. But a member of the team then laid her hands on the lady's stomach and consecrated the water that was now on the inside. There was an immediate reaction, as if the water was boiling in her stomach, and she went into immediate deliverance!

We have found in experience, therefore, that the principle of Numbers 19 holds true for today. The only differences between then and now are that the sacrifice has already been made (Jesus), so, mercifully, no more red heifers are needed, and that he has given to believers power and authority, through the impartation of Holy Spirit power. Because of the cross, Christians can be in a position of victory.

Because of the possibility of demonisation, death is a time of danger to the living. For any spirits that were resident in a person that has just died will seek to find a new home as soon as possible. This point only serves to emphasise how vital it is that we do not have ungodly soul-ties with anyone and that we are always living spiritually clean ourselves.

When counselling people, especially those with long-term problems, we will make enquiries of deaths in the family as a matter of routine. Often, by dealing with things that have transferred from certain individuals, we have been able to short-circuit many hours of ministry as people have been set free from the powers that had been controlling them.

What we have found in experience is that there is often what we call a 'guiding spirit' of the person who has died attached to the person we are praying for. This is a demon which has taken on the characteristics of the deceased. Such a spirit has often been with the person throughout their life. These guiding spirits are the ones that spiritualist mediums summon up when a person consults the medium with a view to speaking to someone who has died.

The guiding spirit, who knew the deceased extremely well and is, therefore, able to deceive with an amazing degree of cunning and accuracy, leads people into false beliefs about the nature of life after death and into the deceptions of spiritualism. By addressing and casting out the guiding spirit of a dead person, we have seen very significant things happen in the person's life as they are healed of the conditions and symptoms which have come down the generation line through the deceased.

ii) Related issues

There are several other aspects of death which the demonic can latch onto which need to be noted when ministering to the living. These have been touched on in other sections, but for completeness of this section I will repeat them here briefly:

a) Grief

This is a necessary process. Without the expression of grief there cannot be full healing from the bereavement. But sometimes a demon will ride in on the emotional trauma and then the person never seems to recover from the bereavement. If, after three months or so, there is not a marked change in a person's condition following the grief of bereavement, it is not unreasonable to suspect that there may be spirits of grief operating. One lady I knew was still grieving the loss of her husband fifteen years later. The grief being expressed at that time was totally demonic. After deliverance she was healed.

b) Shock

This is especially relevant in the case of sudden deaths. The trauma of being bereaved without warning affects people deeply, so emotionally they are wide open to demonic attack. Even if people have been ill for some long time before dying, the effect on the living can still be just as great as if the person had been suddenly killed in a car accident. From the moment they first knew that their loved one was dying, some people have the capacity to put all their emotions 'on hold' so as to support and encourage the one who is actually dying. When it is all over, the shock of not having a patient to sustain can be very traumatic.

c) Loneliness

This is particularly common when a long-standing and devoted marriage is ended by bereavement. The loneliness felt is very intense and demons will ride in on the emotions, especially if the one who is left behind does not have the support of children or other close members of the family to encourage them at that time.

d) Rejection

For some people (especially children), losing a loved one is nothing less than being rejected by that loved one. It's almost as if they feel the person has died deliberately and left them behind. When this happens there is usually a deep root of rejection already in the person, which the demonic takes advantage of to bring in a spirit of ultimate rejection through the death of the person on whom the bereaved depended.

11. Curses (including inner vows, pronouncements, and wrongful praying)

Curses are words which are spoken against another person with intent to harm. The words in themselves have no authority to hurt anyone; it is the spiritual power behind the words that enables the terms of the curse to be fulfilled.

i) God's curse

Before looking at the consequences of curses spoken by human beings, we need to ask what it means in the scriptures when they refer to God's curse being upon someone for breaking particular aspects of the law (eg. Deuteronomy 28:15-68). In these cases the curse is a form of judgement for disobedience and rebellion. When we sin we move outside God's covering and we place ourselves, therefore, under the covering of Satan. Generally speaking, God's curse is the loss of his protection as a result of our own wilful decisions.

In some cases, however, God may act summarily to execute judgement on certain individuals. Scripture says clearly that vengeance belongs to the Lord (Romans 12:19) and that we are not to take judgement into our own hands. In cases where God acts in this way, the actual fulfilment of the 'curse' is probably executed by angels, as is specifically stated in the case of Herod (in Acts 12:23), who chose to allow the people to worship him as if he was God. In the Old Testament an evil spirit is also described as having being sent by the Lord to trouble King Saul (1 Samuel 16:14), indicating that ultimate power, even over Satan's forces, is still in the hands of God and that God can, if he wishes, use an evil spirit to fulfil his purposes.

With regard to the curse of God, Paul said Jesus became curse for us (Galatians 3:13) and redeemed those who believe from the curse of the law. The way God's curse is lifted from mankind is through the cross. Confession, repentance and then forgiveness are the basic requirements for being set free from the general curse that is upon mankind because of sin. They are the specific requirements for each one of us if we find that we have sinned specifically and, as a result, have put ourselves once again under God's curse through further rebellion.

Thankfully it is very clear that John was writing to believing Christians when he said that *"if we confess our sins to God ... he will forgive us our sins and purify us from our wrongdoings"* (1 John 1:9 GNB). John expected that believers would sin, and he made certain that they knew there was a remedy for sin. The process of sanctification sometimes seems long and hard. Paul cried out in anguish that the good he wanted to do, sometimes he couldn't, and in contrast he would find himself doing the bad things which in his heart of hearts he did not want to do! (Romans 7:14-25). Paul's experience was the same as that of all who would set their hearts to follow Jesus. The closer we walk with God, the more conscious we become of sin within. The greater the intensity of the light, the more easy it is to see the dirt!

There are some Christians who, because of sins they have committed in the past, read Hebrews 6 and finish up in deep despair and condemnation. This is a common experience of elderly people who have strived all their life to serve God, often against overwhelming temptations which they have struggled with desperately. They can look back on a life which has been well-spent in God's service, but the closer they come to the end of their days, the more aware they become of their failures.

One of Satan's names is 'accuser of the brethren', and he loves to send an evil spirit to do just that – accuse the saints of God of every misdemeanour they have committed and refer them to scriptures which are devastating if taken out of context and away from the balance of scripture – especially to those who long to be pure in heart and are the most desirous of serving God.

But Satan always has been an expert at quoting scripture. That was the technique he used with Jesus. How easy it would have been for Jesus to have heard scripture being quoted and deduced that what was being implied through the scripture must, therefore, be true. Satan is a liar and he will not hesitate to read, interpret and use even the word of God, if it suits his purposes. How careful we must be in the way we use scripture, and how discerning we must be when other Christians (or non-Christians for that matter) quote scripture to us. It is not so much the words that are quoted that matter, but the spirit that lies behind the words. No wonder it is necessary for one of the gifts of the Spirit to be the ability to discern the difference between those things that come from God and those things that don't (1 Corinthians 12:10).

The Hebrews 6 passage, which those who do not fully appreciate that they have been freed from the curse of the law so often stumble against, is specifically directed at those who have abandoned their faith, not those who are still battling and pressing on, notwithstanding the occasional fall or problem on the way. There is a wealth of difference between those who have abandoned their faith and those who are struggling with the realities of their faith in the midst of a fallen world and within a body of fallen flesh! I would far rather have an employee who makes mistakes, learns by them, and keeps pressing on, than an employee who sits back and does nothing in case he might make a mistake. As the wisdom of the world would confirm: 'The man who makes no mistakes does not make anything'!

It is important that we encourage those who are still battling on for God and remind them that because of Jesus, they are redeemed from the curse of the law. They have been snatched out of the hand of the devil, whatever a lying spirit might try to whisper in their hearts!

If we capitulate to the taunts of the enemy with regard to our past, then we give rights to the enemy to demonise us through doubt and unbelief. We have delivered people from many spirits that have taken advantage of such situations - spirits that have named themselves as despair, fear of God (not the holy fear of God, but a wrongful fear arising out of not being able to trust in the blessings of salvation), unworthiness, guilt etc.

Paul tackles the problem of Christians who have sinned (not built rightfully on the foundation of Jesus) in 1 Corinthians 3. There he likens what we do with our Christian lives to a building and says that there will even be some whose whole building will be destroyed in the fire of God's judgement, because there has been nothing worthwhile to preserve, but even so *"he himself will be saved, as if he had escaped through the fire"* (1 Corinthians 3:15 GNB).

ii) Satan's curses

When it comes to curses that are not of God, we are dealing with something very different, namely evil spirits which have specific job functions to fulfil the terms of the curses that are made by men against their fellows. For those who feel that no curse that anyone else can place against them could ever hurt them, there is encouragement to be found in the Proverbs, where it says *"A curse without cause does not alight"* (Proverbs 26:2 NASB). Broadly speaking, this means that if we ourselves are not giving any rights to the enemy in our lives, then no matter what Satan, demons or malicious people might throw at us, the curse cannot affect us spiritually.

The caution I would issue with respect to such a verse is this: Who of us is so confident of our walk before God that we are absolutely certain we are not giving any cause to the enemy to land a curse on us? Pride is a deadly enemy! Remember what the scripture says about the heart and its deceitfulness.

I believe that other than the fear of God, there are few greater inducements to living a holy life than the fact that our behaviour and the attitudes of our heart can open the door for the enemy to gain access. Praying the Psalmist's prayer of self-examination, *"Test me, and discover my thoughts. Find out if there is any evil in me and guide me in the everlasting way"* (Psalm 139:23-4 GNB) is an important discipline for the believing Christian.

Remember, also, that the ongoing attacks of the enemy can have the effect of wearing us down and making us less resistant to his taunts and testings. We need to be on our guard that we do not let our defences slip and give the enemy grounds for curses to be able to land on us and make their demons stick!

Having ministered to many hundreds of people who have been the victims of curse, I know from much experience that the wiles and the determination of the enemy to neutralise the power of the Body of Christ is such that he will stop at nothing to fulfil his purposes. Curses are one of his favourite means of operation, especially by using areas of vulnerability and channels of curse that we would not normally suspect as being dangerous.

Most people who use curses against others are not aware of the damage they are doing. Very few appear to understand that when they speak wrongfully against someone they are creating an opportunity for the enemy to attack and possibly demonise the person they are speaking about. Those are strong words, and they are not said lightly.

I will never forget the minister who had to resign his living on health grounds, or so he thought. He suffered a breakdown and could not carry on. Little did he know at the time that the vehemence of the words being spoken to him and about him by members of the congregation was such that he was the victim of cursing from the moment he walked into the parish. He was a Godly man, and determined to give the Holy Spirit freedom to operate in the church. But the opposition that came from the members of the church, who had so recently appointed him, was vehement. They wanted a pastor who would do what they wanted, not what God wanted.

After a time he began to react against some of the things being said. His emotions were raw and he and his wife did not know how to protect themselves or have the wisdom to move to a place that did want to hear the message God had called them to proclaim. Other problems in their lives, which had been dormant for years, began to raise their heads, and after a few years they resigned, not only from that church, but from the ministry. Satan had cursed them and they were now in need of more than just a period of tender loving care.

They were both in need of major deliverance from all the spirits of curse that they had taken on board through the words of the some of the congregation. When they came for deliverance both they and we were shocked at the strongholds that the enemy had managed to put upon them through what they had suffered.

We have seen on many occasions how the curses spoken by Christians give even more power to the enemy than those which are spoken by unbelievers. Such curses give the demons rights which directly undermine the life of the Body of Christ. Wrongful praying (when we are asking God to do things which are motivated by wrong desires) is a particularly powerful form of cursing, which other writers, with more experience than me have also given testimony to. For further understanding of this important area, I suggest you read Derek Prince's book, *Blessing or Curse*.

Curses from men fall broadly into two categories. Firstly, there are deliberate curses applied by those who are working within the occult, know exactly what they are doing and, whether they appreciate it or not, are using demons to invoke harm upon the victim of the curse. Secondly, there are those which may not be placed deliberately, but are curses nevertheless, because they fall into the general category of words spoken against another person which are contrary to God's plans and purposes for that person.

iii) Deliberate curses placed by men

We can learn much from the ways those who place curses deliberately operate. They cannot generally just choose someone at random and speak a curse against them. In order to be effective they have to have some form of link with the person which can be used as an access point to the victim. It's almost as if the demons which will fulfil the curse have to have knowledge of the victim or a means of identifying him. That is why they try to obtain something which belongs to the person to use in the cursing ritual.

An object which the victim owns (see also the next section) is frequently used, such as an item of clothing or a piece of jewellery. When an object or a piece of clothing is stolen, for example, it can be used to try to curse its owner. Alternatively a curse (demon) is attached to the object and then it is returned to the owner so that the demon of curse is able to operate directly against the victim.

Something of the person's flesh is especially powerful. Nail clippings, hair trimmings and blood are frequently used. The scripture talks about *"the life being in the blood"* and the use of someone's blood in the cursing ritual, as a means of linking a curse directly to the victim, seems to be one of the most powerful means of controlling people through demonic cursing. We have come up against numerous examples of this.

Another method of linking the curse to the victim is by the use of their photograph. This is more commonly a voodoo practice, where the photograph is used instead of a voodoo doll to put physical pain and symptoms into the victim. For example, by stabbing the doll or the photograph in specific places, the voodooist can use demons to induce identical symptoms in the body of the victim.

In countries where voodoo is a basic practice of native witchcraft, people are often in great fear of the voodooist, for they know what has happened to other people who have fallen victim to his activities. The voodooists are often used in a commercial way and are employed by people to place curses on victims - even competitors in business.

Whenever occultists are used like this to curse victims, whether through voodoo or some other occult practice, they will invariably need something of the person in order to establish a spiritual linking with the intended victim so that the demons will be able to identify the victim and do what is asked of them.

What the above discussion establishes for us is that a linking is required between the one who curses and the victim who is cursed. Without that linking the curse cannot be directed to the victim and it will not work. Even with such a linking, however, it will not necessarily work. I have heard those who have been involved in the evils of the occult say that they found that it was harder to put curses on some Christians than others. Reduced to a simple rule, the closer a person walks with the Lord, the less landing ground there is for the enemy's curses!

We have found in some ministries that when people started to develop strange symptoms for no apparent reason, sometimes these were the consequences of occult curses. At other times people suddenly started having strange accidents or things would be going inexplicably wrong with their relationships or their work.

Ministry in this area has often depended on having a correct word of knowledge about the person being prayed with. At other times when we have suspected a curse and challenged the spirit of curse causing the problems to surface, the demon has often spoken out how it got into the victim. Once the person has forgiven the person, known or unknown, who placed the curse (or who paid the occultist to do so), then deliverance can take place, and usually there is an end to the signs or symptoms that were indicative of the curse being present.

When ministering to people who have been actively involved in false religions or occult practises which, as part of their rituals, invoke curses on others, one can expect to have to deal with many, many different curses of a wide variety of types during the course of the ministry. All witchcraft, satanism, freemasonry and other secret orders (of which there are many) have built curses into all their rituals to try to prevent people from either leaving the organisation, or, if they do so, to hold them into the bondage they willingly entered into whilst a member of the group.

Some of these curses are of death, so it is not unusual to find that after someone has been delivered of a spirit that was attached to a particular ritual, the spirit of curse that was a guardian of the ritual immediately comes into action, and can sometimes try to make the person stop breathing or want to commit suicide. The demon has a right to do this, given by the individuals themselves when they willingly spoke out their acceptance of the terms and conditions of membership or of power elevation within the organisation.

For example, the curses of freemasonry are different at each degree to which the participant rises. We have seen that these curses can be passed on to the children in accordance with the words of Exodus 20:5 - the sins of the fathers are visited on the children unto the third and fourth generations. Daughters of freemasons that we have ministered to have often manifested symptoms of the masonic curses precisely in line with the actual words of the curses invoked by their fathers as part of their ritual initiations into each degree.

Another aspect of cursing through freemasonry is that these curses seem to particularly affect Christians who renounce either their own freemasonry or that of their ancestors. Freemasonry is a form of a 'prosperity cult' for those involved, whereby one freemason is pledged to help their brother freemasons. When people renounce freemasonry, the spirit whose job function it was to encourage prosperity reverses its role in order to fulfil its anti-Jesus objective. Prosperity becomes a curse of poverty which acts against financial interests, especially of believers. We have found in ministering to those affected by freemasonry that there is often a spirit attached to this. We can also testify that with some of these people, when that curse of poverty was broken there were noticeable differences from then on!

As people are set free from all these things and delivered from the demons that have been at work in their lives, the wonder of the cross comes more and more sharply into focus. When Jesus died he made it possible for people to be set free from every curse, because the consequences of all curses were laid upon him, and it is as a result of what he suffered that we can be healed. Isaiah's prophecy (Isaiah 53) in which he describes how the one who was to come would make healing possible, was amazingly accurate.

iv) Non-deliberate curses

By 'non-deliberate curses' I mean curses that are spoken by people against others, but not with the specific intention of bringing harm to the person in the sense that is described above. But our ignorance of how the demonic takes the things we say and do does not prevent the demons from using us to hurt others through our words. For example, the enemy can latch on to what we may say in a fit of temper and make it stick in the mind and the emotions of the person spoken to. If the words are believed and accepted, the demonic can then establish itself, holding the victim to the words that have been said.

However, for this to happen, as with the deliberate curses described above, there has to be some connection between the one who curses and the victim. This brings us back to the importance of soul-ties. More often than not, when people say things to us that really hurt us, they are said by people with whom we already have a soul-tie. It is only because we are close to the person that the words have any power to affect us.

If someone we have never known swears at us abusively for no apparent reason, we will normally just shrug it off. Whilst we may remember the incident, there is no power to hurt or control us implicit in the words. But if a man comes home from work one day and abusively attacks his wife for something she is supposed to have done (or not done!) she is likely to be devastated by the encounter and the wound will go very deep.

If she dwells on what has been said and begins to believe the lies that have been spoken about her (eg. *"you are useless"*), then the enemy can use the soul-tie between her and her husband to lodge a spirit of failure deep inside. Once there, it will do everything it can to make the poor woman live up to the expectation of being a failure, and she will be made to experience on the inside what the spirit keeps on telling her, until she has so convinced herself that she is a failure that her whole world begins to fall apart.

Sometimes in public meetings I have taught on this whole subject of failure and sensed that many people present have been labouring, not just under the problems they have encountered in life, but from the effects of a spirit of failure that has been inducing much of the damage. When the demons behind this are addressed and ordered out, it is not unusual for quite a large percentage of the people to go through deliverance as they are set free from the bondage they have been in.

So what we are looking at in this whole discussion are negative and destructive words spoken (and even prayed!) by people close to us with whom we have a soul-tie. Such words, when believed and accepted, become a landing ground for the demonic.

Children are especially vulnerable to the criticisms spoken over them by parents because they instinctively believe what parents and other adults who have some responsible care for them say. They accept the good and the bad without question. They are encouraged by the good. They are destroyed by the bad. Some of the things people have told us about which were said to them by their parents have appalled us as we have stood by them in their walk towards wholeness. The pain of remembering things that had been said was sometimes so great that it was hard for them to forgive, even though they realised that without such forgiveness the demonic power behind the words could not be broken.

Actual examples of things we have come up against, as a result of which people have needed both deliverance and healing, are as follows.

Said by parents to children

You are useless.

You'll never be any good. You're just like your mother.

Big boys don't cry (accompanied by a beating for crying even though there was a good reason for crying, when aged 7).

You'll never get married. Who would want to live with you?

You're ugly.

You'll never get a job.

Never trust men. They'll only get you into trouble.

You're really wicked, you're evil.

You'll never change, you'll always be the same.

It's in the family - you're bound to get it.

Said by husbands to wives

Why can't you cook like my mother?

You are pathetic.

You dress like a clown.

When I see you in bed I feel like sleeping in the spare room.

Why can't you be like John's wife?

Said by wives to husbands

I wish I'd married a real man.

All you're interested in is sex (to a man who was heart-broken by his wife's total lack of interest in him as a person).

It's a pity the children haven't got someone they can look up to.

You're just like your father - useless.

No wonder you can't get a job. I wouldn't employ you for anything.

Said by a congregation to their minister

It's a pity Mr. Jones had to retire.
   (Mr. Jones was the previous minister)

I used to enjoy visits from the previous Pastor!

We'll pray him out of here, he's not for us!

Don't think you can change anything here.

If you preach more than ten minutes, we'll all walk out.

We pay you to do what we tell you.

Said by a minister to his congregation

You're all dead.

I wish I'd never come here.

If you think you can change me, think again.

Said by an employer to employee

You never do anything properly.

If you carry on like that you'll make me bankrupt.

I'll run my company, my way. Stuff your Christianity.

A monkey could type quicker than you.

How we respond when things like the above are said to us determines what hold, if any, the enemy is able to exercise over us in our lives. These are some of the possible arrows that Paul was talking about when he wrote in Ephesians 6 about fending off all the fiery darts from the evil one with the shield of faith. We can either hold up our shield of faith and, with Godly authority, refuse the influence of such words in our life, or we can accept the words, dwell on them and believe them. As soon as we do this we have given the enemy a right to walk all over us, and at some time in the future we may need deliverance.

v) Self-cursing and inner vows

Unfortunately, children rarely know how to handle the sort of situation when cruel words are spoken against them. The arrows usually find their target. Inside, the child (and often the adult) will make an inner vow. This is a form of self-curse through which we determine not to let these things happen again, whatever it may cost us.

For example, a natural response to the beating given to a seven year old boy because he was crying is to say, *"I will never cry again"*. One man of 46 I ministered to had done just this, and from the age of 7 until the age of 46 he never cried. But the price he paid for such control of his rightful emotions was high. Because his emotions were now demonically controlled through the curse and the consequent inner vow, he finished up in deep depression and had to have medication for most of his life. He only half-lived, such was the crippling effect of both the depression and the drugs. Healing for him began with forgiving his father and renouncing the inner vow he had taken.

When we make an inner vow against ourselves, which means that some part of our lives will be lived in a way that is contrary to God's plans and purposes, then not only do we limit our potential as people, but we invite the enemy to control us in that area. Many people have subsequently realised how stupid it was for them to say such a thing and then find that they could not break free from the situation. They did not realise that they were then fighting the demonic, and it was only after deliverance that they were able to begin the long process of restoration of rightful thought patterns and behaviour.

For example, one girl who had been heavily abused had made many inner vows, two of which were *"I will never sleep in a bed again"* (she had concluded that beds are dangerous and decided not to use them again) and *"I will never trust a man again"* (because men do nasty things to you). Whilst she had tried to overcome these things of her own accord, she had found it to be quite impossible. It was only after she had been delivered of the spirits that were controlling her, as a result of the self-cursing through inner vows, that she could be healed. She was eventually set free from the bondage and was able to both sleep in a bed again and, after a period of time, began to see that not all men would abuse her and that she could look forward to having a loving relationship with a man.

Some of the inner vows that we have had to set people free from are as follows:

> *I'll never forgive myself*
> A very common response to a situation which
> might have been avoided, but something went
> wrong. People can then blame themselves for
> the rest of their lives.

> *I'm ugly, thick, useless, a nuisance etc.*
> Inner vows which are a direct response to
> believing that what others have said against them
> must be true.

> *I'll never speak to .... again*
> Inner vows which are a direct response to damage
> caused by a certain individual.

> *It's not safe to look attractive*
> If I make myself look attractive I may get
> abused again. Deliberately getting overweight,
> or becoming anorexic, are typical responses
> which can hide the sexuality in such cases.

No-one loves me, so I won't let anyone get close to me

The pain of having trusted someone who let them down makes them conclude that no-one can really love them, so they become emotionally reclusive and live behind sealed walls.

I want to die; I'm better off dead

When the pain of living is so great that people conclude the only sensible answer to their situation is to take their own life. This is far more common than most people readily admit. When I ask in public Christian meetings how many people have felt like committing suicide at some time in their life I usually find that at least half the people put their hands up!

I'm not going to grow up

Response of a child who fears the world of grown-ups because of what some of them have done to her.

Parents can't be trusted

Response from a child when betrayed by a parent. One person we prayed with was left for 'five minutes' by their parents, who went off and enjoyed themselves for five hours. The distress caused by this one incident had been life-long.

Sex is dirty

Response of a child who asked her parents questions about the facts of life. Her response to her parents' embarrassment was to conclude that sex must be very dirty. Sexual problems in marriage had their origin in demonic control of her sexuality through this inner vow.

All dads hurt children

Response of a physically abused child to an eventual foster parent. The demons attached to the inner vow prevented relationships with the man who was trying to rescue the child from the past.

190

For those who are trapped in life by the spirits of curse that have been put upon them through the deliberate malicious intent of occultists, the thoughtless verbal attacks of those who oppose us in various ways, or as a result of our own making of inner vows, it is encouraging to remind ourselves of the truth stated so clearly in God's word:

"You believed in Christ, and God put his stamp of ownership on you by giving you the Holy Spirit he had promised. The Spirit is the guarantee that we shall receive what God has promised his people, and this assures us that God will give complete freedom to those who are his ... (and) you will know what is the hope to which he has called you, how rich are the wonderful blessings he promises his people, and how very great is his power at work in us who believe." (Ephesians 1:13-14, 18-19 GNB).

12. Cursed objects and buildings

When we understand that the way a curse is applied to a person is through the agency of unclean spirits, it is easy to understand that unclean spirits could also be attached to objects and buildings, so that those who come under the influence of such places and objects will also come under the influence of the demons attached to them.

Those who have come under the influence of cursed objects have sometimes become the victims of deliberately applied occultic power, but often the victim has come into the ownership of something that has been cursed or been to a cursed place, and they have no framework of understanding to see how it is possible for them to be suffering as a result.

2 Chronicles 29 is particularly significant as a point of scriptural reference in this respect. After the temple in Jerusalem had fallen into pagan occult use, King Hezekiah came to the throne and determined to clean up the situation. Not only did the priests have to make themselves ritually clean after the time of apostasy, but they also had to make every object in the temple ritually clean so that it would be freed from all the powers that were inevitably attached to the objects which had been so defiled.

Occultists attach great power to objects which have had a Christian use and are then stolen and given a pagan use. They recognise that the demonic power that can be wielded through the blatant misuse of objects that were formerly consecrated to God is far greater than with any other object. That is why there is a thriving black market in stolen religious objects and why, in recent years, when there has been such a rise in satanism and witchcraft in the western world, there has also been an enormous rise in the theft of religious objects from churches - especially chalices and other church silverware. As a result, many churches in the UK, which were formerly able to be left open for people to use as a sanctuary at any time, have had to be locked at all times other than when services are taking place, as a deterrent to thieves.

Ministers, and all those responsible for church buildings, not only need to be guardians of the fabric, but need to be spiritually discerning people who will sense when something is not right and exorcise the building of anything that has either been left behind by visitors ('worshippers') to the church or that has been done deliberately through rituals taking place in or around the church at night. This gives an additional modern-day insight into how important it is to follow the early church's example and only appoint to offices in the church men who are *"full of the Holy Spirit"* (Acts 6:3 GNB). How else could they discern those things (of a spiritual nature) which are not of God?

When God gave Moses the instructions for dedicating the Tent of the Lord's presence, he was told *"dedicate the Tent and all its equipment by anointing it with the sacred oil, and it will be holy"* (Exodus 40:9). The implication of this significant verse is that all the objects that were used for the tent and its contents were un-holy, and they needed to be consecrated so that they would become holy.

This is a fallen world, in which, for the time being, everything is under the control of the god of this world (Satan). Prior to consecration, therefore, all the materials which had been used for making the tent and its contents were subject to the influence of the enemy. In order to remove the right which Satan would otherwise have had over the objects used in the worship of the true and living God, there had to be a ritual cleansing (exorcism) of everything so that Satan could have no influence over the worship of God by his people.

This is the origin of services consecrating buildings to be used in the worship of God. This is an important area of study which is too extensive to cover in detail in a general book such as this.

With regard to the ground on which churches are actually built, it is interesting to note that in Exodus 3:5, Moses was told to take off his shoes because the ground he was standing on was holy. It had been made holy by the presence of the living God who spoke to him out of the burning bush. The most interesting point about this encounter is not that the ground on which God was standing would be holy (that, I presume, is obvious!) but that the ground on which Moses had been standing was unholy by comparison. So, it is not only objects and buildings which need to be made holy by consecration, but also the ground on which the building is standing.

Such acts of consecration deal with the claim that Satan would otherwise have (as god of this world) to the land and buildings involved. But where objects, land and buildings have, additionally, been used by man in any form of occult worship, there is additional direct demonic power which has been attached to the site through the agency of man's sin. So not only do they then need consecrating to God, but first they need to be exorcised of all demons that have been attached to them through the sins of those who have used them previously.

I use the word exorcism here deliberately, to distinguish it from the word deliverance which I have used for setting people free from the presence of evil spirits. The word exorcism is not used anywhere in the scriptures to describe the deliverance of people from demons, but it does have a specific and very relevant meaning in this whole area which seems to be much more appropriate for the specific deliverance of inanimate objects and places.

Many of our ancient churches, following the instructions of Augustine, were built on the ancient pagan worship sites in the villages and towns of our land. Whilst the buildings will have been rightfully consecrated to God when constructed, I do wonder if the ground on which the churches were constructed was exorcised of the demons which had been given specific rights there, often through human and animal sacrifice to the demonic deities and ultimately, therefore, to Satan.

There are a number of buildings in which Christians had continued to have problems over a long period of time and which we have dealt with in this way. When the powers attached to the land were challenged, it was not unusual for there to be some very considerable demonic power unleashed as a result, especially on sites where sacrifices had taken place. The demons that were tied to the land through such acts were vociferous in their objection to being removed, and on some occasions tried to enter the people who were involved in the ministry. We have found that when the ground has been thoroughly and rightfully dealt with that there has usually been a marked change in the spiritual atmosphere inside the buildings.

Returning now to cursed objects, we have sometimes found that some people we have tried to help have struggled to get free, and we have struggled to set them free! In a number of these cases we have come up against objects they own which have been cursed and which, therefore, hold an enormous amount of demonic influence over them. Usually the objects involved are items of jewellery, or, if not jewellery, items of significant value. This is one way of ensuring that the person will think twice about throwing such items away and will want to hang onto them for their monetary value. We have found that the only wise policy with all such objects is to adopt the procedure followed by Paul in Acts 19:18-19 with regard to occult books, which, in those days, were exceedingly valuable. They had a bonfire and destroyed them.

You only have to see once the response from the demons inside a person when it is proposed that we destroy the object which has been used to give them power, to realise how vital a part of the ministry this is for those who have either been in the occult or who have been cursed through owning occult objects. The demons will scream out in terror, produce all sort of 'rational' arguments why the objects shouldn't be destroyed and, in the end, when they see that the person's will is set towards getting rid of the accursed objects, the demons will sometimes resort to physical violence to try to prevent what is going on!

Cursed jewellery is often inherited, so one of the questions that we need to ask people who have suddenly started strange problems in their or their family's lives is *"Have you inherited any objects which might have an occult background?"* We have found that sometimes people have kept freemasonry objects belonging to a deceased relative and the demonic resistance to the destruction of these has been as great as if the objects had been used in witchcraft.

For this sort of reason I would never advise anyone to purchase second-hand jewellery of any kind (one has no idea what curse might be attached to them), and to enquire very carefully about the provenance of gifts that are handed down the family line before accepting them! Second-hand engagement rings, for example, can bring with them a curse on the whole marriage, if they have been wrongfully used by previous owners. If they were sold by the previous owner because of a broken engagement or a divorce, a ruling spirit of division could affect the next person who wears the ring. At the very least all second-hand jewellery should be exorcised and re-consecrated to the Lord.

Cursed objects are not necessarily jewellery. Children, for example, place far greater value on a favourite toy than on a piece of gold! We have seen how children brought up in homes steeped in witchcraft are sometimes given a special toy, which has first been demonised by cursing. This toy then acts like a demonic watcher and comforter for the child, and an unnatural attachment to the toy will hold the child in bondage, not just in childhood, but later in life as well.

Ungodly soul-ties of domination and manipulation are encouraged and strengthened by special gifts from the one who dominates through obligation, guilt and weakness. They have often been hand-made, with many hours of work being put into the toy, so that the recipient would feel guilty about ever treating such an object as 'just another toy'. I am not saying that all such toys are given in this way. But the objective of making and giving give is not always as pure as we may be led to believe!

In general, it is only objects that have been specifically used in occult practice that would need to be physically destroyed, but I would strongly recommend that if there is any unnatural attachment to any gift or object, then it should certainly be prayed over and any ungodly soul-tie there may be between the owner and the giver should be cut. I have seen that when this is done the gift can then be viewed more rationally and whilst it may still be appreciated for what it is, it no longer holds the dominating and manipulating power which it did previously.

Finally in this section, I must refer to buildings which people have visited, through which they have inadvertently been demonised. Sometimes it is simply that people have been unwise, not realising the demonic danger they have been in by visiting, for example, the temples of other religions, or other places where demonic power has been given rights through the false worship that has been offered there.

Sometimes visitors are asked to take off their shoes before going in such temples. If people do that, they are in effect offering worship to the demonic deity that reigns over the temple! Therefore, it is not surprising that many people, even committed Christians, who visit such places can pick up a spirit which has been given a right through their action. We need to be on our guard against such possibilities.

At other times people have been demonised through a house they have owned (or sometimes just visited). The previous owners of the house gave rights to the demonic through the things they did in the house, and subsequent owners then walked into the spiritual tidal wave of opposition that was left behind. This would especially be the case if the new owners of the house were Christians, whose very presence is quite naturally a threat to the demons.

This underlines the importance for Christian families to treat their own homes as a temple (in the Old Testament sense) and dedicate both the ground and the building to the Lord, having first cleansed them of any demonic power that has been in residence as a result of the activities of previous owners. We also know of instances where the previous owner died in the house, and although they may not have been into anything particularly occult, their association with the house was so strong that the demons who left the body at death remained tied to the property and continued to 'own' the property, as it were, on behalf of the person who had just died.

Sometimes the guiding demonic spirit of the person has even manifested in the house as a ghost. This can also happen if there has been any past tragedy in the house, especially sudden violent deaths or suicides where the demonic power has been operating powerfully as a result. In some of these instances we have found it helpful to have a communion service in the house as part of the re-dedication of the property, making a statement to all the powers of darkness that it is because of the death and resurrection of the Lord Jesus Christ that Christians need not fear the activities of Satan and can live in freedom from the ongoing influence of his demons in the house.

13. Addictions

There are three main categories of addiction. The first two could also be described as compulsive behaviour patterns.

Firstly, there are addictions which are totally unrelated to the chemical constitution of the body, because they are not connected in any way to the intake of either foreign substances or excessive amounts of substances which are only normally taken into the body in small quantities. The addiction is not to a substance but to a particular behaviour characteristic (such as washing the hands, looking at pornography etc).

The second category of addiction is to the intake of food substances which are not themselves chemically addictive in the way that drugs are (there are no chemical withdrawal symptoms if the addictive material is not available), but without which the victim cannot cope.

The third category of addictions is to those substances, such as drink, drugs and cigarettes, which contain chemically addictive substances for which the person develops a craving, as a result of the withdrawal symptoms that are experienced if the body does not have further supplies. In addition to the chemically based addiction there is also the addictive behaviour associated with taking in the substance - eg. going to the pub, associating with smokers etc. The behavioural addiction reinforces the chemical addiction and vice-versa.

With all three of these addictive patterns we have encountered demonic control which makes it very hard for the individual to renounce and walk away from the addiction. When there is a demon inside, whose job function is to control the person through the addictive pattern, it is that much harder for the victim to break free from the addiction.

Addictions do not normally start by someone choosing to become addicted to something. They are usually a reaction to something else that is going on in the person's life or a response to someone else who encourages the behaviour in question. Almost all the third category of addictions are of this latter type, where there is social pressure to conform to whatever the group are involved in. If one smokes, it is hard for any of them not to smoke. If one takes drugs, then all give it a try.

Once a person has started on an addictive lifestyle, be it behavioural or chemical, then the enemy will do all he can to tie the person into the lifestyle demonically. But there is no point in just trying to cast out whatever demon may have got in. First of all, the right which the enemy has been given needs to be undermined. Sometimes this will be a case of confession, repentance and forgiveness, but rarely is it so simple!

Addictive patterns are almost always a reaction to gaping holes in a person's life which are not being filled in a rightful way. A person may be deeply rejected and craving for acceptance, so he will keep the company of drug addicts who accept him unconditionally as one of them. A person may be going through a breakdown in the marriage relationship and seek comfort in eating chocolate because there is no comfort to be found in relationship with their marital partner.

Much obsessional addictive behaviour also has roots in emotional damage which will need healing. Demons will also be present but unless healing is brought to the emotions deliverance will not be a fully effective means of healing.

Another example of how addictive behaviour demons enter is, say, when a young man is first curious, and then fascinated, about sex and he begins to look at pornography. Before long his craving for heavier and heavier pornography is such that he cannot stop. A demon has filled his eyes with lust. He is addicted to the desire and is now controlled by the demonic.

When helping addicted people, the root must be identified and the real need met, otherwise one could spend hours in ministry trying to cast out demons of this addiction and the other without ever touching the real problem at all! The main problem areas that need to be examined when looking for the roots of addictive behaviour patterns are as follows:

Rejection

Fear

Loneliness

Sexual problems

Relationship break-up

Abusive background (especially sexual)

Control and domination

It will be obvious from the above short list that when dealing with addictions one may be tapping into the demonic at a much deeper level than the superficially obvious. Unless this is done, whatever ministry that is given is likely to be only top-dressing, with little lasting consequences.

Whilst the above does often apply to cigarette smoking and drinking, with this addiction the peer pressure to smoke and drink may have been the only reason that it was commenced. Often people really do want to give up, especially smoking, and they have tried everything they know. With them, ministry can be relatively simple and effective as the demonic which controls the lungs and the need for nicotine is addressed and expelled. The spirits usually come out on the breath from the lungs, often with much coughing and spluttering!

Those who have been delivered of addictive spirits attached to smoking, however, do need to be very disciplined when it comes to their behaviour from then on. For it would not take much to descend once again into a behaviour pattern which would allow the demonic to re-enter. Once there is a weakness, that area has to be doubly protected through obedience and strong Holy Spirit inspired self-discipline.

14. Fears and phobias

The scripture tells us that *"There is no fear in love. But perfect love drives out fear"* (1 John 4:18). The converse of this would seem to indicate that unless we are living in the experience of the perfect love of Jesus we are vulnerable to fear. And there is much truth in that statement also. For it is only the perfect love of Jesus, and the total security that he gives to members of his family, that will protect us from all the crises and difficulties of life.

There are many experiences of life that can cause great fear to come upon us. Many of the things that have been discussed in the previous sections, such as sexual abuse, accidents, rejection, witchcraft etc., are all potential entry points. Young children are especially vulnerable to fears and find it hard not to dwell on the things that have happened to them, but worse still, on what might happen in the future! Fear of the dark, fear of waking up, fear of not waking up, fear of men, fear of women, fear of failure, fear of spiders - the list is endless.

For a fuller understanding of the whole area of fear, and how to be free from it, I would strongly recommend you to read Graham Powell's book, *Fear Free*. Graham's personal testimony of how God set him free adds much to the teaching content of the book.

Not all fear is demonic, for rightful fear is a God-given gift, which is designed to protect us from harm. It is right that we should be afraid of crossing the road in front of a double-decker bus or of putting our hand in a fire. Fear of things like this is critical for the preservation of life.

But Satan will always take what God has given and distort it for his own purposes. For example, God created sex, but Satan encourages the abuse of sex. Similarly, God created fear, but Satan tries to control our lives through fear. If we give way to the fears that we experience from time to time and dwell on them, the enemy will make the most of the situation and give us a spirit of fear which will then hold us in bondage, even in circumstances when, rationally, we know there is no reason to be afraid. The way out of irrational fears is to confess them as sin, invite Jesus to replace the fears with his perfect love and deal directly with the demonic through deliverance. There is an answer. God has promised to provide us a way out.

15. Fatigue and tiredness

Whenever we get overtired we are vulnerable both to temptation and to demonisation. There are many people who claim encouragement and protection from that wonderful verse of scripture: *"They that wait upon the Lord shall renew their strength; they shall mount up with wings as eagles; they shall run, and not be weary; they shall walk, and not faint"* (Isaiah 40:31 AV).

God has promised that he will strengthen us and enable us to cope with whatever pressures we come up against. So why, if that is God's promise, should tiredness and fatigue be a demonic entry point? One reason is that many of us are tired because we are doing things that God has not asked us to do! We cannot claim the benefits of God's promises without also walking in the way of the Godly.

So often people will try to use God's promises as a cover up for their sin, thinking that everything will be alright. Not so. If we are filling our lives with activities and programmes, which may in themselves be good, yet are not the will of God for us, then we should not be surprised if, when we are tired and exhausted, the enemy walks all over us and we end up falling into sin and being demonically affected as a result.

God has given us bodies that need rest and sleep. God has promised to sustain us, so that whatever the pressure we are under, he will enable us to cope. But my understanding of scripture is that this only applies if we are doing those things that are of him. The fact that we may be busy doing things that sound good and occupy our time to the full does not necessarily mean that they are right. Let us be careful not to fall into the sin of presumption and become vulnerable to the enemy as a result.

In Conclusion

In this part of the book we have seen that there are many different entry points that the enemy uses to infiltrate our lives. The list covered is by no means comprehensive, and in the course of ministry people will come up against many other possibilities, although most will fit into one of the above categories.

We have found that one of the most effective means of satisfactorily completing deliverance ministry is to deal with the entry point and remove the rights on which the demon is depending for its security. In this way one is not only dealing with the deliverance but removing the access route by which a further demon might try to enter. Healing can then follow, so that the objective of ministry can be fulfilled - that the people of God should be able to walk in obedience, fulfilling God's divine purposes for their life and enjoying the blessings that he desires to give liberally to his children.

For Caution and Encouragement

Because this book's focus is on demonic activity and entry points, we must be very careful not to take on board fear or become obsessed with the idea that everything is demonic! Remember Satan would want to take us way out of the balance intended by God in this area.

Physically, if we could see all the germs surrounding a cup, we would not drink from it, but we do because in practice we are naturally immune and in part we are protected by hygiene routines. So it is with the demonic, believers have a Godly in-built resistance and we also have God's word which if adhered to keeps us healthy and clean. Above all we depend on Jesus and the finished work of the Cross which will protect us, cover our mistakes and warn us of all impending danger if our hearts are turned towards him.

"And so, in honour of the name of Jesus, all beings in heaven, on earth, and in the world below will fall on their knees, and all will openly proclaim that Jesus Christ is Lord, to the glory of God the Father."

(Philippians 2:10-11 GNB)

PART C

THE PRACTICE OF DELIVERANCE MINISTRY

The final part of this book explains the practical ministry of healing through deliverance in a way that can be easily understood and applied. The ministry procedures emphasise how important it is to see that correct foundations are in place in the lives of those in need, as well as to see people set free from all that oppresses or controls them.

The healing ministry has many parts, deliverance being just one. Emotional and physical healing often go hand in hand with deliverance. As Paul mentions in 1 Corinthians 12:9, there are gifts (plural) of healing and it is important that those who minister deliverance should always maintain a wise balance between the different aspects of healing that an individual may need.

Chapter 5

Preparing a Person for Healing through Deliverance

Introduction

When a person asks for counselling and prayer ministry, it is often as a last resort. By the time most people seek such help, they have usually exhausted all other possible sources of available assistance, ranging from advice from a neighbour to seeing their local doctor or being referred to a consultant at the local hospital. Many will also have tried various alternative medicines and some will have dabbled in remedies and treatments of dubious origin or even consulted an occult practitioner such as a spiritualist healer or a new age therapist.

In the local church there will also be those who have been prayed for by the fellowship (at a distance) because they are sick, or have been to the communion rail for prayer during a communion service, or had the laying on of hands at a healing service, but appear to be no better.

In our experience the most common reason why so few people get healed through these more routine opportunities for healing prayer is that those who are praying are praying about the symptoms, whereas they should be praying about the situation that underlies the symptoms. Quite simply, they may be praying for the wrong thing! However, there are many people who only want prayer for their symptoms. They are not at all interested in God bringing order to all areas of their life and it is not surprising, therefore, that healing through prayer usually eludes them.

Each time a person asks for prayer, no matter how low-key the request may be, it is a cry for help. The sensitive minister will respond to such cries by making an opportunity to talk personally with the individual and gradually find out what is lying behind the sickness or circumstance which has prompted the request for prayer. If a church has a ministry team, then members of the team can be asked to spend time with each person who asks for prayer, so that there is no danger of people being uncared for and slipping through the ministry net.

In churches where there is already an established healing ministry, asking for prayer with members of the healing team should be a normal and wholly acceptable part of the ministry of the church. Even then, however, there will still be those private or shy people who would find it very hard to share their problems and their needs - especially with someone they have to worship with week by week! Great sensitivity is needed to encourage them to be open to God as they share their situation with someone they can learn to trust.

At the other end of the scale will be those who want to share a fresh need every week! Whilst some people do have more problems than others, sometimes it will be necessary to encourage them to walk in the healing that God has already given and grow stronger in their faith before proceeding to the next stage of their healing. Godly discipling is a very important dimension to the whole process of Christian healing.

When asked questions by the rich young ruler, Jesus had no hesitation in telling him that if he was going to progress with his faith he had to do something about his wealth, for this was getting in the way of his relationship with God (Luke 18:18-23). And when Jesus talked with Nicodemus, he side-stepped the theology and made sure that Nicodemus realised he had to put things right in his own life first and be born again of the Spirit of God (John 3).

Jesus never displayed hypocritical respect for a person's position or standing in society. He spoke the truth about their situation, irrespective of whether or not they wanted to hear it. Just after Simon Peter had that amazing revelation about the very character of Jesus as the Messiah, he started speaking words which were prompted by the devil. Jesus did not ignore these words, as we might have done out of deference to Peter's position as a leading disciple with very special giftings (Matthew 16:13-23), but publicly rebuked the enemy, who was now using Peter to speak out lies.

There are times when we might be tempted to avoid speaking the truth out of deference to, or fear of, the person being prayed for. In the local church, it is especially difficult for people to face potentially embarrassing personal issues, for they fear their local reputation may be sullied if they are really truthful about themselves.

It is clear from the contents of this book that it is important to assess any potential demonic dimension that may be contributing to a person's sickness, especially in the case of longer term conditions. However, when ministering to people in need it is also important to remember they are people and not just objects out of which you are going to try and cast a demon!

Any demons present in the person have gained access through specific rights given during the person's lifetime or through their generational line. Unless those rights are properly dealt with, any deliverance ministry may only be short-term in effect, and the long-term consequences could leave the person in a worse state spiritually than they were before ministry! Preparing a person to receive ministry is, therefore, a vital part of the process of seeing people set free from the powers of darkness. Hence the importance of this chapter.

When one is dealing with a specific physical symptom it is often possible to minister directly into that situation alone and to limit any questioning to things that may be directly associated with the condition. But in the following guidelines for preparing a person for ministry it is assumed that the person is willing to get his whole life in order and is not just asking for prayer for healing from flu!

1. The ministry team

Over the years Ellel ministry teams have ministered to many thousands of people. Based on that experience, we would want to underline the value of adhering to the following basic guideline - never minister alone! If we step outside of what is both scriptural provision and common sense we run the risk of putting ourselves and the ministry of healing in danger.

Why is this so important?

i) This is what Jesus told the disciples to do

Jesus sent the disciples out to minister healing and deliverance in pairs (Luke 10:11). There is no doubt that he did this both for their encouragement and protection. We should be careful not to do otherwise. It is different if ministry is taking place in the context of a large public meeting when there are many people around. In these circumstances, we allow one-to-one ministry, since there are plenty of people around to bring extra help if necessary, but in all other circumstances it is a rule of Ellel Ministries that when ministering to individuals it is vital that the ministry team consists of at least two people.

ii) There is the power of agreement in prayer

Jesus further encouraged his disciples to minister in pairs when he said, *"And I tell you more: whenever two of you on earth agree about anything you pray for, it will be done for you by my Father in heaven"* (Matthew 18:19 GNB). This scripture has been taken wildly out of context by some people who think that if they simply agree (in the flesh) about anything they might want (rather than need), God is duty bound to supply!

It is necessary to understand the true meaning of agreeing together in prayer. The psalmist states *"Delight yourself in the Lord and he will give you the desires of your heart"* (Psalm 37:4). The key to blessing lies in the relationship each one has with the Lord. It is only as we delight ourselves in him that the desires of our heart will become those that are on God's heart also.

Each of the two who are agreed together in prayer need to be delighting themselves in the Lord and hearing from him for themselves as to what God's will and purpose is. When they find that they have independently heard the same thing from the Lord, they can agree together about what God is saying, and go to the Lord with tremendous confidence and faith, asking him to fulfil those desires that have come from him in the first place. When praying for an individual, the strength that is given to the prayer when two are agreed together in this way has to be experienced to be understood.

Jesus goes on to say in Matthew 18:20 that wherever two or three are gathered together in his name, he is present with them. Again, this requires understanding. It does not mean that God is not with individuals when they pray alone! I believe this scripture can only be fully understood in the context of spiritual warfare where two fighting together are infinitely stronger than two separate people fighting alone.

There is a special blessing from the Lord upon those who come together in prayer, fellowship and warfare to both uplift Jesus and to bring down the work of the enemy. The combined power of two people counselling and praying together is very much more than the simple addition of one plus one.

iii) Two counsellors provide protection for each other and security for the person being prayed for

When praying with people who are empowered by the demonic, the demons occasionally rise up within the person to physically, emotionally or verbally attack those who are praying. There is great security in not being alone when these sort of things happen. Indeed, two together in ministry is a very effective preventative against anything untoward happening.

The protection needed is for more than just the time of ministry. For if the ministry has been one-to-one, when it is all over there is no independent witness to what actually happened in the counselling room. One of Satan's names is 'accuser of the brethren' and he delights to try to destroy people through gossip, rumour, scandal and lies. Whilst these are tactics that he will always try to use against any Holy Spirit led ministry, we should try not to put weapons in Satan's hands which could be used against us!

If we minister alone, who is to say what really happened behind the closed door of a counselling room? We have had to pray with ministers whose very reputation has been at stake as a result of things that have been said about them in the community. In one particular case a Pastor had prayed with a woman in his study. No-one else was present at the time. He rightfully confronted her with things that were going on in her life, encouraging her to put her life in order. She did not like the advice, went away and then made an official complaint to the effect that he had sexually abused her in his study. She told others in the community and, before many days had passed, it had become a major scandal. I am absolutely convinced that nothing untoward happened in this case. She was aggrieved by the straightness of his advice to her and because she was not willing to bring her life into Godly order, the demons had a free opportunity to use her to try and destroy this man's Godly ministry.

He had made a mistake by ministering to her alone and in so doing had handed a primary weapon into the enemy's hands. If he had taken the simple precaution of having somebody else with him then none of this would have happened. There would have been an independent witness to everything that had been said and done.

Sadly, we have also had to pray with women who actually have been sexually abused by their Christian counsellor, who had used the confidentiality of the counselling room to allow sexual desires to gain the upper hand. Again, if a third party had been present it would never have happened. The damage done by incidents such as this is incalculable. When people have had their lives torn apart by the very people they thought, before God, they could trust, it not only has the effect of making them run from Christian counselling and ministry, but frequently makes them run from God as well, believing it is he that has betrayed them. No wonder Jesus said that *"If anyone should cause one of these little ones to lose his faith in me, it would be better for that person to have a large millstone tied round his neck and be drowned in the deep sea"* (Matthew 18:6 GNB).

We have also had to minister into situations where a man being ministered to by a male counsellor came under a homosexual threat from his counsellor. So, especially in the current sexual climate, it is not even safe to minister alone with someone of the same sex for danger of any subsequent homosexual or lesbian accusations. The counsellee also needs to be protected from possible danger.

One of each sex ministering to a counsellee is probably as near to the ideal as is possible. There are situations, however, where the counsellee may not be ready to cope with this. For example, a woman who has been sexually abused by men could find it very hard to receive ministry from a man in the first instance, notwithstanding the fact that one aspect of the ministry that will need to be walked through is the forgiveness of men for what they have done.

Often, in such circumstances we have begun the ministry with two women ministering, and a man has been introduced at a later stage to help with the healing of relationships to men. In general, ministry by a man to an abused woman and by a woman to an abused man (when the abuse has been carried out by a member of the opposite sex) is an important part of the ministry process.

In summary, my advice to those who would get involved in the counselling ministry or in praying for healing and deliverance is as follows:

a)   Never minister alone.

b)   Always have someone on the ministry team who is the same sex as the counsellee. (It is alright for two men to minister to one man and two women to one woman; but never for two men to minister to a woman or two women to a man. The best combination is for one of each sex to be involved in the ministry.)

c)   If the ministry team is a husband-wife team, then, in the case of heavier ministries (especially where there has been serious abuse or involvement in occult activities), it is always advisable to have a third person present also. The main reason for this is that with some married couples one partner may so submit themselves to the other, that they effectively suspend their independent judgement of what is happening, and the couple end up acting as one person rather than two. It is then possible for the husband-wife team to be deceived into a wrong course of ministry and a third member of the team will help provide a balance or corrective should this be necessary.

d) Caution should however be exercised with regard to men and women ministering regularly together who are not themselves married to each other, so that no ungodly relationships develop between the counsellors.

e) Always seek the Lord together for the counsellee before meeting with them for counselling and prayer.

f) Always agree together about the course of action before commencing prayer and ministry. There is nothing worse than the counsellors being divided about what to do next. Satan thrives on division!

g) Ministry can be spiritually, emotionally and physically exhausting. So, after ministry, pray for one another so that each one will be strengthened, restored and built up for whatever is to follow, and any particular hurts that may have been received during the ministry can be brought to the Lord for healing. For example, it is not unusual for some things said by a counsellee to be speaking unknown to them right into the pain of the counsellor's own personal situation. Clearly this cannot be discussed in the ministry time, but afterwards a few minutes prayer will go a very long way towards restoring the bruised heart.

This has happened to me personally. I was praying into the details of a person's family situation, when I realised I was talking as much to myself as to the person I was praying for! Immediately after the ministry time, I was the one who received further healing and deliverance!

If people follow the above basic guidelines, they will find that:

a) The combined power of two people counselling together in Godly order is much greater than ministering alone.

b) There is protection from subsequent misrepresentation or accusation, or from being misquoted.

c)   There is always someone present, of the same sex as the counsellee, to help with personal and intimate ministries and the laying on of hands during prayer.

d)   There is a Godly check on the course of the ministry which prevents them going off track.

e)   There will be a rightful holding back from new avenues of ministry until both are agreed that it is right.

f)   The ministry can change from one counsellor to the other with regard to taking the lead. The one who is not directly ministering at any one time can be praying for the other.

g)   They can test and pray about particular words of knowledge that the Lord might give before applying them in the ministry.

h)   They can encourage each other to grow in faith and expectation.

i)   They can take time out to talk and pray with each other about the ministry at any time.

j)   They can remind each other of relevant scriptures. One can be looking up appropriate scriptures whilst the other is continuing with the ministry.

k)   The mixture of gifts and abilities that two people bring to a ministry enables a wider perspective on the situation.

l)   It provides physical protection for each other.

m)   They can recognise times when the enemy may be particularly attacking their co-counsellor and pray for protection.

n)   It avoids the counsellee becoming too dependent on one person. Spreading the ministry amongst others provides for more balanced relationships subsequently.

o)   It provides for ministry continuity in the event of one of the counsellors becoming ill, or being called away from a ministry appointment for an unavoidable reason.

p)   It enables a ministry team to train up other members in the security of a learning situation alongside more experienced counsellors

Counselling Questionnaire

The remainder of this chapter outlines the more commonly encountered areas of investigation which will help counsellors to uncover areas of possible problem. To help with this aspect of prayer ministry, Ellel Ministries has produced a comprehensive *Counselling Questionnaire* which many have found to be extremely helpful. (Copies of this copyright publication are available at a small charge directly from Ellel Ministries - for address see the appendix).

The questionnaire is not just designed to expose potential demonic problems but aims to expose the root cause of a whole range of healing needs.

2.   Getting started

When a person has plucked up the courage to ask for prayer it is important that a start is made as soon as possible in beginning to tackle the problem. If the situation is a complicated one it may be a little while before in-depth ministry is possible, but at the very least a meeting should be arranged to make an initial assessment of the situation. This will encourage the person to know they are being cared for. It is likely that in a preliminary meeting some things will emerge which will encourage the person being prayed for to do a bit of spiritual homework!

In recent years we have found that making an initial assessment of the person's needs and situation has been a valuable part of the ministry procedure. This ensures that the best possible ministry team can be arranged for the person and the condition in question. Also, the person will have an opportunity to bring answers to any important questions on areas that were brought to light during the time of assessment.

Before any assessment of ministry is commenced be sure to encourage the person to be totally honest – with God, themselves and their counsellors. This will be hard, initially, for some. Often people have woven a complex web of 'white lies', half truths or self-deception which can camouflage their past. It may take a little while before the person realises that they are not going to be rejected by being honest about themselves and that they are not going to be disapproved of if things are exposed which they had hoped to keep hidden, or just did not want to face up to.

It is also vital to assure the person that whatever they say will be kept totally confidential and that there will be no danger of private information becoming public knowledge. Over the years we have had a significant number of people who have come to Ellel Grange for help because it is seen as a confidential and neutral source of help. Private details about individuals have been passed round in their local church on the 'prayer grape-vine' (often known as the gossip-line) and, because of this, those with real problems have declined to seek help from those who could help them locally, but who can no longer be trusted with confidences.

Satan loves to destroy the healing ministry through breaches of confidentiality. When you assure someone that your word is trustworthy, be sure to never let any confidential details about any other person ever get into the public domain. It is different if the people themselves choose to tell something of their story by way of testimony. That is their privilege, but we should never do it for them!

If a person has a relatively complex history, it will be essential to take notes. If you don't, you may find your memory fails you at the critical moment and you won't be able to remember what to pray for. Even worse, you might start praying with a person about something which has nothing to do with them but with someone else you were praying with last week! Again, always ask permission and do assure the person that any notes you take are always kept very securely under lock and key. Locked filing cabinets, to which only those authorised as members of the ministry team have access, are absolutely essential.

3. Whose agenda?

When a person asks for prayer, find out why they are asking for help. Generally speaking their agenda for God will be the healing of the presenting symptoms.

Whilst God is, of course, concerned about the symptoms a person is suffering from, he also sees them from a different perspective. There may well be a different agenda that God needs to deal with first. In Luke 5, for example, the man who was paralysed was brought to Jesus through a hole in the roof by four friends. He had a specific item on his agenda - to be healed of the paralysis. When Jesus looked at the man he realised that his Father's agenda for the man was initially different - to deal with the sin.

Almost certainly the paralysis had a root cause which lay in unconfessed and unforgiven sin and Jesus was not just interested in dealing with the presenting symptom of the paralysis, but in dealing with the sin, so that the symptoms would not come back again at a later date with the possibility of the man then turning his back on Jesus who had healed him. Jesus was undoubtedly concerned for the man's physical welfare, but he was even more concerned for the man's spiritual well-being. And that is something which we must never lose sight of when ministering healing.

As we counsel and talk with each person it is vital to seek out God's agenda for them and to encourage them to lay down their agenda for the time being. What we have found is that as people do this unconditionally, God is able to meet them exactly where they are. The more open a person is to God, the more powerful the anointing of the Holy Spirit will be upon them during ministry, and the deeper will be the blessing that God gives.

As you talk with the person, explore the causes and situations that lie behind the presenting symptoms. Many of the possible ones are specifically described in later sections of this chapter. What you will find is that there are likely to be a number of situations contributing to the condition and it may be necessary to unravel quite a tangled web of personal history, so that when it comes to prayer and ministry you will be able to tackle each situation that has been exposed through the counselling in a specific way.

Ultimately God wants to restore his order into a person's life. That is a vital part of the process of healing. In many situations people struggle with all that this entails, but it is necessary for people to willingly bring their lives under the Lordship of Jesus and into a right relationship with God. God is a God of order.

It is clear from Leviticus 26 (verses 14-17) that one of the consequences of breaking God's covenant is disorder, which can lead to a breakdown of health. So it is not surprising, therefore, to find that when people bring their lives into harmony with God's covenant that they start to get healed. The older a person is the more things there are likely to be that might need to be brought into order. And for many, there might be quite a few practical things that will need to be put right - such as forgiving people who have hurt them. Essentially, counselling people as a preparation for healing and deliverance is a process of uncovering the holds that the enemy has gained over their lives and then dealing with them.

A person's spiritual situation needs to be assessed in the light of all the foundational teaching contained in Chapter 2. Getting to grips with vital issues such as acceptance, forgiveness, the Lordship of Jesus etc., will significantly ease the actual process of deliverance. You will find that some of the people coming for help do not really know Jesus, so it may be necessary to lead the person into the Kingdom of God before starting to pray further with them. Those who enter the healing ministry must also be willing and able to be evangelists and lead people to Christ. Over the years there have been many hundreds of people who have become Christians through the work of Ellel Ministries. They have come with an agenda for healing, but have discovered that their primary need was a relationship with Jesus, the one who is able to heal.

It is very hard to pray for people for anything, let alone deliverance, if they are still bitter and unforgiving in their hearts. It is vital to ensure that there is no unforgiveness that can stand in the way of God's blessing and the anointing of the Holy Spirit.

If this groundwork is not done, and an obviously manifesting demon is addressed by the counsellor, a considerable battle may ensue if one tries to cast the demon out whilst it still has rights to be there. The end result may be to disillusion the counsellee, so that they will be tempted to reject deliverance ministry; and exhaust the counsellors because they are attempting to cast out demons before ensuring that they are in a position of authority. Do not be tempted to go straight into deliverance without first undermining the rights of the demons through good spiritual house-keeping and cleansing.

4. Note any symptoms of possible demonisation

Some of the observable symptoms of demonisation are described in Chapter 3. These will provide you with an outline of the sort of things to look for as you counsel those who come for prayer. Those who pray for healing and deliverance need to model their ministries as closely as possible on the ministry of Jesus. This may sound like an impossible ideal, but the clear evidence of the Gospels is that when Jesus met and prayed for people he had clear insight about what was going on in their lives. He not only knew about their symptoms, but he knew also what they were thinking about and what was in their hearts (Luke 5:22, John 2:25).

When Jesus sent out the disciples to preach, heal and deliver (Luke 9), he gave them his power and authority, which must mean that they were also gifted with his ability to see what was wrong with those they were praying for. In 1 Corinthians 12, Paul formalises a description of the ministry gifts of the Spirit. The gifts that God has given through the Holy Spirit to his people are to help Christians to be dynamically effective in the ministry of the Gospel.

After Jesus was baptised by John the Baptist in the river Jordan he was dramatically filled with the Holy Spirit and the crowds heard a voice from heaven saying, *"You are my own dear Son. I am pleased with you"* (Luke 3:22 GNB).

From that moment on Jesus moved in the miraculous and day-by-day manifested in full measure the ministry gifts of the Holy Spirit. After Jesus went back to heaven he promised to send the Holy Spirit, and at Pentecost this promise was fulfilled. Those who were filled with the Holy Spirit were then able to move in the gifts of the Spirit as Jesus had done.

To be baptised in the Spirit is a vital step towards an effective healing ministry. Unless one is moving in the gifts of the Spirit, the potential for healing prayer could be severely restricted to the routines of religious expression. Some people will, of course, be healed in this way, but in general it will only be those who, by the grace of God, have prepared their own hearts for ministry, have dealt with all the obstacles in their life to the work of the Spirit and are ready to receive.

In our experience it is only a small percentage of those in need of healing who come fully prepared to receive healing from the Lord. I have often found that in the lives of even the most saintly of people there have been strongholds that the enemy has gained, sometimes early in life, which have held power and control. People have needed help to see these things and take the appropriate action to undermine the work of the enemy in their life.

We should expect that the Lord will reveal his heart to us about those who come for prayer. Sometimes he will give a word of knowledge. At other times, through the gift of discerning of spirits, one will have an immediate sense of the presence of the demonic, and at other times God will raise up that wonderful gift of faith to believe for the seemingly impossible. But we should expect that as we wait on the Lord he will speak to us so that those who are truly seeking him can walk towards the healing that Jesus offers to those who come to him.

The restoration to the Body of Christ of the full use of all the gifts of the Spirit is a vital step towards the restoration of the healing and deliverance ministry. Teaching that says the gifts of the Spirit are not for today closes the door on so much blessing that God wants to pour out upon his people.

There will be times, however, when we do not seem to have an answer. One longs for a word from the Lord to help with a ministry but nothing seems to happen. At times like this I have come to understand that there can be a number of different reasons, one or more of which may be relevant at any particular time:

a) The person's will is out of line and they are unwilling or don't know how to bring their life into line with God's will and truth.

b) Intercessory prayer (or fasting) may be required to overcome the enemy's strategy and release the anointing of the Holy Spirit.

c) There may be other areas that God wants to deal with in the person's life before he is able to bring healing, (eg. unforgiveness).

d) The counsellors may themselves be overtired and not alert in the Spirit to what God might want to say.

e) The situation being dealt with may require others with particular experience to be present for the next stage of ministry, (eg. someone with an understanding of false religions or occultic matters).

Satan is opposed to the deliverance ministry because in essence it is this ministry that exposes his plans and purposes for the individual and the corporate body.

It is important to persevere and not give up. The ministry of healing is often an intense battle against the work of the enemy, not just in the person's own life, but also in the family line they belong to. There are times too when the warfare is especially strong because Satan does not want to see a whole church fellowship opened up to the healing and deliverance ministry, and from this point of view some ministries might be more strategic than others.

So as we minister it is vital to listen to the Lord as well as the person and to seek God for specific revelation as to what strongholds the enemy has in the person's life, which will be strategic in the ministry of healing and deliverance.

5.   Investigate false beliefs and occult involvement

Satan is behind all false forms of worship whether they are open false religions or occult (hidden and secret) practices. He also rejoices when Christians favour heretical beliefs and reject the foundational truths of the Gospel. This is an important area of investigation when counselling people, for when people get involved in any of these activities they are opening themselves up to the enemy and, through false worship and beliefs, make themselves vulnerable to demonic power which lies behind the false religion.

Scripture contains numerous warnings against occult (pagan) practices of worship (eg. Deuteronomy 18:9-14) and is equally condemnatory about religious routines which appear to be worship of the living God but which are filled with hypocrisy because of the secret sin in the heart of the worshippers (Isaiah 1:10-20). When self is on the throne of a person's life they are practising self-idolatry. God clearly says in his word that *"you shall worship no God but me ... for I am the Lord your God and I tolerate no rivals"* (Exodus 20:3-5 GNB).

Whenever we place ourselves, another person, an object, a religion, heretical beliefs, a secret society (such as freemasonry) or anything else before worship of the true and living God, we are indirectly elevating Satan. Just as God has promised to inhabit the praises of his people (Psalm 22:3), so Satan will take specific advantage of such sin and inhabit the 'praises' (worship) of those who give place to him on to the throne of their lives. Demons will attach themselves to areas of false worship, eg. oaths, idols, statutes, rituals, etc. and will seek to invade and occupy the person who makes himself vulnerable through known or unknown sin.

In ministering to many different people we have found that the beginnings of a particular problem has often been some form of occult involvement or heretical belief or practice. The involvement can be as low-key as visiting a pagan temple while on holiday overseas and taking shoes off as a mark of respect to the worshippers. In Exodus 3:5 God speaks to Moses out of the burning bush and tells him, *"Take off your sandals, for the place where you are standing is holy ground"*. The principle established here is that ground, which was made unholy through the fall and the temporary rulership of Satan over the world, is made holy by the presence of God.

When people take off their shoes at a place of worship, they are acknowledging that the ground has been made 'holy' by the presence of the 'god' which is worshipped at the temple. True holiness, however, is only a hallmark of the one true God, not of the false gods that have deceived the peoples of the world into giving homage to the demonic and ultimately to Satan, the fallen god of this world. So, in taking off their shoes like this they are in effect giving credence to the belief system and in so doing can open themselves up to the possibility of being demonised. We have seen many people set free from demons that gained access in this way and had cursed them with all manner of bondages and ill-health.

A few years ago I ministered to a Christian pastor who had formerly been a Sikh. Whilst in many ways he had been a very effective pastor, he knew he was being held back in his ministry. It was only when he renounced the spirits of deception which lay behind his former religious life that the demonic power which was still controlling him could be cast out. The anger and threatened violence of the demons was such that he realised in a very dramatic way how it was that he was being held back in his ministry.

Often the Lord has drawn our attention to particular items of jewellery. When we have asked about them, there has invariably been some strong occult association with either the jewellery itself or the person from whom the jewellery came. At times there has been tremendous demonic resistance to removing the jewellery because of the power of the curses that have been attached.

Similarly, occult objects may be kept in the house. Usually the person who owns them is totally unaware of the power of the demonic to use such objects as channels into their home and, sometimes, into members of their family. Masonic objects of deceased relatives are typical items of this nature to find stored in the attic. I will never cease to be surprised at what is brought to light by a few carefully directed questions about either dead relatives or living ones who are involved in some odd practice or other!

Of a similar nature to spirits that become attached to occult activity are all the religious spirits associated with other religions or heretical pseudo-Christian beliefs. Scripturally they all come under the general description of "lying spirits" which Paul warns us people will be deceived by. *"The Spirit says clearly that some people will abandon the faith in later times; they will obey lying spirits and follow the teaching of demons*" (1 Timothy 4:1 GNB). They can bind the mind and the understanding so that the person is closed to the work of the Holy Spirit.

In ministry I have had to deal also with many spirits, that have held people in bondage, which have responded directly, when named correctly, according to the name of the denomination they have been attached to! Whenever love for the dictates of a denomination becomes more important than love for and obedience to Jesus then we should be aware that people can make themselves vulnerable to the possibility of being controlled by religious demons.

That is not to say that there isn't a rightful place for order and discipline within a denomination, there is. But let us be sure that we don't make heavy burdens for people to carry (like the Pharisees did) that God is not asking them to bear!

Finally in this section, we have found in practice that there is a demonic stronghold behind each of the major heretical beliefs and when people give credence to any of these beliefs then they are in danger of receiving a spirit of deception, which will then start to affect other areas of their Christian life. It is hard, sometimes, for people to see this, but when they do there can be quite a battle to set people free. The demonic power behind such beliefs can be very subtle and it sometimes requires finely tuned discernment to understand what is happening.

In the Appendices to this volume is a brief checklist of the primary occult and non-Christian religious systems. Involvement with any of these is likely to be the source of demonic control. It may be helpful to have each person work through this list as a preparation for ministry.

6. Check out the generational lines

In Chapters 3 & 4 it was explained in detail how and why demonic power is able to pass down the generation lines so that one generation can be demonised as a result of the sins of earlier generations. When counselling people, especially those whose problems would appear to have been long term, it is vital to look carefully at the possibility of generational sin being the source of the present problem.

When doctors investigate a medical condition, one of the questions they are trained to ask is about the generational history of the disease, *"Did either of your parents or any of your grandparents have this?"* The medical profession recognises that in many cases there is a family susceptibility to a condition which can be transmitted from one generation to another. Whilst in some of these conditions there is a well-defined genetic pathway, that is not always the case. And even in the case of genetic transference one has to question what happened in the first place to create the defective condition which has come down the family line?

We have sometimes found it helpful to prepare a simple family tree of the previous two or three generations, indicating on this those who have died and when and what they died from. The correlation between the death of one person and the onset of related or similar symptoms in another member of the family is often very close. Frequently we have seen people set free from the demons that have transferred at death and then seen the person healed of the condition. We not only ask about physical conditions, but also behaviour characteristics. Behaviour of the person can also be influenced by the demonic through the sins of the fathers in the same way as can the condition of the body.

Sometimes we have seen how a demonically induced condition has missed a generation. For example, when grandparents die any demons that have rights to the family will pass to whoever they can get to in order to maintain their presence in the family.

7. Explore the sexual history

A person's sex-life is generally considered to be forbidden territory for open discussion! People are embarrassed by the subject and fear gossip. And if they are involved in Christian ministry or leadership they fear that if dark secrets were brought to the light they may lose their position and reputation. Pride and fear keep many a person away from the doorway to healing. Satan rejoices in this, for it means that the most powerful means he has of controlling a person by the demonic (through ungodly soul-ties) is territory which remains a forbidden subject.

Often we have to explain in detail how Satan can use sexual sin to affect a person by the demonic, before they will see the wisdom of bringing everything into the light. I am sure that Jesus knew the full significance of what he was saying when in his answer to Nicodemus he said, *"Anyone who does evil things hates the light ... because he does not want his evil deeds to be shown up"* (John 3:20 GNB).

In general, people will be more open about confessing and dealing with sexual sins that were committed before they became a Christian. But as Christians are 'not supposed to do these things', to face up to reality when there has been post-conversion sexual sin takes an enormous amount of courage. But we must face up to it. For, sadly, many Christians have taken the world's standards into the church, instead of taking their Christian way of life into the world. As a result, in the present generation we probably face the greatest incidence of sexual sin in the body of Christ that there has been since Pentecost.

Counsellors cannot afford to be prudish or ill-informed about the whole range of possible sexual sin. Neither must they be condemnatory or judgemental when things do come to the light. It is absolutely vital that those who may be sharing long-hidden secrets for the very first time do so in an atmosphere of trust, love, non-judgementalism and respect.

The soul-ties which people have established through sexual sin can be used by Satan for the rest of the person's life, or until the tie is broken through confession and repentance, and deliverance of any demonic powers that took advantage of the sin has taken place. Wrong sexual soul-ties can also be established between sexual participants without full intercourse having occurred. For some people the emotional involvement of an illicit relationship can be a significant a channel for the demonic.

But when intercourse takes place, the act is recognised by Satan as if it was the physical consummation of a 'marriage'. For in a Godly relationship, once the marital vows have been made, the full marriage is initiated with intercourse. The church has always recognised that where intercourse subsequently proves impossible (for whatever reason), the marriage can be annulled if the partners so wish and the 'husband and wife' be absolved of their marital vows and be considered as single people.

Conversely, when two people have intercourse together it is as if they are married to some extent because the sexual act which scripturally consummates a marriage has actually taken place. So Satan has rights to hold these people together through a 'physical marriage' for the rest of their days. This tie can act like a demonic tube through which Satan can affect a person. What has been established in the heavenlies in this way can only be undone through confession and repentance and asking God himself to break the soul-tie through the work of the cross.

When God does this, the healing and freedom from bondage that can result is remarkable! Satan loves to keep people chained to the sins of their past, but Jesus came to set the captives free! Similar chains will need to be broken when a person has suffered sexual abuse. For even though they did not choose to have the sexual relationship they have usually been tied to the abuser through trauma and fear, even if intercourse has not taken place, and by the act of intercourse as well in the event of uninvited intercourse or rape.

Where there have been many sexual partners we have sometimes asked the person to make a list of the first names of all those they can remember. If they can't remember names, we have asked them to try and remember something about that person so that when we pray through the list we can be specific about each relationship. On occasions when there have been too many partners for memory to cope with we have dealt with those that come readily to mind (usually the more significant ones) and then prayed about the others in a group!

We have seen through much experience the wisdom of James' advice, *"so then, confess your sins one to another and pray for one another, so that you will be healed"* (James 5:16 GNB). When people have the courage to bring to the light those things that have been hidden, God is able to heal us of the consequences. Is this not what Jesus was doing when he confronted the paralysed man in Luke 5 with his sin before praying for healing from the paralysis?

8.   Look for signs of rejection

I strongly recommend all those who are seeking to bring healing to hurting people to first read Steve Hepden's book, *Explaining Rejection* (Sovereign World). This will help counsellors to understand how it is that demonic powers can so effectively control the lives of those who have been rejected.

Unhealed hurts from the past caused by rejection are primary entry points for the enemy. Whilst the pain is unhealed, and those who have done the rejecting are unforgiven, healing can be an elusive target that is never quite reached. The demons will hang on until there is no longer any ground left for them to stand on.

The most common demons encountered in this area of ministry are those which respond to the names of rejection, fear of rejection and self-rejection. These three often operate together in the rejected person in an unholy trinity of demonic control. They have the effect of isolating the person from quality relationships with those they know and love, and preventing the person from realising their full potential under God.

Spirits of infirmity and sickness and a range of other demonic beings seem to be able to enter on the back of this group of rejective demons. Whilst I do not want to give more credence than is necessary to the holds which rejective demons can have, I do want to emphasise that dealing with the emotional roots of rejection and making right choices with regard to ongoing relationships will remove much of the ground on which these demons stand. I would rather spend a few hours bringing deep inner healing to hurting and rejected people before attempting to cast out the demons than risk hurting the people more by trying to cast out the demons at a time when doing so may cause them considerable distress.

9.   Investigate other ungodly soul-ties

In addition to the sexual soul-ties, Satan can use people who dominate and control to hold us into the bondage of an ungodly soul-tie which was established by other than sexual means. Demons can then use this relationship as a point of transference. When counselling people, I often ask if there is anyone they are so afraid of that they feel obliged to get their permission before embarking on something new.

If there is fear then there is likely to be an ungodly domination by that person, and if people are afraid to make normal decisions for themselves without reference to someone else, it is likely that there is some ungodly manipulation.

I remember telling one lady that she needed to go home and tell her mother that she loved her, but that this did not mean she had to refer every decision to her for consideration. Her immediate words spoke volumes, *"I can't do that. She'd kill me!"* Mothers and mothers-in-law can sometimes be very controlling and have the effect of dominating the whole family.

It is right and necessary for parents to hold up Godly authority in the family, but when young people grow up they should develop more mature relationships with their parents. The parents should relinquish their desires to control their children, although much loving advice and support may often still be necessary. Parents can still continue to provide advice and help if it is wanted, but that is not the same as insisting that the 'children' do what the parents want!

10. Find out about accidents and traumas

Accidents and sudden traumas have the effect of putting all the body's systems into a state of shock. The physiological effects of shock are well known and defined and there are established methods of care and, sometimes, treatment to cope with the after-effects.

What is less appreciated, however, is that the person suffering the accident is also spiritually vulnerable when trauma takes place and there is a danger of potential demonisation - often through the fear which is associated with the traumatic experience.

For example, I have delivered many people of spirits of fear associated with car accidents. These have sometimes been so powerful as to prevent the person from living a normal life. One lady, who suffered a near-miss whilst on the pillion of a motor-bike, had been fearful for nearly forty years before she was delivered of the spirit that had come in at the moment of near disaster. The effect of the deliverance was to release her into a much more active life in many areas of her daily routine. Fear had robbed her of doing many things which she would otherwise have enjoyed.

There have been times, also, when we have been unable to bring deliverance to a person who has been demonised through trauma without leading them through the process of forgiving the person who caused the accident and, in some cases, breaking the soul-ties between the people involved. There may also be sin involved which needs to be confessed, repented of and forgiven. When dealing with the consequences of accident and trauma one cannot overlook any of the foundational principles of ministering healing - they are all potentially relevant.

If the accident or trauma was very severe, the effect on the personality can be such that there is an inner broken-ness of the spirit and soul. This can mean that any demons that entered with the accident may be lodged in the broken part and are not easily delivered. The consequence of this is that a person may have pain arising from injuries which should have healed years ago, but never have. The body, which God designed to heal, remains stubbornly afflicted with the consequences of the accident - even ten or twenty years after the event!

Isaiah 61:1 tells us in prophecy that one of the healing works of Jesus would be to *"bind up the broken-hearted"*. In some cases healing prayer (as opposed to deliverance) is necessary for the binding-up (healing) of the person - even for traumas that happened many years previously. In experience we have found that many people were not able to be fully delivered from the demonic which came in through the trauma, until the Lord brought healing to the broken-ness on the inside.

As a general rule, I will ask most of the people I pray for if they have ever suffered any major shocks or traumas. There has been great blessing when ministering in these situations as people have been both healed and delivered. I have come to the conclusion that this is one area of ministry about which Satan has tried to keep the church ignorant. The effects of such prayer can be dramatic as long-lasting symptoms are finally dealt with and people can be released into the fulfilment of their Godly gifts and callings.

In Summary

These aspects of counselling are all important as a preparation for deliverance. The order in which these matters are tackled, however, is not usually significant. In a person with many problems it is not unusual to find that demonic power is attached to many, and sometimes all, aspects of personal need described here. It is important not to forget that for many people healing is a process, as bit by bit the strongholds of the enemy are eroded through prayer and deliverance.

There are times when I have talked the person through many areas needing healing and then ministered into each area after the interview stage was over. At other times I have opted to minister into some areas before moving on to investigate other areas. The choice is yours. The most important thing to do is to listen to God about what is best for the person you are trying to help. There are no rules - just guidelines. It is vital that we are sensitive to what God is doing in the person and allow the Holy Spirit to direct the ministry.

Some people find it hard to be so flexible in their approach to personal ministry, but if you study the Gospels you will find that Jesus dealt with people differently every single time. He listened to the Father and did only what the Father told him to do (John 8:28). As far as is possible we should follow this same 'Jesus model' of ministry.

Chapter 6

Foundation Prayers

The earlier parts of this book have explained how demons can influence and enter a person. The last chapter described important groundwork that should be covered as preparation for deliverance. We now turn our attention to the actual process of deliverance.

During the counselling interview, the counsellors will have been taking notes of those areas where there is likely to be a demonic problem. It is these areas that must now be addressed. Whilst the person ministering will normally be the one who speaks to the demons and tells them to leave, it is vital to have the active participation of the person being delivered. The counsellee should not passively expect someone else to do all the work. Each of us has a will, and if that will is not actively involved, then the deliverance is likely to be incomplete and short-term in its benefit.

The demons know whether or not a person's will is really cooperating with both God and the counsellor. The man who wanted to be delivered of a spirit of lust so that he could give up his sexual sin did not receive successful deliverance. If he had been really serious about putting God first in his life, he would first have exercised his will, and brought his life into order by giving up his sinful lifestyle, before seeking deliverance. The demons would then know that his will was in line with God's will and that, when ordered to do so, they would have to leave. When Jesus healed the paralysed man (Luke 5) he first dealt with the sin before ministering healing. That is a position of potential victory.

It is necessary for the person to have exercised his will by choosing to make Jesus Lord of every area of his life, by living in a way that would not continue to give the demons further rights through sinful behaviour and by wanting to be set free of any demons that have entered.

Assuming now that the necessary groundwork has been done and that the person seeking help is ready to proceed, we have found it necessary for the person to pray about those things that have been brought to light through the counselling. Whilst it is possible for people to pray silently, we have found that praying out loud is more helpful. It strengthens the counsellee's determination to overcome demonic powers in Jesus' name and ensures that the counsellor knows that important things are not being forgotten.

As part of their training, Ellel Ministries' counsellors learn to use prayers such as those detailed below at this stage of ministry. Please note, however, that this is not a liturgy of healing which will guarantee that a person receives automatic deliverance! God looks on the heart, and if the person is saying prayers with the lips, which are not a genuine expression of the heart's desire, then any related deliverance is unlikely to take place.

There are many different forms of prayers such as these, and it is helpful if counsellors get to the point of so understanding the foundational principles involved that they can construct appropriate prayers at the time to exactly suit the situation of the person they are praying for. These prayers will, however, provide a suitable framework on which to build other prayers for particular situations.

To invite Jesus to be the Lord of each area of the counsellee's life

We recommend praying in this way to all those seeking help, even for apparently mature Christians. Our experience has proven time and time again that, for many people, the reason they have not been set free previously is that there are areas of their life which are not rightfully submitted to the Lordship of Jesus, but are firmly under the control of either self or the demonic.

Prayer:

Lord Jesus, I confess that I have sinned and acknowledge my need of you. I thank you for dying on the cross for me and accept you as my Saviour. I invite you now to be Lord of every area of my life - Lord of my mind and all my thoughts, Lord of my emotions and all my feelings and reactions, Lord of my will and all my decisions, Lord of my body and all my behaviour, Lord of my spirit and my relationship with You, Lord of my time, my work, my home, my family, my possessions and all my relationships. Thank you that your blood was shed that I might be set free. Amen.

To break the links with previous generations

Praying in this way does not cast out spirits that have come down the generational lines but the effect of the prayer is to cut them off from their generational root.

Prayer:

I unreservedly forgive all my ancestors for all the things they have done which have affected me and my life. I specifically renounce the consequences of their sins in Jesus' name. As a child of God I now claim that the power of the blood of Jesus is setting me free from the consequences of generational sins. I claim my freedom from the consequences of all occult activity on either my father or my mother's family lines (at this point it is important to specifically name any known occult activity, eg. spiritualism), from curses and pronouncements that have had an effect on my life, from hereditary diseases and from the effects of any of their sins which have influenced me. I pray this in the name of Jesus, who became curse for me on Calvary and died that I might be set free. Amen

To forgive others for what they have done to us

Forgiving others is a vital step towards deliverance. Unless people are willing to forgive others they are not able to receive forgiveness for their own sins (Matthew 6:15). In the middle of the prayer is a space for the counsellee to speak out loud the names of all those they know of that they need to forgive. Some names will be harder than others to say.

You may need to help the person to persevere as they apply their will to getting through the list. Such is the significance of forgiving others that you may also need to bind any demons that begin to manifest at this point, in order to try and stop the process of forgiveness taking place. The demons will do everything they can to prevent the person from clearing this important ground for deliverance.

Prayer:

Thank you Jesus for dying that I might be forgiven. By an act of my will I now choose to express the desire of my heart and forgive those who have hurt me.

(At this point name out loud the people that need to be forgiven). I release each and everyone of these people into the freedom of my forgiveness. In Jesus' name. Amen.

For some people, before they are able to forgive certain individuals, it may be necessary to repent of harbouring hidden anger, resentment, bitterness etc. against them. This is sin - even if it appears that such anger and bitterness is justified by what the person has done.

Prayer of repentance for harbouring thoughts against someone:

Father, I confess that, as a result of being hurt, I have allowed myself to hold anger, resentment and bitterness in my heart against (insert here the names of specific individuals). I acknowledge this as sin and I now repent and turn from this behaviour. I ask that you will forgive me and cleanse me. In Jesus' name. Amen.

To forgive oneself

Often people blame themselves for what was obviously someone else's sin and continue to live in false guilt and bondage. People can also hold themselves responsible for things, such as accidents where no-one was obviously to blame, instead of placing the blame on Satan through whose temptations man became a fallen race and brought upon himself the consequences of sin.

Prayer:

Thank you father for forgiving me for things that I have done. I now choose to forgive myself for the things which I know you have already forgiven me for. In Jesus' name. Amen

'Forgiveness' of God

God cannot do wrong, hence the inverted commas around the heading. But some people blame God for things as if they are his responsibility. They are really blaming God for things which are ultimately Satan's responsibility and this needs to be repented of.

Prayer:

I confess that I have blamed you Lord for things which are not your responsibility. I recognise this to be sin and I ask you to forgive me. I know that you hate what Satan has done in my life. Thank you for loving me and promising to set me free. In Jesus' name. Amen.

To confess personal sin that may have given rights to the demonic

a) Occult sin

Prayer of confession:

Father, I confess that I have sinned against you and your word by my involvement with the following occult practices (speak out here all known involvements). I acknowledge that ultimately all these practices are the worship of Satan and I choose now to place Jesus on the throne of my life. I ask you now to forgive me for these and any other occultic involvements that I may have knowingly or unknowingly entered into. In Jesus' name. Amen.

b) Sexual sin

Prayer of confession:

Father, I confess that at various times in my life I have been powerless against the continuing attacks of the enemy on my sexuality. I have chosen to sin in various ways and ask you to forgive me for the following: (specifically speak out loud here all the sexual sins that the Lord brings back to the memory. Be patient as it may take the counsellee some time to get through the list.) I now agree with your verdict on my sin. I renounce all pleasure associated with these sins. I ask you to cleanse my memories, heal the hurts and forgive me. In Jesus' name. Amen.

c)   All other besetting sins

Besetting sins are those sins which seem to continually trip someone up. They will be different for each person according to their own particular pilgrimage through life.

Prayer of confession:

Father I ask you to forgive me for my continual vulnerability to the sin of (insert here the specific sin or sins involved). I recognise my own part in choosing to sin in this way and ask you to set me free from the chains that have bound me to this sin. In Jesus' name. Amen.

Repentance from sin

Confession of sin and repentance are not one and the same. The prayer of confession is a recognition of the nature of the sin and an admission of responsibility. Repentance, however, is the expression of willingness to turn from the sin. Many people know exactly what they are doing, and may even go to confess their sin regularly, but if they are not turning from the sin also, their prayer of confession is simply a string of empty words that have no effect or power.

Prayer of repentance:

I now turn from my sin. I ask you Father to forgive me for all that is past, give me the discernment to recognise temptation when it comes and the strength to resist it. Thank you that Jesus' blood was shed that I might be made clean. I ask you to cleanse me now from all uncleanness. In Jesus' name. Amen.

When people have confessed and repented of sin, it is important that we speak the truth of scripture into their lives afresh and affirm them with the words:

"If we confess our sins, he (God) is faithful and just and will forgive us our sins and purify us from all unrighteousness." (1 John 1:9)

and remind them that God has said, *"Confess your sins to one another, and pray for one another, that you may be healed"* (James 5:16 NASB).

Renunciation of Satan's works

Provided there has been true confession and repentance of the above sins, formal renunciation of Satan's works in the life of a person is not a requirement for forgiveness. Such a renunciation is implicit within the prayer of making Jesus Lord.

With regard to deliverance, however, we have found it to be helpful and significant for the counsellee to speak out to Satan and all the powers of darkness a formal renunciation of their influence. It is one more step towards undermining the hold that demons may have on the individual. We do not pray to Satan (we should have no desire to ask him for anything), but we can address him in this way - rather like Jesus did when addressing the powers of darkness that were speaking through Simon Peter that tried to divert Jesus from going up to Jerusalem (Matthew 16:23).

Personal declaration:

Satan, I hereby renounce you and all your works in my life. I, by an act of my will and in the strength that Jesus Christ of Nazareth gives me, close the doors of my life to all the entry points you have previously gained through my sins. I speak out, in the name of Jesus who defeated you at Calvary, that you no longer have any right to trouble me on these specific issues - which have now been confessed, repented of, and forgiven, and from which I am now being cleansed by the shed blood of the Lord Jesus Christ.

To break ungodly soul-ties

The interview stage will normally have revealed any ungodly soul-ties that Satan will have used to bring in the demonic. It is helpful to systematically break these as you minister to the individual. Deliverance may occur after each one of these has been broken, so be prepared. This is a prayer of command that is normally prayed by the counsellor for the counsellee.

Prayer:

In the name of the Father, the Son and the Holy Spirit, I break all ungodly spirit, soul and body ties that have been established between you and (speak out here the name of the individual involved). I sever that linking supernaturally and ask God to remove from you all influence of the other person (name the person again here if you prefer) and draw back to yourself every part which has been wrongfully tied in bondage to another person (again name the person here if you prefer).

This prayerful statement may then be followed up by a prayer for deliverance of any demons that entered through the particular soul-ties being referred to at each stage. If you are ready to move straight on to deliverance, continue as follows:

I now speak directly to every evil spirit that has taken advantage of this ungodly soul-tie. You no longer have any rights here and I order you to leave now without hurting or harming (name here the individual being prayed for), or any other person and without going into any other member of the family. In Jesus' name. Amen.

Infilling with the Holy Spirit

At this stage it is often helpful to stop for a moment and ask the Lord to anoint the person afresh with the Holy Spirit. It is the anointing that 'breaks the yoke'. Stop and wait patiently as you observe what God is doing in the person's life. Remember that this is God's work and it is our privilege to cooperate with whatever he wants to do at this moment.

Sometimes I bless some oil and anoint the person. The effect of this is always to bless the person, but on occasions we find that there is a very strong demonic reaction to the anointing with oil. It seems that when the Holy Spirit comes on a person the primary point of access to the life of the individual is through the spirit. To anoint a person with consecrated oil, however, is to extend that anointing to the flesh, wherein the demonic normally resides.

It is not unusual to find that at such times the demons will even speak out through the lips of the person saying things like, *"it burns, it burns, get it off!!"* There is no doubt that demons do not like consecrated oil and, equally, that they are not overly concerned about unconsecrated oil. However, it is not the oil, but the presence of the Holy Spirit in the oil, that causes such distress to the demons.

I have found on some occasions that it is helpful for the counsellee to speak out a prayer of consecration to the Lord, asking to be filled with the Holy Spirit. At times like this we have seen people baptised in the Holy Spirit for the first time. It is much easier for people to receive the Holy Spirit in this way when they have brought their life into order.

Prayer of consecration:
Lord Jesus, I give my entire being - spirit, soul, body - into your hands. I invite you now to fill me with your Holy Spirit, that I may be totally yours. In Jesus' name. Amen.

Of course there will be occasions when a person is ready for deliverance ministry without it being necessary to pray through all, or even any, of the above prayers. This is especially the case in a public meeting, after people have been convicted by the Holy Spirit through the teaching and, as a result, have put that particular area of their life in order. Then it is generally a very simple matter to address and deliver the individual of any demons whose ground has now been removed through repentance.

But when a person comes for counselling and help we have found that to try and short-circuit important preparatory stages has, in the long term, been a false economy. It is important to realise also that not everybody will need to deal with all the above areas in their life at the same time. On one occasion the counsellor might be dealing with occultic sin and so will use the prayer (or a similar prayer) to deal with this matter alone, and follow through with deliverance in this area. Other matters will then be dealt with at another time.

However, if the occultic sin is linked with an ungodly sexual relationship it is unlikely that deliverance will be successful unless both the sexual and the occultic sin are dealt with together. So it is necessary for the counsellor to both seek the Lord for wisdom and apply common sense! There are times when discernment is not so much a supernatural gift of God but the practical application of the information we already have!

Chapter 7

The Ministry of Deliverance

Exercising Authority

The key to the actual process of deliverance is authority. Demons are living beings who are in the service of their master Satan. Jesus never joined in the rebellion which we know as the fall and, therefore, never came underneath Satan. Satan is the ruler of this world, but Jesus is high over all (Eph. 1:18-23) in a position of authority and with the incomprehensible power of the Almighty. Satan is under his feet.

Jesus gave the disciples his power and authority to go and cast out demons (Greek: *ekballo*, meaning to throw out forcibly). In the Great Commission Jesus told the disciples to teach new believers to do the same things he had taught them to do. Believers are therefore operating underneath the same commission that Jesus gave to the disciples.

God also gave freewill to mankind. If a person chooses to continue in a wrong heart attitude, an ungodly belief system or the practice of sin, then any demons present as a result of these things have been given rights to stay by the person involved. That is why repentance is such a vital part of the process of healing through deliverance. The rights the demons have must be removed.

It is only exceptionally (see Acts 16:18) that deliverance without the cooperation of the individual is permitted. And even then the implication of Matthew 12:43-5 is that unless the doors are closed to the enemy through faith in Jesus, the latter state of the person could be even worse if more demons subsequently re-occupy the territory.

Assuming, however, that all the groundwork has been done and the person's will is in line with God, then the process of deliverance should be the relatively simple one of exercising God-given authority over a spiritual being which, in terms of authority, is beneath us and whose source of power (Satan) is ultimately under the feet of Jesus. To exercise authority one needs to be in a position of authority. It is vital, therefore, that those ministering deliverance should truly know who they are in Christ.

If Satan will allow those operating in the occult to cast out demons (which he does) through occult exorcism, so that people will be yet further deceived, he can certainly instruct some demons to come out in response to the commands of 'Christians' who may be operating in deliverance, but who do not truly know God. After all, Jesus did say that there would be some who had cast out demons in his name to whom he would have to say, *"I never knew you. Get away from me ..."* (Matthew 7:23 GNB).

The process of deliverance is sometimes accompanied by a variety of physical manifestations, but it is important to stress that a person does not have to experience manifestations in order to be delivered. Response to being delivered varies enormously from person to person. The only general rule that we have found applies is that the more thoroughly the ground work is done, the easier the deliverance eventually is.

For example, if a person is truly forgiving and repentant, that will ease the process of deliverance. But if there is still a lot of unhealed emotional pain or buried anger, then the demons can use this to resist deliverance and the effect can be a display of violence fuelled by this source of emotional energy.

Some critics of deliverance naively suggest that inner healing is all that is needed. On the contrary, some practitioners of deliverance disparage the process of inner healing, saying that it is unnecessary. In practice both are essential if full healing is to take place. Whilst inner healing can take place before or after deliverance, our experience is that if none takes place before deliverance then the process of deliverance is made harder for both the person being delivered and the person praying for deliverance. Sometimes, the demons are able to use this pent-up energy to magnify the strength of the manifestations. Unhealed and buried emotions are like food for the demonic and if there is 'stored' anger and emotional pain, release of this will be necessary alongside the deliverance.

At other times the manifestations that are observed during deliverance are helpful in discerning what is actually going on in the person - especially if it is clear that the person needs deliverance but it is not immediately obvious what right they have to be there. This is especially the case when dealing with generational demonisation. In these cases the person is largely ignorant of what may have happened on the ancestral line and cannot, therefore, easily 'confess the sins of the ancestors' in order to undermine the rights of the demons.

When the demons are spoken to and ordered to leave, they can manifest in the person without actually coming out. The way they manifest often provides clues to their nature. If, for example, there has been generational witchcraft, the body of the person can involuntarily take on a position indicative of a particular ritual. Another person might develop a sudden pain in a particular part of the body and this can indicate a generational sickness of demonic origin which is being forced to manifest itself prior to being delivered.

At other times we have reminded the demon that it is under the authority of the Lord Jesus Christ and ordered it to speak the truth which Jesus Christ himself would confirm as truth. This puts the demon in the same situation as the demon which controlled the Gadarene demoniac. This demon was obliged to answer Jesus' questions and speak the truth. Whilst I do not recommend talking to demons as a normal means of deliverance, we have found that in some cases (as with Jesus and the Gadarene demoniac) it was a necessary part of the process of healing through deliverance. One should always remember that the only reason for speaking to demons is to effect deliverance.

The range of possible manifestations is wide and varied. However, one should never be diverted by the manifestations but rather press on with the deliverance until either the deliverance is complete or it is clear that the demon is not readily coming out. When this happens it is necessary to go back to the Lord and ask him if there is anything else that needs to be done first, and to go back to the person and ask them what is happening (the Lord will often speak to them directly at this point showing them any rights the demon still has).

When deliverance is taking place the person being delivered is generally aware of something happening at the spiritual level, even if there are not any obvious manifestations. It is important to reassure the person when there are manifestations. The person can feel defiled or embarrassed by the demons, especially if they come out with vomiting, or some other painfully obvious exit route. It is the spirits that are evil and unclean - not the person.

When the demons begin to exit, any of the following manifestations are possible. The first five are manifestations that can also be experienced during an anointing of the Holy Spirit and it is important to discern what is actually happening. Sometimes, it is the anointing of the Holy Spirit which stirs up the demonic and initiates the process of deliverance.

None of the following manifestations are unusual, although the more thoroughly the groundwork is done, the less likely it is that there will be any serious manifestations. It is important to keep the eyes open when ministering deliverance - both for the sake of discernment and, sometimes, self-protection!

Some Possible Demonic Manifestations

Cold
Especially when spirits associated with death or serious evil practices begin to manifest

Trembling
Either a part of the body can begin to tremble or the whole body can tremble gently

Shaking

When trembling becomes more powerful, specific parts of the body in which the demon has had a strong hold can shake, sometimes powerfully. The shaking can be so strong that the person is thrown to the ground.

Falling to the ground

In the Gospel accounts of the healing ministry of Jesus, it is only when demons were encountered that people were thrown to the ground. This contrasts markedly with the phenomenon whereby the Lord causes people to fall gently to the ground and rest in His presence. When this happens demons can be stirred up by the presence of the Holy Spirit and even take control. Hence the importance of discernment and monitoring what is happening.

Palpitations

These can cause a sense of panic in the person. This is either natural fear, or a consequence of the demonic reaction of having to leave.

Pressure

Especially on the head or the shoulders.

Physical pain

When a demon is forced to manifest it will sometimes cause pain in the part of the body which it has influenced. This can be the case with spirits of infirmity or spirits which are attached to the consequences of accidents or traumas of the past.

Lumps in the throat

The most common exit point for demons is either on the breath or through the throat. It sometimes feels as though there is a physical lump when the demons are on the way out.

Deep breathing

When demons exit on the breath there is usually a deepening of the breathing cycle which can sometimes develop into yawning or coughing. Interestingly, spirits of death usually live on the lung area.

Stirring in the stomach

A demon which has lodged here will sometimes move around shortly before deliverance takes place, giving the feeling of something going round and round in the stomach. At other times a person may feel they are going to be physically sick although they rarely are. A type of vomiting (or retching) may take place.

Feeling ill or faint

The experience of feeling sick can be felt in various parts of the body (especially the head) and is not just limited to the stomach area. See also 'stirring in the stomach'.

Sudden headaches

A common symptom, especially when dealing with mind control spirits or religious spirits or false religions and idolatry. A tight band is sometimes felt around the head, as if the demon is trying to compress the brain.

Unnatural movements

The hands, arms, legs and feet can sometimes move wildly as demons are being expelled. On occasions the movements betray evidence of how the demons got in. At other times the movements may indicate release of pain at the same time as deliverance is taking place.

Contortions of the body

When spirits are coming off the spine, for example, the back can be arched backwards like the sting of a scorpion. The foetal position may also indicate long buried pain and it is important to discern correctly what is actually happening.

Screaming

A scream will often indicate a demon leaving but if it continues without release, there will be emotions involved that need healing.

Pupils dilating

The eye is the lamp of the body. Where light comes in the demons may also look out. The effect can be for movements of the pupils to be independent of their normal response to light and dark as the demons manifest.

Squints and Convergence of the eyeballs

During deliverance it is sometimes helpful to look the person (and the demons) in the eye. There is something about a look which implies authority. The demons will do all they can to avoid eye contact. The commonest tactic is to make the eyes diverge or converge so that it is impossible to look into both eyes at the same time.

Pupils disappearing upwards

When only the whites of the eye are visible, the demon has taken the eyeball upwards so that it is not possible to look the person in the eye. This power is commonly encountered when there is any form of witchcraft in evidence.

Sexual movements (or feelings)

When sexual spirits manifest they can sometimes make the person have feelings and responses in the sexual area.

Demonic tongues

Not all tongues are of the Holy Spirit. It is relatively easy to sense the harshness of a demonic tongue which is in conflict with the tongues which are a gift of the Spirit.

Sudden violent actions

When ministering deliverance there can be a sudden violent reaction, when a particular demonic stronghold is mentioned - as if it has been suddenly awakened from a long sleep! Be on your guard - especially when dealing with heavily demonised people.

Running away

Sometimes people will be tempted by their demons to get up and run when deliverance is near. People need to be encouraged to know that their body is their own and they don't have to obey what the demons are telling them to do.

Hissing

Hissing is a characteristic of the snake. It is not surprising, therefore, that demons who are subject to 'that old serpent, the devil' should manifest in this way. Hissing can also indicate spirits that imitate members of the cat family.

Burping
Where demons have been present on the digestive system, there may be manifestations of the above.

Swearing
People who do not normally swear at all can suddenly break out into the foulest language when a demon is exposed and forced to the surface. They do not like being expelled.

Snarling and Barking
These are characteristics of animals, usually dogs. Where animalistic spirits manifest it is usually indicative of false religions, witchcraft or satanism having some influence on the person or their generational line.

Roaring
Usually characteristic of spirits associated with the larger cats (lions, jaguars etc). Again, most often associated with the higher occult powers.

Bellowing
Sounds like an angry bull. Usually evidence of strong rebellion.

Pungent smells
When some demons leave there is a nasty smell left behind. Again this is only normally experienced when dealing with high powers of occult rituals.

Claw-like actions
Evidence again of animalistic spirits. These spirits might have accessed the family line through bestiality, or through idolatry of the animals or their images.

Slithering across the floor like a snake
A more powerful demonstration of a snake-like spirit than hissing.

As soon as any of the above manifestations occur, quietly exercise the authority you have in Jesus Christ and order the demon to leave without hurting either the individual or anyone else. There may be resistance, but if all the rights the demons had have been undercut there should be no reason why they won't leave.

If, after a little while, the demon is seen only to be manifesting and not actually leaving, backtrack and ask the Lord to show if there is anything else that needs to be done before the demon is free to leave. It sometimes happens that there is another demon holding in the one that is manifesting, and this will need to be delivered first.

When dealing with heavily demonised people the control spirit will sometimes manifest in order to distress the person and try to terminate the ministry. It will only do this when it has a well-organised defence, and this may have to be unpicked before the strong-hold can be demolished. When the defences are down, even apparently powerful demons are reduced to size and are not stronger than others. A demon is only as strong as the defence or rights that it has.

There is no scriptural precedent for telling demons where to go, so I usually tell them to go to the *"dry and waterless places"*, which is the place Jesus said they would go to when they come out of a man. We do not have authority to cast them into the abyss. Even the demons that faced Jesus knew that there would be an appointed time for this to happen and they challenged Jesus as to whether or not he was going to deal with them in this way before their appointed time! If Jesus chose not to send them into the abyss, we shouldn't even try!

We can banish them from the person who has just been delivered and we can banish them from our own local space (home, church etc.), which should be cleansed territory, but we have no authority to take demons out of circulation! They have chosen to be under Satan's authority and there they will remain until Satan himself, with all his demons, is thrown into the lake of fire at the end of time as we know it.

If no obvious manifestations or deliverance occurs, yet you are convinced there is a demonic presence, then pray determinedly into the situation. Some demons will try to hide in order to avoid being delivered. Address yourself to the particular area of sin (or problem) through which the demon came in and ask the Lord to expose any darkness that is there.

Remember also that the angels are *"ministering spirits sent to help those receiving salvation"* (Hebrews 1:14). Deliverance is but one aspect of our great salvation, so ask the Lord to send his angels to minister to the person you are praying for. We have sometimes heard the demons cry out in terror when we have prayed in that way! We do not have authority over the angels - they are at the disposition of the Lord - so we must ask him to send them.

Quietly, but firmly, remind the demons that they are under your authority, and that their master (Satan) is under the feet of Jesus, and command the demon to leave in Jesus' name. It is not necessary to raise the voice unduly or get agitated, although when exercising authority it is not unusual to find that most people raise their voice a little.

Exit Routes of Demons

The exit route of the demons is sometimes indicative of the way the demons came in. When the demons are cast out they generally leave in one of the following ways:

a)   Lift off with no obvious manifestations

b)   Through the throat and mouth (occasionally nose) with deep yawning, burping, coughing, vomiting, choking, breathing, etc.

c)   Through the eyes - the eyelids sometimes flick noticeably during deliverance of demons that have come in through the eyes

d)   Through the ears

e)   Off the top of the head

f)   Through the hands and fingertips

g)   Through the feet and toes

h)   Through the sexual orifices

i)   Through the back passage

Post-Deliverance Care

After deliverance has taken place, it is very important to stay with the person for a while to encourage and reassure them. Sometimes they feel defiled by the experience, even though they feel clean inside as a result of the deliverance. Ask God to send the Holy Spirit to come and fill every area that has been vacated by the spirits.

Deliverance will generally go in stages. The Lord will bring healing to one area and then allow a space before the next area of ministry is begun. In this way the person is strengthened and encouraged to press on to victory. Don't forget that very normal things like cups of tea and coffee are an important part of keeping people encouraged during ministry - as well as keeping the counsellors refreshed! In the case of heavy deliverance it may be a little while before the person can be left alone.

After ministry is over you may find it helpful to arrange to see the person again fairly soon so that you can monitor progress and the person has something to look forward to as the next stage of their healing. For some people also you will find that the advice of Chapter 9 a helpful way of encouraging them to live in such a way that they will remain free in the future.

When people become experienced in ministry they will interchange freely between deliverance ministry and prayer for inner healing or physical healing and then back to deliverance. Healing is a process involving all the different aspects of personal ministry. Flexibility is important so that we are able to respond quickly to what God is doing and help the person to flow with the leading of the Holy Spirit.

Chapter 8

Why Some People are Not Delivered

Throughout this book there is extensive teaching on how to prepare someone to receive healing through deliverance. Implicit within this teaching are reasons why people may not be healed. The following is a checklist of reasons which the counsellor may find helpful when ministering healing through deliverance:

1. The counsellee does not really know Jesus

2. There is no faith that God is able or willing to heal and deliver

3. There is no belief that Jesus wants to heal the counsellee

4. Life is out of balance - in disorder or spiritual chaos

5. Bitterness and unforgiveness

6. Unresolved pain or guilt

7. Praying for the wrong thing

8. The counsellee believes that 'Christians can't have demons' or is possibly under a spiritual covering that holds such a view

9.   There is unconfessed sin which the counsellee is wanting to keep hidden

10. Ungodly soul-ties are still in place

11. The counsellee is either under, or using, ungodly domination or control

12. There are occult powers in place whose control has not been broken either in the counsellee or in those with whom there is a close linking

13. There is little or no anointing in the place of ministry - due to uncleansed ground, buildings or organisations

14. There is hidden or unrecognised abuse or emotional damage that still needs healing

15. Curses of sickness or death are still in place

16. Generational sin and/or demonisation has not been dealt with

17. There is an inner broken-ness through trauma and deeper healing is needed

18. The counsellee is living in denial of the real problem

19. The counsellee has made inner vows which need to be renounced

20. The counsellee is in disobedience over something God has already told them to do (which they are not agreeing to)

21. The ministry team need to seek the Lord for specific revelation about hidden demonic controls affecting the individual concerned

22. The counsellee doesn't really want to be healed

23. Counsellee is not under Godly authority

24. Lack of discipling in the local church

25. Legalism

26. Blocked memories that need to be released

27. Passivity

28. The ministry team are not in a right relationship with each other and are blocking the anointing

29. God's timing

30. The person is suffering from a sickness that is unto death and needs to be prepared to meet the Lord

Chapter 9

Advice to the Delivered

Ten Major Keys to Staying Free

After surgery, a patient receives a list of things they should and should not do. In just the same way, after deliverance ministry, there are things we can do to ensure that people grow strong again and are able to withstand the many ongoing attacks of the evil one. Satan does not give up territory lightly and whilst he does have to bow the knee to the name of Jesus, he will usually try to regain ground that has been lost.

The following guidelines have proved helpful to people who are determined to walk in obedience to the Lord Jesus Christ. In reality they are things that we should all be aware of as part of our normal Christian walk and experience:

1.　The Lordship of Jesus must be central in your life

The number one priority must be to ensure that Jesus is given his rightful place in every area of our lives. If there are things we think, say or do that cannot be shared with Jesus, then we are on dangerous ground which Satan will want to take advantage of.

2.　Be continuously being filled with the Holy Spirit

Whilst the first time someone is baptised in the Holy Spirit is a very special experience, we must not limit our experience of being filled with the Spirit to this occasion. We need to be continuously being filled with the Holy Spirit. This is the full meaning of Ephesians 5:18. The Holy Spirit is our counsellor, comforter, exhorter and strengthener. We need him at all times to be able to live effectively as servants of the Lord Jesus Christ.

3.   Read the word of God daily and allow it to minister to you

The scripture contains everything we need for Godly living. It is a helpful discipline to follow a Bible reading programme on a daily basis, with some explanatory or devotional notes. But it is also important that we read through scripture for ourselves and allow God to speak to us directly through his word.

4.   Wear the armour of God at all times

The armour is for our defence and protection. Study what Paul teaches in Ephesians 6:10-18 and remember that the Holy Spirit will enable us to maintain a Godly stand against all the attacks of the evil one. If during the day there have been moments of failure, confess these immediately, ask God for forgiveness and repair the armour ready for the next encounter. God does not condemn us for moments of failure, but he does expect us to use the means of grace available to us when we have made mistakes so that we can continue to walk tall and strong.

5.   Be on your guard against the enemy's counter-attacks

If we have taken ground from the enemy through receiving healing and deliverance ministry, then be sure that Satan will try to win back some of that ground as soon as possible. Regaining lost ground is one of the first lessons of warfare and Satan knows that only too well! Watch out for temptations, especially in the areas where sin has had to be radically dealt with prior to deliverance. Ask others to pray for you if you are feeling particularly vulnerable at any time. Be aware that the habit needs to be dealt with as well.

6. Be in good fellowship with others

If we remain in good fellowship with other Christians, we will always have a body of believers around us to continue to minister to us as and when necessary. We also need help to see ourselves as others see us and to pinpoint any areas of our life where we may be giving Satan some unnecessary leeway. Small fellowship groups within the life of the church are the ideal venue to grow stronger as faith develops. If no such group meets in your own church, see if there is an inter-church group meeting locally or a group from another church that might be willing to have you share in one of their mid-week meetings.

7. Allow the Holy Spirit to produce the fruits of the Spirit in your life

There is no law against Godliness! The fruit of the Spirit is the outworking of God's Spirit in our lives. If we allow him to nurture and encourage us, we will quickly find that positive changes begin to happen in our lives. If we struggle with a particular area, then we can ask for further prayer, for there may be another demonic stronghold that needs to be broken or more inner healing that is necessary to provide a foundation for progress.

8. Walk continuously in forgiveness

There is no shortage of opportunities to forgive people! We must maintain a Godly attitude towards all those who offend us and not let any more roots of bitterness grow up in our hearts.

9. Praise God in all circumstances

Praise is a vital part of Christian living. God does not change in his character, so there is no need to allow changes in our circumstances to change our attitude towards him. We should not fall into the trap of thinking we should praise God for everything that happens, though, otherwise we could find ourselves having to praise God for something that Satan has prompted someone to do against us. We should not be praising God for these things as they are not his choosing for us. But we should never stop praising God for who he is.

10. Keep the right company

The company we keep can strongly influence the things that we do. If a certain group of people have led us into a way of life that has been bad for us, then we should think more than twice before renewing those relationships. We do not want to cut ourselves off from others, but there are times when for a season until we are stronger, it may be necessary to be very disciplined as to our lifestyle, the company we keep and the places we go.

Postscript

*"Jesus welcomed the people, taught them about the
Kingdom of God, and healed those in need." (Luke 9:11)*

I did not enter the ministry of healing through any personal
desire. It was simply in response to the call God put on my life
back in 1974. At that time, through a very clear word, I knew
that I was to spend the rest of my life ministering in
evangelism and healing to those in need and teaching others
how to heal the sick.

I did not read the small print of the contract at the time, I
simply set out to fulfil whatever it was that God would have
me do! However, when I read the 'textbook' (compulsory
reading for all disciples!) I found that the healing ministry of
Jesus contained some dimensions about which I was ignorant.
Yet I could not ignore the facts of deliverance as described in
the Gospels, so I began to explore this area and see if it had
any relevance to the church in the latter years of the
twentieth century.

Twenty years later I can now look back and see how
absolutely vital it was that I did not try and practice the
healing ministry in isolation from all that Jesus said and did.
Without the keys of deliverance most of what God has fulfilled
through Ellel Ministries could never have happened. Many of
the people who knocked on our door for help in those early
days had been prayed for many times without any noticeable
effect - deliverance was the primary missing ingredient.

The pilgrimage God has taken us along, as we have
ministered to and taught many thousands of people, has not
been an easy one, but there are now many people across the
world who have taken these keys for themselves and are
applying them effectively in their local church situations.

Deliverance and healing has been such a neglected part of scriptural truth that most believers, and unquestionably most leaders, need further training in order to move forward with confidence in this area. To meet this growing need, the staff of Ellel Ministries (which numbered about 150 people in the middle of 1995) are committed to teaching and training at our own centres and in other places across the world as the Lord leads. We see the importance of presenting a balanced Gospel in which evangelism, healing and deliverance are all primary ingredients.

The whole work of Ellel Ministries is a faith ministry which means that we are unreservedly committed to fulfilling the vision that God has given for the work. We are not a church, but a servant body to the churches for equipping and training in evangelism, healing and deliverance. We have no major endowments to fund the ministry and are dependent on donations and income from training courses to meet all expenses. Course fees are generally fixed at about half their real cost so that price does not become a major obstacle to training for those who cannot readily afford such expenditure.

Right from the beginning the work has been encouraged by a committed group of prayer supporters. Each centre has a regular meeting of the Prayer Support Group where the needs of the work are shared.

It is our prayer that wherever this book is read Christians will catch catch the vision for establishing the healing and deliverance ministry in the lives of their local church and so fulfil the Great Commission to make disciples of the Lord Jesus Christ.

Appendix 1

Qualities of a Christian Counsellor

The opportunity to minister into the lives of others is a privilege that should not be taken lightly. The following list of qualities of a Christian Counsellor is not meant to be a counsel of perfection, but an objective towards which we should aim, so that we can seek to be as effective as possible in the work God has called us to do.

If God waited until we were perfect before he could use us, none of us would be acceptable! Clearly no-one can be a truly Christian counsellor unless they are born again (No.1)! It is important that our hearts are right towards God and that we are willing to allow him to change and develop us so that we choose to become willing servants, whose calling in life is to bring healing to the hurting and broken 'sheep'. These notes were originally compiled for the use of Ellel Ministries Associate Counsellors and ministry teams, but the principles embodied in these notes are applicable to those ministering healing all over the world.

1. **Born again** (John 3:3, Rom. 6:23)

   Unless we are born again, we, like Nicodemus, will not be able to understand spiritual matters such as the truths about God, man, salvation, healing and deliverance. Our efforts will be powerless without a living relationship with the Lord Jesus Christ.

2. **Spirit filled** (Eph. 5:18)

   The Holy Spirit is the comforter and counsellor. It is he who will enable us to counsel with the compassion of the Father and the uncompromising love of Jesus.

3. **Exercising the gifts of the Spirit** (Rom. 12:6, 1 Cor. 12)

Without the gifts of the spirit we will not be able to fully discern spiritual matters. It is vital to know in counselling what God is doing in the life of the person, what their human spirit is doing and what the evil spirits are doing. The other gifts are also vital for an effective healing ministry.

4. **Manifesting the fruits of the Spirit** (Gal. 5:22-25)

It is the love, joy, peace, etc. of God, which should be manifest in the lives of those who truly know him, that will help people to trust their counsellors and receive all that God has in store for them.

5. **Walking in the Jesus model** (John 2:25)

Jesus always listened to what the Father had to say. So must we when ministering to people in need. What God is saying about the person is more important than what we might think!

6. **Willing to receive ministry as well as give it**
(Prov. 3:11, 12:1, 13:1, 15:32; John 21:15-19)

None of us is perfect! Therefore, we must always be willing to let God move in our own lives. Anyone who is not willing to receive ministry for themselves, when appropriate, is not suitable to minister to others.

7. **Well-versed in the scriptures** (1 Tim. 4:6-7, 2 Tim. 3:16)

The Bible is our workshop manual for life. It contains insights that will continually illuminate the counselling situation. If we ignore the reading and study of the Bible, we will not be in a position to use this most precious of weapons in the fight to bring healing and deliverance to the hurting and wounded.

8. **Active members of a local church** (Heb. 10:25, Rom. 12:4)

It is essential that we work from a rightful God-given base of authority and order, and not act as lone rangers in the community. We also need the strength and encouragement that comes from corporate worship, teaching and fellowship. If we cease to meet together we may soon grow cold toward the Lord and/or wander into deceptive beliefs without there being any Godly accountability.

9. **Denominationally neutral in ministry** (Rom. 12:1)

   All denominations have their own particular structures and related beliefs. Within this, it is important that we do not minister a denomination but we minister a relationship with Christ. Do not be judgemental or condemnatory about anyone's church or denomination.

10. **One hundred per cent committed, ready for anything, wholly available to the Lord** (Heb. 12:1-2)

    If we are less than whole-hearted we will be vulnerable to the enemy's attack and more likely to give up when things get tough.

11. **Obedient to the Holy Spirit** (Rom. 12:2, Gal. 5:25)

    Many people are willing to teach truth, but there is a big difference between truth that is known in the head and truth which is applied in our lives. Obedience is one of the major keys to the anointing of the Holy Spirit.

12. **Forgiveness is a way of life** (Matt. 6:14-15)

    As counsellors we will find there are many opportunities to forgive! For example, hurting people say things when under pressure and, if we do not forgive them, we could be blocking the anointing through the attitude of our own heart. We cannot teach forgiveness without a forgiving heart ourselves.

13. **Be a man or woman of prayer** (1 Thess. 5:17)

    One of the temptations that faces counsellors is only to pray for others and never to seek God in prayer themselves. It is vital that our own relationship with the Lord does not get swamped by the burden of helping others.

14. **Know who you are in Christ**
    (Rom. 8:1, 1 John 4:4, Eph. 1:19-20)

    Our security is in Christ. If we are not familiar ourselves with all that Jesus has done for us on the cross, and the consequences of our salvation, then it is possible that the demonic powers will be able to exercise authority over us! It is vital that we are aware of our position in him.

15. Be sacramentally sensitive
(James 5:14-16, 1 Cor. 11:26 32)

Some Christians come from a tradition that has little use for the sacraments. In the scriptures, however, anointing with oil, baptism and communion are all significant. We have found all of these to be important on occasions as part of healing through deliverance. Be sensitive to what God may be asking you to do in this respect.

16. Be anointed for the task (2 Tim. 1:6-7)

The anointing of God is more important than the appointment of man. We should continually seek the Lord for a fresh anointing for each ministry we begin, so that we will be able to be for that person everything that God wants us to be.

17. Know how to lead a person to Christ
(Phil. 4:9, 1 Cor. 2:1-5)

There will be many times when we have to become an evangelist in the healing ministry, for we will discover that some of the people who come for help do not know Jesus. The most important healing of all is healing of the spirit, that it may be born again and restored to life in relationship with God.

18. Look after your body - keep it as fit as possible
(1 Cor. 3:16)

The body is the temple of the Holy Spirit. We need to be available to help others - unless we look after our bodies our lives could be limited in their effectiveness.

19. Be clean, well-presented, with no abnormal body odours! (1 Cor. 14:40)

If our body is offensive to the counsellee we may find them backing off from prayer because our proximity is off-putting.

21. Willing to eat anything and sleep anywhere
(Rom. 14 & 15, Matt. 18:18-32)

When our teams go out on ministry trips it is important that they are grateful for whatever their hosts are able to provide. Ingratitude gives the enemy a stronghold.

20. Willing to fast (Matt. 5:16-18, Acts 13:2-3)

Fasting sharpens the spiritual appetite and make us more sensitive to God. Make sure you use the time you would have been eating for praying.

22. Willing to prefer others above yourself (Rom. 12:10)

It is important that we don't let pride and self-importance get in the way of helping others. Scripture encourages us to humble ourselves!

23. Be sexually well-informed

Many of the people who come for help have problems associated with their sexuality. We must not show shock or surprise when they talk about this area. We need to be well-informed so that we will be able to understand just what their problem is.

24. Be occultically well-informed (2 Cor. 2:11)

There are many Christian books these days which provide up-to-date information about the occult. We need to be familiar with what Satan is doing in this area and understand the importance of dealing with the occult when seeking to bring deliverance.

25. Be well-read on the healing ministry (Prov. 8:1-10)

God is gifting and equipping many different people with experience of the healing ministry. We need to read what others are doing so that we can all be built up by the Godly teaching and experiences of others.

26. Be unshockable (John 4:17-18, 8:1-11)

Whilst the experiences of others may be radically different from anything we have done, we must be careful not to alienate the counsellee by over-reacting to what they have done.

27. Be morally above reproach (1 Tim. 3:1-7)

If we open the door to the enemy through our own sin, then it will affect our ministry. If we are in deception ourselves, then there is both the danger of further deception and of that sin being exposed and used by the enemy to undermine the validity of what you are doing and bring dishonour to God.

28. Willing to speak the truth in love (Eph. 4:15)

It is sometimes necessary to confront a person with truth about themselves, but it must be done in a way which demonstrates love without compromise.

29. Not afraid of physical affirmation (Rom 16:16)

The encouragement of a gentle touch can be a precious part of the healing ministry. We must be careful, though, to discern when a touch might be offensive (eg. to someone who has been sexually abused) and refrain from causing more problems by our enthusiasm.

30. Be prepared not to project your own opinions
(Prov. 3:5-7)

Our opinions in a conversation must always be secondary to the truth of scripture and the needs of the counsellee. We must be careful not to let the counselling interview become a platform for our own points of view!

31. Be prepared not to let your own problems interfere in the ministry (2 Cor. 12:9-10)

Sometimes during a counselling interview things are said which expose hurt and pain in our own lives. Whilst it is right to make a note of these for future prayer, we must be careful not to let the counselling time be reversed by allowing our own problems to become the centre of attention.

32. Be willing to love (and even hug) the unlovable
(Luke 5:13)

Some people do not naturally invite your close attention. But they, perhaps above all others, need to know that you love them in spite of their appearance, situation, or even body odour. Unconditional acceptance is a vital step towards healing for many people.

33. Be flexible!

There will be times when the needs of the counsellee will cut across our own plans and diary. We must be flexible and flow with what God is doing and be willing to change things that might not be as important.

34. **Be a servant of others** (Isaiah 52:13-53:12, Phil. 2:7)
Jesus humbled himself and came as a servant of others. How can we do anything less than follow in his footsteps?

35. **Be willing to take attacks without bitterness or resentment** (1 Peter 3:8-9)
If we allow the criticisms of others to affect our hearts, then they will eventually undermine the fruit of the ministry. When we are taking ground from the enemy, he will usually send some people to make it difficult. It is vital that we do not allow such situations to interfere with our relationship with God or with others. Jesus told us to bless those who curse us (Matt. 5:44).

36. **Be totally confidential**
If we break the confidentiality of the counselling room and speak out things that have been said in confidence we will destroy the trust between counsellor and counsellee and probably alienate the person from all future healing ministry. If we are not able to be confidential we should not be in the healing ministry.

37. **Be non-judgemental** (Matt. 7:1-6)
If a counsellee senses the judgement of our disapproval they are unlikely to be totally honest. If they keep things hidden that need to be brought to the light they are unlikely to get delivered and healed.

38. **Be patient and be a good listener**
If we display impatience, especially with those who are not able to express themselves quickly, people will back off from asking for help. Love must be the source of our patience.

39. **Be polite and courteous at all times**
This may sound obvious, but it is amazing how, when under pressure, Christians can sometimes appear less than polite!

40. **Be willing to give all the glory to God for whatever he chooses to do through you** (Psalm 96:1-8)
God is the healer. Whatever happens in the Christian healing ministry comes from him. So we must not try and take the glory for ourselves. Pride is a dangerous trap for an effective healing ministry.

Appendix 2

Magic, the Occult & the Bible

OLD TESTAMENT

Genesis 41:8, 41:24
This passage shows that the power of God is far superior to that of the Egyptian magicians, as God enables Joseph to interpret the king's dreams.

Exodus 7:10-12
Again God's power is proved greater, as the snake which came from Aaron's staff swallows the magicians' staffs.

Exodus 8:8-19
When the Lord causes a plague of gnats which the magicians cannot imitate, even the magicians recognise the power of God.

Exodus 22:18
Women who practised magic were to be put to death. From this verse it would appear that women were especially involved in magic and sorcery.

Leviticus 19:26
God's law states quite clearly that we should not practise any kind of magic.

Leviticus 19:31, 20:6
The Lord tells the people not to seek out those who consult the spirits of the dead, because they would make the people unclean. He will turn against those who consult mediums and cut them off from his people.

Leviticus 20:27

The law demands that anyone who consults the spirits of the dead should be stoned to death.

Deuteronomy 18:9-14

Just before the Israelites enter the Promised Land, the Lord, through Moses, tells them not to practise those things which the nations there do: sacrificing children in the fire, practising divination, looking for omens, using spells and charms and consulting the dead. God hates it when people do these things.

2 Kings 9:22

In this verse we have the meeting of King Joram of Israel and Jehu (his commander-in-chief). When asked by the king if all was well, Jehu replies that there cannot be peace while all the witchcraft and idolatry that the king's mother Jezebel started was still around. NOTE: See all of 2 Kings chapters 9 and 10.

2 Kings 17:17

In a description of the fall of Israel to the Assyrians in 721 BC we find that part of the reason for the fall was that they still consulted mediums and fortune-tellers, provoking God's anger.

2 Kings 21:2-6

Here we find that Manasseh, king of Judah (687-642 BC) reintroduces many evil, pagan practices. He sacrificed his son as a burnt offering, practised divination and magic and consulted of mediums and fortune-tellers. This disobedience to God's law led to the eventual fall of Jerusalem in 598 BC.

2 Kings 23:24

King Josiah of Judah makes many reforms towards returning to God, including banishing all mediums from Jerusalem and Judah. But it did not abate the Lord's anger or stop the fall of Jerusalem.

1 Chronicles 10:13-14

Saul dies because he was unfaithful to the Lord and consulted a medium for guidance rather than the Lord.

Isaiah 2:6

In his prayer, Isaiah implies that due to the Israelites' following of superstitions from the East and divination from Philistia, God has forsaken them. In Isaiah 3:2-3 he predicts the downfall of the nation due to practices which anger God, and which the leaders of the nation would appear to ignore.

Isaiah 8:19-20

The Israelites are told to refrain from consulting mediums and fortune-tellers, even though it had been a custom through divination to do so. Emphasis is to listen to what the Lord has to say and not the mediums. The people were to consult God, not the dead.

Isaiah 44:25

The pagan oracles were proved false in their predictions about Babylon and this verse emphasises God's power over the predictions of astrologers and fortune-tellers.

Isaiah 47:11-15

In this passage Isaiah foretells the downfall of Babylon, and says that no magic spells, charms, astrologers etc. can save them from disaster.

Isaiah 57:3

Sorcery is put on the same footing as any other sin against God.

Jeremiah 27:9

In this passage the Lord was telling the Israelites to submit to the king of Babylon but prophets, sorcerers, and mediums were falsely prophesying and telling them not to submit.

Ezekiel 13:6-9

The Lord denounces the false prophets of Israel because they claim to come from God but he has not spoken to them. Their visions are false and their predictions are lies. The Lord cuts them off from citizenship of Israel and proclaims that they will never again enter the land of Israel.

Ezekiel 13:17-22

Here false prophetesses are condemned because of their use of magical charms and their attempts to lure people away from the ways of the Lord. They were controlling people by means of these charms.

Daniel 1:20

Daniel and his friends had ten times more wisdom and understanding than all of the magicians and fortune-tellers in the kingdom.

Daniel 2

No fortune-teller, magician, sorcerer, astrologer or wizard could explain the meaning of the king's dream, but Daniel could because God revealed the meaning to him. King Nebuchadnezzar realised that God is the greatest of all gods and the one who reveals mysteries.

Hosea 4:17

The people of Israel had fallen under the influence of pagan worship, here referred to as under a spell of idols.

Micah 5:12

When the Lord rescues Israel from the Assyrians he says that he will destroy their magic charms and fortune-tellers.

Nahum 3:4

In the fall of Nineveh the Lord punishes the people for, amongst other things, the use of charms by which they had enchanted other nations.

Zechariah 10:2

In this verse we are told that the answers given by fortune-tellers are lies and nonsense, and interpreters of dreams only mislead. The use of these things is a sign of a lack of spiritual leadership.

Malachi 3:5

On the Day of Judgement the Lord will testify against those who practise magic.

NEW TESTAMENT

Acts 8:9-24
The story of Simon the magician. Simon, on seeing the gifts of the Holy Spirit, wishes to buy the gift, even though he has been baptised. This shows that evil powers can still have hold of a believer.

Acts 13:6-10
The story of Bar-Jesus (Elymas) on Cyprus. He had magical powers and claimed to be a prophet, but he tried to stop the spreading of the word. Paul, then filled with the Holy Spirit, discerns the evil in him and brings about a temporary blindness on him.

Acts 16:16-18
The slave girl was only able to tell fortunes because of an evil spirit within her.

Acts 19:19
Newly converted Christians who had practised sorcery brought their scrolls and burned them publicly, indicating their complete renunciation of magic.

Galatians 5:20
Those who practise witchcraft will not possess the Kingdom of God.

Revelation 21:8, 22:15
Those who practise magic will be thrown into the lake of fire and sulphur and will not be allowed to enter the city.

Appendix 3

Glossary of Occult Terms

Acupressure/Acupuncture
An ancient Chinese philosophy and medical technique which defines disease as an imbalance in the flow of 'life energy' and redirects this flow by applying pressure or inserting needles on particular points of the body to bring about healing. It is believed that the body has twelve meridians divided into two groups of six lines. One is called Yin and the other Yang. The life force Ch'i is believed to flow along these lines.

Amulet
An object, normally worn or carried, used as a charm to ward off evil spirits and spells. A popular amulet is the proverbial rabbit's foot.

Ankh
A cross with a loop on the top; this ancient Egyptian symbol of life is often associated with fertility. Images of Egyptian gods are sometimes shown bearing an ankh. The symbol is widely used in modern-day occult circles.

Apotropaion
A charm to ward off evil spirits or the evil eye.

Apparitions
Spectres of dead people, ghosts or phantoms.

Astral projection
When part of a person travels outside of their own physical body and operates on a different level of consciousness. Adepts are able to travel considerable distances and report accurately things they have seen in other places, before returning to their body.

Astrology

The belief that celestial bodies influence people; predicting the future by reading the stars - especially the arrangement of the stars, planets and constellations at the time of birth. See signs of the Zodiac.

Augury

The use of signs and omens to foretell the future. Divination by observing the flights of birds, or studying the droppings or entrails of animals and birds.

Automatic writing

Messages written by an individual whilst in a trance-like state. The hand is driven by spiritual forces to write down messages from 'the other side'. A similar phenomenon to automatic writing is automatic drawing, painting and speaking. The drawings and paintings can look remarkably like original works of well-known artists. Mediums believe that the dead are expressing their giftings through the living.

Birth signs

The twelve astrological signs, known as the signs of the Zodiac, representing the divisions of the heavens, which are used for predictions based on birth dates.

Black arts

General name of malicious practices associated with a variety of occult activities.

Black magic

Magic performed for evil purposes, summoning demons and evil spirits and performing ceremonies in order to bring harm to another person.

Black mass

A satanic parody of the Roman Catholic mass, where communion is desecrated, the Lord's prayer is recited backwards, and animals or humans (often unbaptised infants) are sacrificed. Blood from the victim is used as a substitute for the communion wine in the parody of the mass as an offering to the devil.

Blood subscription
A pact made with Satan in blood in which promises are made to serve evil in order to gain power.

Cartomancy
Using playing cards as a means of divination or fortune-telling.

Chain letters
A letter which promises good luck to the recipient if it is copied and sent on to more people. There is a curse of bad luck if the recipient refuses to cooperate.

Channelling
A New Age type of spiritism where channellers open themselves up to the supernatural realms (sometimes in a trance) and become channels for the communication of messages which are often designed to teach, guide or direct the recipient. The source of the information is sometimes referred to as an "ascended master".

Charm
An incantation or object in the occult world which, like a talisman, is believed to contain supernatural powers.

Clairaudience
The extra-sensory ability to hear sounds made in the spirit realm or from a distant time or place.

Clairvoyance
The extra-sensory ability to see images that are beyond the physical realm and not ordinarily visible. Also the alleged ability to see events that took place in the past or are yet to happen.

Colour therapy
A method of treating disorders using colours which are believed to have 'corresponding vibrations' which are claimed to have healing potential.

Conjuration
The act of summoning up a demon from the supernatural realms

Coven
A group of witches or satanists traditionally thirteen in number, although there can be as few as five or as many as fifty. The coven meets together to perform rituals and ceremonies, especially at special festival times (sabbats). The coven is under the leadership of either a high priest or high priestess.

Crystal ball gazing (crystalomancy)
The practice of staring into a ball shaped glass object for the purpose of fortune-telling. The practitioner goes into a trance-like state and foretells future events.

Crystals
Some advocates of the New Age believe that crystals have the power to cleanse, heal and restore the flow of energy in the body as well as bringing self-transformation and enlightenment.

Death magic
Evil magic used to bring death to an intended victim. Most closely associated with voodooists, but also practised by other occult groups.

Deja Vu
The feeling of already having experienced a new situation or place, even though it is physically impossible for the person to have been there before.

Demon worship
The practice of appeasing the demons in order to earn their protection. Once started, failure to continue to worship turns the 'blessings' into 'cursings'.

Disembodied spirits
Believed to be the spirits of dead people that are unable to find rest.

Divination
Collective name for various occult techniques used to gain information about people and situations, or events past or future.

Divining rod
A forked wood or metal rod used to locate underground sources of water. When the rod passes over the water the rod moves.

Dowsing
The process of finding underground water supply using a divining rod.

Dream interpretation
The process of using dreams for the purpose of divination

Dungeons and dragons
An occult fantasy role-playing game where the players closely identify with their characters who engage in murder, witchcraft, torture, rape, demon-summoning, voodoo, cannibalism and various occult powers to advance in the game. The game has been a significant factor in many documented suicides and murders.

Ectoplasm
A cold, slightly luminous, whitish substance which comes from a medium's body which is believed to indicate the presence of a disembodied spirit

Enchanting
Exerting magical influences on a person so as to manipulate them to your own ends.

Erhard seminar training (The Forum)
A religious venture for those wanting to fulfil the new age quest of self-image enhancement

Extra sensory perception (ESP)
The ability to perceive an event or an idea through a means other than the five senses. Practitioners of divination use ESP.

Fetish
An inanimate object believed to be inhabited by a spirit.

Findhorn
A New Age community in the north of Scotland which offers teaching in the principles of New Age Spirituality.

Fire-walking
The ability to walk through fire or on hot coals without being physically harmed in any way.

Fortune-telling
The practice of using various methods of divination to foretell future events.

FHU (Foundation of Human Understanding)
An institution founded by Roy Masters, an early devotee of hypnotism and mind control. The disciple of FHU teaching ultimately seeks answers to life in the exercises and techniques offered by Masters.

Guided imagery
Directed visualisation exercises resulting in a relaxed or trance-like state. Possibly includes astral projection and the meeting in the supernatural realms with spirit guides.

Guru
A spiritual master, guide or teacher.

Hand-writing analysis (Graphology)
A form of divination through which aspects of character, career future, trustworthiness, emotional development, personality type, etc. are believed to be revealed by analysis of the hand-writing.

Heavy metal and rock music
The main message of this music centres around drugs, sex, violence, murder, degradation of women and serious involvement with the occult, witchcraft and satanism.

Hepatoscopy
Divination through examination of the liver.

Hex
To hex someone means to put a spell on them, usually with the objective of causing them misfortune.

Hexagram
Two triangles inverted one on top of the other to form a six-pointed star. In witchcraft the sign is used to harness and control the power of demons.

Homeopathy
The alternative treatment of a disease by the administration of minute doses of drugs which in a healthy person would produce symptoms of the disease. The principle stated by its founder Samuel Hahnemann is, *"like is healed by like"*. The drug solution is often so diluted that it may no longer contain any of the actual remedy. More of a belief system than a genuine medical practice.

Horoscopes
Charts which predict peoples' destinies, based on astrology. Horoscopes are also used to predict favourable times and seasons for important events.

Horse brasses and horse shoes
(Placed over a door or given as a sign of good luck)
Amulets which are used to fend off evil spirits. The iron of a horseshoe is believed to provide protection against witchcraft.

Hypnotism
The practice of putting a person in a trance-like state in order to probe the unconscious or recover memories of the past. Also used by doctors who do not realise the nature of the spiritual powers they are using.

Hydromancy
The practice of divination using observations of water.

Idol
An image of a deity which becomes an object of worship and adoration. A person or thing that is an object of excessive or supreme adulation.

Incantation
A magical formula produced by repeating certain words, phrases or sounds.

Incubus
An evil spirit which sexually violates a woman.

Iridology
The process of diagnosing sickness by using the eye like a crystal ball. Changes in the appearance of certain sectors of the eye are believed to correspond to sickness in various parts of the body.

Jonathan Livingston Seagull
A book by Richard Bach, allegedly channelled by a spirit and based on New Age philosophy.

Kabbalah
Jewish mystical tradition based on a mathematical interpretation of scripture. Various magical and occult practices stem from the Kabbalah.

Levitation
Raising people or objects into the air by using supernatural power alone.

Lucky charms and charm bracelets
A form of amulet worn by people who are largely ignorant of the spiritual nature of the charm.

Magic
Dominating or manipulating people or circumstances through occultic power and evil spirits. Sometimes spelt magick to differentiate from the 'magic' which is the sleight of hand of entertainers.

Mantra
A word given to a transcendental meditation (or yoga) devotee, which they must repeat and meditate on even though they do not know what it means. It serves as a vehicle through which the person gets into contact with the spirit realms.

Martial arts
The various fighting sports such as karate, kung-fu, t'ai chi ch'uan, judo, jujitsu and aikido. The spiritual centre of all these martial arts is in taoism and buddhism. The religious

significance of martial arts is the harmonising of yin and yang and the ability to harness the power of ch'i, enabling enormous physical feats. Many who practise martial arts are not aware of the religious nature of the sports.

Medium
A person who is open to being used as a channel to communicate with the spirit realm.

Mesmerism
An alternative name for hypnotism, named after Anton Mesmer who experimented a great deal with using hypnotic powers.

Metaphysics
A philosophy of principles relating to the supernatural. The scientific study of supernatural things.

Mind control (Silva)
Started by Jose Silva. It has now become a major form of self-help therapy which draws on eastern religious techniques and occult powers. It opens the door to mediumship in the mind and being controlled by spirits.

Mind science
The practice of metaphysical science in order to prescribe therapy for the betterment of the individual. God is believed to be a concept and evil a state of the mind which can be changed.

Mind reading
The practice of exploring what another person is thinking by using occult powers.

Moon-mancy
The practice of divining using the moon as a divining agent.

Mysticism
The belief that spiritual union with the ultimate reality can only be achieved through an empty mind and intuition, because God transcends human knowledge.

Necromancy
Communication with the spirits of the dead or the practice of divination by consulting them. Often used in seances by spiritualists.

Neopagan
A follower of a western religious system which is associated with the worship of nature and the lunar goddess, the occult, ancient Greek or Egyptian religions, ceremonial magic, witchcraft or druidism.

New Age movement
Originated in the early seventies, it is linked with the beginning of the age of Aquarius. An amorphous spiritual movement standing at variance with the Judeo-Christian heritage and, indeed, secular humanism. Beliefs associated with New Agers are generally rooted in eastern religions such as: pantheism (God is all and all is God); reincarnation (with rewards, justice and judgement being enacted on people through the nature of their reincarnated self); universalism (all the diverse religions of the world are simply alternative paths to the same goal - hence the conflict between New Agers and Christians who believe that Jesus is the only way); personal transformation (through mystical experiences and contact with the source of divine energy). New Agers believe in a higher self which they refer to as the Christ so that Christ is within all people and all people are potential Christs. The ideas of New Agers are mostly ancient occultic beliefs updated for modern-day consumption.

Numerology
Divination based on the use of numbers. Specific values and meanings are assigned to numbers, and letters are each given a numerical value. The numerical values of peoples names and their birthdates are used to make predictions.

Occult
Secret, mysterious beliefs and practices involving supernatural powers which oppose the Kingdom of God. The occult is generally divided into the three broad categories of spiritism, fortune-telling and magic.

Omens
Uncontrollable or unusual events which are then interpreted as a means of divination.

Ouija board
A board used for communication with the spirit world. Communication is via a pointer which moves round pointing to letters, numbers or 'yes' and 'no'.

Palmistry
Divination by examining the lines on the palms of the hands in order to determine the future.

Parakinesis (PK)
The control of objects by the power of the mind and will.

Parapsychology
The pseudo-scientific study of phenomena of the human psyche which are not interpretable according to normal scientific methods: eg. telepathy, clairvoyance, ESP etc.

Pendulum
A small object on a string which is used for dowsing, diagnosis (especially of the sex of an unborn child) and fortune-telling. Involuntary movements of the pendulum are believed to have specific significance.

Pentagram
A five pointed star which can be arranged with three points upwards or three points downwards. If up, it generally symbolises human spirituality and is a witchcraft symbol. If down, it indicates darkness and is associated with black magic and satanism. In witchcraft four of the points represent the four elements of earth, air, fire and water and the fifth represents the spirit that controls the elements.

Phrenology
Divination by examining the shape of the skull.

Physiognomy
Observing the features of a person's face in order to determine their character.

Planchette
A board on which lines, letters or sentences are spelt out without direction from the person resting their fingers on the board.

Precognition
Foreknowledge of events.

Psychic birth
The occult experience of rebirthing out of which people awaken to the realisation that 'all is one'.

Psychic healing
The use of occult power to bring healing.

Psychic sight
The ability to see things even when the eyes are closed or, in some instances when the person is blind.

Psychography
Spirit writing through the hand of a medium.

Psychometry
Receiving psychic knowledge about a person or events in their life from handling an object which belongs to them.

Punk rock
Music which carries with it a message of rebellion against established society - especially against law, religion and tradition.

Pyramidology
The use of a pyramid whose shape is believed by some New Agers to balance energy and bring spiritual enlightenment.

Reflexology
An ancient Chinese and Egyptian practice which involves massaging the feet to restore the 'energy flow' in corresponding zones of the body.

Reincarnation
The belief that a man's soul never dies but passes from one body to another in a cycle which does not end until the person reaches perfection and no longer needs physical existence.

Rhabdomancy (see dowsing)

Rhapsodomancy
Looking for omens in random passages read from a book, often poetry.

Satanism
The worship of Satan and the practice of rituals carried out in obedience to Satan.

Seances
Meetings where people come together to contact the spirits of the dead through a medium.

Silva mind control (See mind control)

Sorcery
The power to change events and to influence people or situations for harm or good through the control of spirits by the use of black magic.

Soul travel
When the soul moves outside of the body and is able to look down on the body from above and move short distances away. Less powerful, though similar in nature, to astral projection.

Spell
An incantation used to harness magical power.

Spiritism (spiritualism)
The conjuring up of demons and the communication with the spirit realms in the belief that the dead can communicate with the living - usually through a medium.

Spirit guide
A spirit known to a medium or channeller who regularly provides information from 'the other side'.

Stichomancy
A form of rhapsodomancy.

Stigmata
Marks resembling the wounds of the crucified Christ which supernaturally appear on the body.

Superstitions
Irrational beliefs or practices resulting from fear of something unknown, mysterious or imaginary.

Table tipping
A process of divination through the supernatural movement of a table by spirits.

Talisman
An engraved object believed to harness magical powers to protect the owner or bring prosperity.

Tarot
The occult practice of using a set of 22 cards for fortune-telling. Each card has a pictorial meaning, one of which is in the form of a skeleton representing death.

Tea-leaf reading
Attempting to find meaning through patterns left in the bottom of a tea-cup by the residue of tea-leaves.

Telekinesis (TK)
The ability to move or control objects using spiritual powers only.

Third-eye
The eye of spiritual vision, said to be located on the forehead between the two physical eyes.

Transcendental Meditation (TM)
A religious system which stems from Hinduism whereby a mantra (a secret sound) is repeated during meditation and the mind is said to be in the deepest level of consciousness. The awakened kundalini power in transcendental meditation is the same as that in yoga.

Trance
A mental state where the conscious mind rests, leaving the person open to control by a spirit.

Translocation
The movement of a person from one place to another by supernatural means.

Voodoo
Voodoo is a form of religious witchcraft involving rituals, sacrifices, divination and rhythmic dancing. A number of deities are worshipped, and magick is used to help the sick or bring harm and death to a victim through the use of potions, incantations, dolls and various rituals.

White magic
Magic that is said to have helpful and positive purposes. However, the spiritual powers used are evil spirits and the Bible makes no distinction between black or white occult practices - all are wrong.

Witchcraft
The harnessing of supernatural powers for the malevolent purpose of practising black magic. Witches generally believe in the great mother goddess and her consort Pan in contrast to satanists who believe in and worship Satan.

Yoga
One of the oldest words in the Hindu religion. Yoga is the path followed so as to realise god within you. A spiritual discipline aimed at controlling the physical, spiritual and psychic. In the Indian religious tradition, the goal is loss of individual identity and union with the universal one; the aim is to awaken the kundalini power of the serpent lying dormant at the base of the spine.

Zodiac
The twelvefold division of the sky into signs. The word zodiac simply means the 'circle of animals'. Astrologers believe that the sign a person is born under largely determines the make-up or character of that person.

Appendix 4

Alternative Medical Practices

Alternative medical practices are not necessarily spiritually dangerous. Whether they are safe or not, usually depends on the beliefs of the practitioner.

The following, however, are some of the alternative medical practices which are known to have spiritual origins or guiding principles of a New Age, Occultic, or otherwise non-Christian nature:

Acupuncture

Aromatherapy

Bach Flower Remedies

Colour Therapy

Crystal Therapy

Faith Healers

Guided Imagery

Homoeopathy

Hypnotherapy

Iridology

Kinesiology

Magnetic Healing

New Age Medicine

Past Lives Therapy

Psychic Healers

Psychic Surgery

Pyramid Healing

Radiesthesia

Rebirthing

Reflexology

Spiritualist Healing

Zone Therapy

Appendix 5

Glossary of Other Religions

Aethurius Society, The
Founded by George King, a student of yoga, who claimed to have been visited by 'Master Jesus' from the planet Venus. This Jesus gave him a new Aquarian Age Bible. The society is now a cult which places much significance on its belief in Unidentified Flying Objects (UFOs) and extraterrestrial visits to earth. New Age and Eastern religious practices dominate the ceremonies.

Animism
The belief that inanimate things such as plants, stones, trees, etc. have a soul or spirit of their own. Animism is an important part of the religious beliefs of primitive peoples.

Anthroposophical Society, The
Founded by Rudolf Steiner who fell out with the Theosophical Society because of their over-emphasis on eastern religious ideas and practices. He called his new discipline of anthroposophy a 'spiritual science'. The theology behind his thinking was a mixture of Spiritism, Christianity and Mysticism. Reincarnation became a central belief. Steiner had considerable influence on education and established many special schools in which his philosophy could be taught as part of the educational process.

Armstrongism (Worldwide Church of God)
Founded by Herbert W Armstrong, this sect has had worldwide influence via its *Plain Truth* magazine, (about 8 million copies were given away freely each month), and his radio broadcasts (in the USA and via Radio Luxembourg) and television broadcasts (largely in the USA).

Armstrong denied the Trinity and believed that he alone was God's true prophet and that all that had preceded him was corrupt and false. He believed that the ultimate objective of man was to progress towards being god. Much of his deceptive beliefs, however, were dressed up in traditional Judeo-Christian beliefs and to the undiscerning it would not have been easy to see through his persuasive writing and speaking.

He attracted many followers and much money into his organisation. Following the death of Armstrong the church is rethinking much of its theology and the doctrine that humans will one day become God has been made redundant!

Baha'i

The Baha'i faith is a 19th century offshoot of Islam. It teaches that all religions contain a degree of truth and that they should all be united into a world religion of universal principles. This universalism is at odds both with both Christianity and Baha'i's Islamic parent. Baha'i teachers also proclaim that the world's nine great religious teachers were all manifestations of God (Moses, Buddha, Zoraster, Confucius, Jesus Christ, Muhammad, Hare Krishna, Bab and Baha' U'llah). These nine are represented in the nine sided Baha'i temple in Wilmette, Illinois.

Buddhism

Founded by Gautama Buddha in about 500 BC. After intense meditation he received the enlightenment that has become known as Buddhism. In 245 BC five hundred Buddhist monks gathered together to write down the collected teachings of three centuries of Buddhist tradition. But in subsequent centuries the unity of Buddhism gradually broke down so that there are a multiplicity of sects forming what the world recognises as Buddhism today.

Buddhists do not recognise a supreme God, and as such their beliefs are more atheistic than theistic. For them God is more a process of being made perfect. Reincarnation is at the heart of Buddhist teaching with salvation being described as the ultimate escape from the cycle of rebirth.

For the Buddhist, salvation is earned by obediently following the eight-fold path of: Right belief, right feelings, right speech, right conduct, right livelihood, right effort, right memory and right meditation. Buddhists believe that this path will ultimately lead to the bliss of Nirvana. The Buddhist way of life includes self-denial and a moral code not dissimilar to some of the teachings of Christianity (such as no lying, fornication, theft, murder etc.). Buddhism is the world's fourth largest religion (behind Christianity, Islam and Hinduism).

Children of God

The Children of God was formed in 1968 by Moses David, formerly David Berg. The church has undergone many changes since then, including the renaming of the church as 'The Family of Love'. However, the love that is advocated is contrary to that which is advocated by Jesus. Whilst David Berg had some mainstream Christian roots, he quickly left these behind with the advocation of free love amongst the members and the use of sexual favours as a means of evangelising.

Christadelphianism

John Thomas founded his teaching through a magazine 'The Apostolic Advocate' in 1834, but the name Christadelphian did not emerge until 1869.

Thomas wrote the Christadelphian classic *Elpis Israel* (an exposition of the Kingdom of God) then *Eureka* (a commentary on the book of Revelation), recognising the supreme authority of the Bible but only as interpreted by him. God exists in physical form and has created men whom he has raised to divinity (pluralism). Jesus is such a man who earned his right to divinity; whilst the Holy Spirit is an unseen power by which God upholds the whole of his creation. All the faithful will be immortalised on earth and the wicked will be annihilated; therefore, there is no heaven or hell for mankind.

Christian Science

Founded by Mary Baker (Eddy) in the late 19th century. It is a mind science of false healing with a doctrine which is declared to be Bible-based, but the teachings of Mary Baker are regarded as revelation, with greater authority than the Bible. God is justified as triune by virtue of being the god of life, truth and love. Jesus is believed to have been human and is now dead, whilst the Christ and the Holy Spirit only exist in the order of 'Divine Science'. Man is deemed as incapable of sinning;

sickness, sin and death are considered unreality; and the one way to heaven is by goodness as taught in the 'Divine Science'.

Church of Bible Understanding

Used to be called the Forever Family and was founded by Stewart Traill. It is an anti-trinitarian movement, rejecting both the word 'trinity' and the concept as unbiblical. Jesus is the Saviour but he is not God. Sin equals 'worldliness' and 'hypocrisy' and Traill equates this with the older generation, unlike the Bible in which both young and old are told to repent of sin because *"all have sinned"*. The church is organised into groups: The guardians are the leaders, the sheep are advanced believers, whilst the lambs are new converts. They meet together in units known as 'communal houses'.

Church of the Living Word (The Walk)

Was founded in 1954 by John Robert Stevens. He was ordained by Full Gospel Temple and his ordination was recognised by the Foursquare Church and the Assemblies of God. However, all of them later revoked such recognition due to 'aberrant' doctrines. Basic to Stevens' understanding is a concept called transference where the person lays aside their personal identity and allows themselves to become Christ. The goal for the church, as well as each individual, to become a god. *"God becoming man means nothing unless we become God, unless we become lost in him."* It is believed that the Holy Spirit enables this to happen. Stevens declares that the Bible is an authoritative but outdated document and that the church needs new and supplementary revelation which is to be channelled through himself as God's apostle.

Confucianism

A humanistic religion founded by the Chinese philosopher, Confucius, in the 5th century BC. His teachings are contained in four books written by his disciples: *The Analects, The Great Learning, The Doctrine of the Mean* and *The Book of Mencius.*

The doctrine of Confucius contains instructions on relationships and the basic nature of man in a six-fold teaching of:

Jen	Rule of reciprocation of goodness
Chun-tzu	Humility, sincerity, magnanimity and graciousness

Te	Inspiration and power needed in virtuous rule
Li	Reverence, courtesy and standard of conduct
Wen	Benevolent acts of peace through music and poetry
Cheng-ming	The correction of roles (eg. Let a father be a father, etc.)

Divine Light Mission

The Divine Light Mission was founded in 1971 by Guru Maharaj Ji who believes he is the incarnation of the divine. What is taught is a derivative of Hinduism and devotees receive knowledge directly from Maharaj Ji. It is claimed that the Holy Spirit is knowledge that flows from Maharaj Ji. He instructs his people to discover the 'divine self'. Humanity is inherently divine and the key to divinity is in being given the proper knowledge to discover the 'goodness within'. Salvation therefore is knowledge, given by the Guru, that leads to enlightenment.

Freemasonry

Freemasonry is a worldwide organisation which promotes the glorification of man by his own achievements, both within and outside masonry, and is supported by a tightly controlled brotherhood of Masons to the total exclusion of a believing faith and trust in the Lord Jesus Christ.

It is a secret society to which members are bound by powerful oaths and penalties sworn on pain of tortuous death at the hands of brother Masons to protect its secrets.

It is essentially religious being a mixture of Hinduism, Kabbalism and Rosicrucianism, with the pagan religions of Egyptian and Greek mythology.

The teachings of Freemasonry bear no relation to, nor are they compatible with, biblical Christianity. Prayers raised in the name of Jesus Christ are forbidden.

Freemasonry purports to be a quest for divine light, but the various ceremonies entered into and oaths taken only serve to cause spiritual blindness and darkness.

There are 3 stages (or degrees) of membership into *Blue Lodge*. A further 10 degrees in the *York Rite* or a further 30 degrees in the *Ancient and Accepted Scottish Rite* lead to the achievement of the title of 'Sovereign Grand Inspector General 33rd degree'.

Hinduism

Hinduism is a modern term to describe the ancient religion of India dating from pre-2000 BC. It has many forms, no formal creed and no one founder. Hindu scriptures are voluminous but the best known are the *Upanishads*, the *Vedas*, the *Puranas* and the *Bhagavad Gita* (song of the Lord). There is only one God, Brahman, a triune god of: Brahma - creator, Vishnu - preserver, and Shiva (Siva) - destroyer. There is a level of nationally recognised gods, such as Krishna, Indra, Agni and Durga; a further level of regional gods sometimes referred to as devatas, and then a lower level of local or village gods, being a vast army of bhuts (spirits).

Hinduism has been termed as more of a philosophy than a creed and is concerned with mystical insights and mythological exploits of the gods.

As with Buddhism, reincarnation is a central belief. The universe is in a series of cycles of growth and decay (Kalpa) and the law of Karma determines one's future life here on earth until Nirvana is reached (the escape from the cycle of death and rebirth). Relationships are vertical with a rigid caste system of priests, noblemen, peasants and servants.

International Church of Ageless Wisdom, The

The church was founded by Beth Hand. In forming the movement she taught and preached a mixture of Hinduism, Buddhism, Spiritualism, Astrology and Yoga techniques, as well as the mystical teachings of Kabbalah. She had previously discarded her Episcopal church roots. The church believes God cannot be a person and therefore Jesus cannot be God incarnate. God is the creator and source of all that is, and as such is the father of all humanity. As a result, all people are brothers and sisters and therefore sons and daughters of God.

International Community of Christ, The (Jamilians)

Founded by Eugene Savoy in 1972 who followed the alleged secret (or hidden) teachings of Jesus as well as those of the ancient sun worshippers. Members of the community are taught that they can experience the redeeming power of the sun, that the power in Jesus' miracles came from the sun, and that Jesus will return as a new and radiant sun *"unlike any sun that ever shone"*. Jesus is essentially one who shows the way to the eternal sun. Savoy also asserts that his son Jamil was a reincarnate Christ.

ISKCON (Hare Krishna)

The International Society for Krishna Consciousness (Hare Krishna) was founded in America in 1965 by the guru Swami Prabhupada, who remained its leader until his death in 1977. Hare Krishna was founded by Chaitanya Mahaprobha in the early 16th century as the Sankirtana movement developed from the Hinduistic worship of Krishna (the reincarnated son of the god Vishnu). Krishnans believe in one god, Krishna, and that Jesus is Krishna's son. Salvation must be earned by a series of good works in a cycle of reincarnation until oneness with Krishna is achieved. Part of this involves chanting a sixteen-word mantra (called Kirtanya) many times a day.

Islam

This religion was founded by Mohammed (Muhammad) among his family in Mecca, Arabia, but did not emerge as a religious power until his emigration to Medina in 622 AD. This year marked the start of the Islamic calendar, known as AH (the year of Hejira).

Islam means submission to the will of Allah and its teachings are principally contained in the Sacred Koran (Qur'an). Allah is the all powerful God, whilst Jesus is among the six major prophets named in the Koran with Muhammed being the last and greatest.

The six articles of faith to which Muslims subscribe are: belief in God, his angels, his books, his prophets, the day of judgement and God's sovereign decrees.

The five pillars of Islam are: confession of the faith, prayer, fasting, giving of alms and pilgrimage to Mecca. All of these are obligatory duties, with the pilgrimage is required only once in one's lifetime.

Jehovah's Witnesses
(Watchtower Bible and Tract Society)

Jehovah's Witnesses (JWs) deny the divinity of Jesus, his eternal existence and his physical resurrection. They believe that the archangel Michael was Jesus Christ in his pre-human state. The Holy Spirit is not recognised as a person but rather as the invisible force of God.

Jehovah's Witnesses believe only 144,000 will go to heaven and that an unnumbered crowd of faithful people will have everlasting life on earth, having proved their faithfulness to Jehovah. Unbelievers and Satan will be annihilated in the end. The JWs believe that they are the one true church on earth, and that all denominational churches will be the enemy of God in the battle of Armageddon.

Materialism

Whilst materialism is not a religion as such, much of the world worships at the altar of materialistic success and makes an idol of wealth. The demonic power behind materialism holds vast numbers of people into a godless lifestyle.

Mormonism
(The Church of Jesus Christ of Latter-Day Saints)

Joseph Smith founded Mormonism in 1830 after claiming that a visitation from the angel Moroni led him to find two buried golden plates on which a book was written in a foreign language. This 'book', which was translated and entitled the *Book of Mormon,* is considered by the Mormon Church to be the word of God. In 1842 Joseph Smith became a Mason and adopted many of the Masonic rituals into the Mormon temple rites.

Brigham Young, second president of the Mormon Church, frequently taught the doctrine of blood atonement, whereby a *"man might be killed to save his soul"* if he committed certain sins such as murder, lying, marrying a black person, apostasy, etc. Young, who had 20 wives, instituted the practice of polygamy in the Mormon Church.

Some of the Mormon beliefs which differ from Christianity include: baptism by proxy for the dead, the assertion that the New Jerusalem will be built on the American continent, and the necessity of Mormons marrying in a Mormon temple in order to achieve godhood in eternity.

Mormons claim to be the restoration of the only true church established by Jesus Christ.

Oneness Pentecostalism

Rejects the traditional Christian doctrine of the Trinity and therefore baptises people once in the name of Jesus Christ. The movement grew out of the Assemblies of God and has had a number of names: the 'New Issue', 'Jesus Only' movement, 'Jesus Name', 'Apostolic', or 'Oneness Pentecostalism'.

Rajneeshism

Bhagwan Shree Rajneesh became a guru in 1966, hailing the benefits of open sex and advocating the dismantling of the family unit. His beliefs mainly stem from Hinduism, asserting that all reality is one. The aim of Rajneeshism is to attain enlightenment through reincarnation, love, sex and meditation. Rajneesh died in 1990, having attracted over 200,000 followers. Many of his followers have joined the New Age movement.

Rastafarianism

Leonard Howell is credited with the 6 principles that are behind Rastafarian thinking.

He stated that:

1. Black men are reincarnations of ancient Israelites
2. Haile Selassie is the living God and the Emperor of the World
3. Ethiopia is heaven, the Jamaican situation is hopeless hell
4. Blacks are superior to whites
5. Blacks will avenge themselves against the whites
6. Blacks will return to Ethiopia.

Father Joseph Owens said, *"The keystone of all Rastafarian theology is the divine supremacy of Haile Selassie, Emperor of Ethiopia."* It claims Selassie is Jesus reincarnate; he is the returned Messiah. Rastafarianism is a rejection of Christianity as the white man's religion.

Reorganised Church of Jesus Christ of Latter-Day Saints

Arose out of a power struggle for leadership of the Mormon Church after Joseph Smith and his brother were murdered. Brigham Young took the larger group to Utah, whilst those who remained under Joseph Smith Jnr. settled in Missouri. Neither church recognises the other.

In contrast to the Mormons, the Reorganised Church does not practice baptism for the dead nor do they believe in polygamy. Sealed marriages are not conducted nor are the secret rites prevalent in the Utah church. Joseph Smith's Inspired version of the Bible is used by the Reorganised Church whilst the Utah Church use the King James Version. In all other aspects they are the same.

Rosicrucianism

Founded by C Rosenkreutz in the early 15th century under the title 'Fraternity of the Rose Cross'. It is a mixture of Hinduism, Judaism, Occult, Alchemy and Hermetism (the relationship between the heavenly and earthly spheres). Basic to the theology of Rosicrucianism is the idea that all knowledge of mankind is made available to those that seek to know and this discovery of the truth comes through suffering, contemplation and various ascents of reincarnation. The *Fama* is the definitive source of Rosicrucian philosophy but its author is not known with certainty.

The triune godhead is comprised of the seven spirits before the throne. *"The Father is the highest initiate among the humanity of Saturn ... the Son is the highest initiate of the Sun ... the Holy Spirit (Jehovah) is the highest initiate of the Moon."*

The 20th century has witnessed the founding of numerous associated orders of which AMORC is probably the best known (Ancient Mystical Order Rose Cross).

Scientology

Founded by L Ron Hubbard in 1955, the Church of Scientology depended heavily on Hubbard's creative imagination. He combined Freudian psychoanalysis with Eastern thought and ideas from his science fiction writings, and produced a religion that has gained a wide appeal with those seeking improved mental health. Scientology conflicts with Christian truth in many different ways. Scientologists believe that there are many gods. According to scientology there is no such thing as sin or evil, and hell is a myth. Scientology embraces the reincarnational beliefs of Hinduism.

Sikhism

Founded by Guru Nanak in the 15th century AD in the Punjab province of India. The teaching of Sikhism is that *"there is no Hindu and no Muslim"*, resulting in a religious combination of both Hindu and Moslem theology.

The sacred scriptures of *Nanak,* the *Granth Sahib* or *'Lord's Book',* having been written by many authors in six different languages and several dialects so that the average Sikh knows very little of its content. The *Granth Sahib* teaches the Hindu doctrines of Karma and reincarnation and that there is one god, Sat Nam. The most obvious sign of a male Sikh is his turban.

Spiritualism

The Spiritualist Church was founded in 1908, although mediums have operated in the spirit realm since Old Testament times. Many people are deceived into attending services by the addition of the word 'Christian' to the title of the Church - especially those who are distressed after the death of a loved one. Many New Age practices such as chanelling are simply spiritualism dressed up in a more acceptable guise for modern day consumption. The whole purpose of spiritualism is to contact the dead 'on the other side'. In practice, people are deceived by evil spirits.

Sufism

The Sufi Order is a branch of Islam which separated in the late 7th century AD, seemingly as a reaction against the formalism and legalism of the early teachings of Islam from the Koran.

Sufi means mystic and Sufists in their quest for a deeper spiritual knowledge of Allah sought a spiritual union with the Divine through meditation and even twirl dancing *(Whirling Dervishes)* rather than by the strict observance of the five pillars or duties of Islam. The sacred book of Sufism is the *Masnavi,* and although some of the teachings are at variance with the Koran, the book still has considerable religious importance throughout Islam.

Sufism teaches repentance of sins, the attaining of religious knowledge, the love that exists between God and man, and finally, the union with Allah which is achieved by annihilation *(Fana)* in him. This latter concept of *Fana* is one of the strongest differences between Sufism and Orthodox Islam (which regards the relationship of Allah with man as one of separation between subject and object).

Taoism

Founded by an enigmatic character called Lao-tzu in the early 6th century BC. He was credited with writing the book entitled *Tao-Te-Ching (The Way of Power)* which was popularised in the in the writings of Chuang-tzu. The teachings of the religion embrace stillness, inaction, placidity, quietude, passivity and communing with nature. Herbal medicines have been a part of Taoism since the 2nd century BC.

The central concept of the *Tao (way or path)* includes the further concept of Yang and Yin, the opposites of male/female, positive/negative, good/evil, light/darkness, life/death, etc. and the invisible life energy force Ch'i.

Theosophy

A society founded by Madame Helena Blavatsky and Henry Olcott in New York in the year 1875. The Society was formed to *"establish a nucleus of the universal brotherhood of humanity; to promote the study of comparative religions and philosophy as well as making a systematic investigation of the mystic potencies of man and nature"*.

The doctrines of Theosophy state that: God is an impersonal divine source; that Jesus was divine in the same way that are divine because we are extensions of God; that God is latent in all of us; and we are saved as we make contact with the deep and hidden knowledge within ourselves. The Society also believes that the latent becomes actual through reincarnation.

Transcendental Meditation (TM)

TM stems from Hinduism. It is pantheistic, maintaining that God is one with the universe and is revealed as Brahman, Vishnu, and Siva. Maharishi Mahesh Yogi founded TM and tailored it to appeal to Americans by focusing on immediate results. The message of peace and love brought popularity in the 1960s, but followers began to fall away in the 1970s. This caused Maharishi to change the name to the *Science of Creative Intelligence (SCI)* and exchange the religious vocabulary with psychology terms, a change which brought many thousands of new followers.

Unification Church (Moonies)

Founded by Yong Myung Moon (later changed to Sun Myung Moon) in 1954 in South Korea. He claimed to have received a vision of Jesus Christ and been told that he was to complete the task that Jesus had left 'undone'. In 1957 he published a book *Divine Principle* which became the chief text for the Unification Church.

The Moonies believe: God the creator exists in dual Yang/Yin form; Jesus Christ's mission was cut short by crucifixion but that he will be born again; the Holy Spirit is a female spirit working on earth; and that the original sin of Adam brought spiritual death to the human race, but as it is God's will that all are restored to him, all go to paradise until the gate of the Kingdom of Heaven is opened.

Unitarian – Universalist Association

A Unitarian believes in one God but holds that Orthodox Christianity has forsaken the real, human Jesus of the Gospel. The Universalist Church seeks to promote harmony between all religious faiths. The Unitarian-Universalist Association, formed in 1961, seeks the development of character and the fostering of the human spirit. Their goal is world community with peace, liberty and justice for all. Reason is the principal authority, rather than the Bible or creeds. They reject the doctrine of the Trinity, the Virgin Birth, and the belief that Jesus is the Messiah and God Incarnate.

Way International, The

Founded by Victor Wierwille after resigning from his ordained ministry in Ohio with the Evangelical and Reformed Church. As with many other religious leaders, Wierwille claims that 'The Way' is the one true church of God and that he alone had been gifted to bring God's truth to the world.

Their doctrine states that God is one and he alone is the creator; Jesus was the son of God but not God the son, he only came into existence when conceived in Mary's womb; and the Holy Spirit is an impersonal presence or power that God gives to believers.

The original success of *The Way* was due to a powerful and fervent evangelistic programme including the study course *Power for Abundant Living* and followed by teaching books of which the best known are *The New Dynamic Church, Jesus Christ is Not God, The Word's Way, The Bible Tells Me So* and *Are the Dead Alive Now?*.

Zen Buddhism

Is a development of Buddhism but its exact origin is obscure. Legend attributes its origin to a wandering Buddhist master, Bodhidharma. It contains Buddha's emphasis on meditation to achieve emptiness and the final goal of enlightenment but it has no sacred scriptures or literature. Its teachings are transmitted from mind to mind, although Zen meditation includes the chanting of sutras, texts that summarise the various discourses of Buddha.

Zoroastrianism

Is an ancient religion founded around 660 BC by Zoroaster. The sacred text is the *Avesta*. The religion contains the dualistic belief that *Ahura Mazdah* is supreme over all other gods and that a cosmic war is being raged between *Ahura Mazdah* and the evil spirit, *Angra Mainyu*. All humanity is involved and has a choice to make between good and evil, with subsequent reward or punishment.

Bibliography

Anderson, Neil T. *Walking in the Light: Discerning God's Guidance in the New Age*. Monarch Publications, England, 1993

Baer, Randall N. *Inside the New Age Nightmare*. Huntington House, Lafayette, USA, 1989

Bubeck, Mark I. *The Adversary: The Christian Versus Demon Activity*. Moody Press, Chicago USA, 1975

Bubeck, Mark I. *Overcoming the Adversary*. Moody Press, Chicago USA, 1984

Chandler, Russell. *Understanding the New Age*. Word Publishing Ltd, England, 1989

Day, Joff. *Settled Accounts: Learning How to Forgive and Release*. Sovereign World, England, 1994

Dere, Dr Jack. *Surprised by the Power of the Spirit*. Kingsway, England, 1995

Ellis, Roger & Andrea Clarke. *The New Age and You*. Kingsway, England, 1992

Ellis, Roger. *The Occult and You*. Kingsway, England, 1994

Finney, Charles. *Principles of Revival*. Bethany House Publishers, Minneapolis, USA, 1987

Gibson, Noel and Phyl. *Deliver Our Children from the Evil One*. Sovereign World, England, 1992

Gibson, Noel and Phyl. *Evicting Demonic Intruders*. New Wine Press, England, 1993

Gibson, Noel and Phyl. *Excuse Me...Your Rejection Is Showing*. Sovereign World, England, 1992

Gordon, Bob. *The Disciple's Handbook for the Spirit-Filled Life*. Sovereign World, England, 1993

Green, Michael. *I Believe in Satan's Downfall*. Hodder & Stoughton, England, 1975

Hammond, Frank. *Overcoming Rejection*. Sovereign World, England, 1991

Hammond, Frank and Ida Mae. *Pigs in the Parlour: A Practical Guide to Deliverance.* New Wine Press, England, 1992

Hammond, Frank. *Soul Ties.* The Children's Bread Ministry, Texas, USA, 1988

Hancock, Maxine & Karen Burton Mains. *Child Sexual Abuse.* Highland Books, England, 1987

Hepden, Steve. *Explaining Rejection.* Sovereign World, England, 1992.

Hobson, Peter. *Christian Deliverance Volumes 1,2 and 3.* Full Salvation Fellowship, Sydney, Australia, 1985-1988

Huggett, Joyce. *Listening to Others.* Hodder & Stoughton, England, 1992

Hurding, Roger. *Bible and Counselling.* Hodder & Stoughton, England, 1992

Hurding, Roger. *Roots and Shoots.* Hodder & Stoughton, England, 1986

Johnson, David & Van Vonderen, Jeff. *The Subtle Power of Spiritual Abuse.* Bethany House Publishers, Minneapolis, USA, 1991

Kjos, Berit. *Your Child and the New Age.* Victor Books, Wheaton, USA, 1990

Koch, Kurt. *Between Christ and Satan.* Kregel, Grand Rapids, USA, 1962

Koch, Kurt. *Demonology, Past and Present.* Kregel, Grand Rapids, USA, 1969

Koch, Kurt. *Occult Bondage and Deliverance.* Kregel, Grand Rapids, USA, 1970

Kraft, Charles H. *Defeating Dark Angels.* Sovereign World, England, 1993

Lea, Larry. *The Weapons of Your Warfare.* Word (UK), England, 1990

Lewis, C.S. *The Screwtape Letters.* Harper Collins, England, 1977

Livesey, Roy. *Understanding Alternative Medicine.* New Wine Press, England, 1988

Logan, Kevin. *Paganism and the Occult.* Kingsway, England, 1994

Logan, Kevin. *Satanism and the Occult*. Kingsway, England, 1994

Marrs, Texe. *Dark Secrets of the New Age*. Crossway Books, Westchester, USA, 1988

Martin, Walter. *The Kingdom of the Cults*. Nova Distribution, Eastbourne, England

Martin, Walter. *The New Age Cult*. Bethany House, Minneapolis, USA, 1989

Mather, George A & Larry A Nichols, *Dictionary of Cults, Sects, Religions & the Occult*. Zondervan Publishing House, Grand Rapids, USA, 1993

Marshall, Tom. *Healing from the Inside Out*. Sovereign World, England, 1988

Marshall, Tom. *Free Indeed!* Sovereign World, England, 1983

Marshall, Tom. *Right Relationships*. Sovereign World, England, 1992

McClung, Floyd. *The Father Heart of God*. Kingsway, England, 1994

McClung, Floyd. *Spirits of the City*. Kingsway, England, 1990

McCormick, W.J. McK. *Christ, The Christian & Freemasonry*. Great Joy Publications, Belfast, 1987.

Miller, Roger. *Curses, Unforgiveness, Evil Spirits, Deliverance*. Trumpet of Gideon Ministries, Germantown, USA, 1994.

Moody, D.L. *Power from on High*. Sovereign World, England 1992

Nee, Watchman. *Release of the Spirit*. New Wine Press, England, 1965

Nee, Watchman. *The Spiritual Man*. Christian Fellowship Publishers Inc, Richmond, USA, 1977

Nee, Watchman. *The Latent Power of the Soul*. Christian Fellowship Publishers Inc, Richmond, USA, 1972

Parker, Russ. *The Occult: Deliverance from Evil*. IVP, England, 1992

Penn-Lewis, Jessie and Evan Roberts. *War on the Saints*. CLC, England, 1973 (Reprint)

Peretti, Frank. *This Present Darkness (Novel)*. Crossway Books, Illinois, USA, 1989 (UK edition: Kingsway, 1994)

Peretti, Frank. *Piercing the Darkness (Novel).* Crossway Books, Illinois, USA, 1989 (UK edition: Kingsway, 1994)

Pfeifer, Samuel. *Healing at Any Price?* Word Publishing, England, 1988

Powell, Graham and Shirley. *Christian Set Yourself Free.* Sovereign World, England, 1994

Powell, Graham. *Fear Free.* Sovereign World, England, 1987

Prince, Derek. *Blessing or Curse: You Can Choose.* Word (UK), England, 1990

Pulling, Pat. *The Devil's Web.* Huntington House Inc, Lafayette, USA 1989

Reisser, Paul & Terri; John Weldon. *New Age Medicine.* IVP, Downers Grove, USA, 1987

Richards, John. *But Deliver Us from Evil.* DLT, London, 1974

Roebert, Ed. Ministering in the Gifts of the Holy Spirit. Sovereign World, England, 1991

Sandford, John & Loren. *Renewal of the Mind.* Victory House Inc, Tulsa, USA, 1991

Sandford, John & Paula. *The Transformation of the Inner Man.* Victory House Inc, Tulsa, USA, 1982

Sandford, John & Paula. *Why Some Christians Commit Adultery.* Victory House Inc, Tulsa, USA, 1989

Sandford, John & Paula. *Healing the Wounded Spirit.* Victory House Inc, Tulsa, USA, 1985

Sandford, John & Paula. *Restoring The Christian Family.* Victory House Inc, Tulsa, USA 1979

Sandford, Paula. *Healings Victims of Sexual Abuse.* Victory House Inc, Tulsa, USA, 1988

Sandford, Paula. *Healing Women's Emotions.* Victory House Inc, Oklahoma, USA, 1992

Seamands, David A. *Healing for Damaged Emotions.* Scripture Press Publications, Wheaton, USA, 1993

Seamands, David, A. *Healing Grace.* Scripture Press Publications, Wheaton, USA, 1992

Seamands, David, A. *Healing of Memories*. Scripture Press Publications, Wheaton, USA, 1985

Sherman, Dean. *Spiritual Warfare For Every Christian*. YWAM Publishing, Seattle, USA, 1990

Smith, F Lagard. *What You Need to Know About the New Age Movement*. Harvest House Publishers, Oregon, USA, 1993

Strohmer, Charles. *What Your Horoscope Doesn't Tell You*. Word Publishing, England, 1991

Subritzky, Bill. *Demons Defeated*. Sovereign World, England, 1992

Subritzky, Bill. *How to Cast Out Demons and Break Curses*. Dove Ministries, Auckland, New Zealand, 1991

Subritzky, Bill. *Receiving The Gifts of the Holy Spirit*. Sovereign World, England, 1986

Wagner, C.Peter (Editor). *Territorial Spirits*. Sovereign World, England, 1991

White, John. *When the Spirit Comes with Power*. Hodder & Stoughton, England, 1992

White, Tom. The Believer's Guide to Spiritual Warfare. Kingsway, England, 1991

Whyte, H.A.Maxwell. *Demons and Deliverance*. Whittaker House, USA, 1989

Wilson, Earl D. *A Silence to Be Broken*. IVP, England, 1987

Woodworth-Etter, Maria. *A Diary of Signs and Wonders*. Harrison House, Oklahoma, USA. (Reprint, originally published 1916)

Wright, H. Norman. *The Power of a Parent's Words*. Regal Books, Ventura, USA, 1991

The inclusion of a book in this Bibliography does not necessarily mean that the author of this book would endorse everything that is said by other authors. Readers are encouraged to use their discernment to "test everything and hold on to the good." (1 Thess. 5:21)

Index

*If you would like further information about the
work of Ellel Ministries, or would like to be placed on
the mailing list, or would like to support the work –*

Please write to:

**Ellel Ministries
Ellel Grange, Ellel,
Lancaster, LA2 0HN
England**

**Tel: (0)-1524-751651
Fax: (0)-1524-751738**

Other centres at:

Glyndley Manor
*Stone Cross, Pevensey,
Nr Eastbourne, E. Sussex
BN24 5BS
Tel: 01323-440440
Fax: 01323-440877*

**Ellel Ministries
Pierrepont**
*Churt Road, Frensham,
Surrey, GU10 3DL
Tel: 01252-794060
Fax: 01252-794039*

Ellel Canada
*RR#1, Orangeville,
Ontario, L9W 2Y8
Canada
Tel: (519) 941-0929
Fax: (519) 941-4062*

**Ellel Ministries
East**
*Veresegyhaza,
PF 17,
2112,
Hungary*